Sir Rowlar

The Story of a G

Eleanor C. Hill Smyth

Alpha Editions

This edition published in 2023

ISBN : 9789357953580

Design and Setting By
Alpha Editions
www.alphaedis.com
Email - info@alphaedis.com

Contents

PREFACE

IN Gladstone's "'musings for the good of man,'" writes John Morley in his Life of the dead statesman (ii. 56, 57), the "Liberation of Intercourse, to borrow his own larger name for Free Trade, figured in his mind's eye as one of the promoting conditions of abundant employment.... He recalled the days when our predecessors thought it must be for man's good to have 'most of the avenues by which the mind and also the hand of man conveyed and exchanged their respective products' blocked or narrowed by regulation and taxation. Dissemination of news, travelling, letters, transit of goods, were all made as costly and difficult as the legislation could make them. 'I rank,' he said, 'the introduction of cheap postage for letters, documents, patterns, and printed matter, and the abolition of all taxes on printed matter, in the catalogue of free legislation. These great measures may well take their place beside the abolition of prohibitions and protective duties, the simplifying of revenue laws, and the repeal of the Navigation Act, as forming together the great code of industrial emancipation.'" To the above the biographer adds that in Gladstone's article in the *Nineteenth Century* on Free Trade, Railways, and Commerce, he divided the credit of our material progress between the two great factors, the Liberation of Intercourse and the Improvement of Locomotion.

In view of the occasional attempts to revive the pernicious franking privilege, and of the frequently recurring warfare between Free Trade and the rival system, whose epitaph we owe to Disraeli, but whose unquiet spirit apparently declines to rest within its tomb, the present seems a fitting time to write the story of the old reform to which Gladstone alluded—"the introduction of cheap postage for letters," etc., the narrative being prefaced by a notice of the reformer, his family, and some of his friends who are not mentioned in later pages.

My cousin, Dr Birkbeck Hill's "Life of Sir Rowland Hill and History of Penny Postage" is an elaborate work, and therefore valuable as a source of information to be drawn upon by any future historian of that reform and of the period, now so far removed from our own, which the reformer's long life covered. Before Dr Hill's death he gave me permission to take from his pages such material as I cared to incorporate with my own shorter, more anecdotal story. This has been done, but my narrative also contains much that has not appeared elsewhere, because, as the one of my father's children most intimately associated with his home life, unto me were given opportunities of acquiring knowledge which were not accessible to my cousin.

Before my brother, Mr Pearson Hill, died, he read through the greater portion of my work; and although since then much has been remodelled, omitted, and added, the narrative ought to be substantially correct. He supplied sundry details, and more than one anecdote, and is responsible for the story of Lord Canning's curious revelation which has appeared in no previous work. In all that my brother wrote his actual words have been, as far as possible, retained. The tribute to his memory in the first chapter on the Post Office was written after his decease.

INTRODUCTORY

THE earliest of the postal reformer's forefathers to achieve fame that outlives him was Sir Rowland Hill, mercer, and Lord Mayor of London in 1549, a native of Hodnet, Shropshire, who founded a Grammar School at Drayton, benefited the London Blue Coat School, was a builder of bridges, and is mentioned by John Stowe. From his brother are descended the three Rowland Hills famous in more modern times—the preacher, the warrior, and the author of Penny Postage. Some of the preacher's witticisms are still remembered, though they are often attributed to his brother cleric, Sydney Smith; Napier, in his "Peninsular War," speaks very highly of the warrior, who, had Wellington fallen at Waterloo, would have taken the Duke's place, and who succeeded him as Commander-in-Chief when, in 1828, Wellington became Prime Minister. A later common ancestor of the three, a landed proprietor, married twice, and the first wife's children were thrown upon the world to fight their way as best as they could, my paternal grandfather's great-grandfather being one of the dispossessed. But even the blackest cloud has its silver lining; and the fall, by teaching the young people self-help, probably brought out the latent good stuff that was in them. At any rate, family tradition preserves memory of not a few men and women—Hills, or of the stocks with which they married—of whom their descendants have reason to be proud.

There was, for example, John Hill, who served among "the twelve good men and true" on a certain trial, was the only one of them who declined to accept a bribe, and, the fact becoming known, was handsomely complimented by the presiding judge. Thenceforth, whenever the Assizes in that part of the country came round again, John used to be asked after as "the honest juror." At least two of my father's forebears, a Symonds and a Hill, refused to cast their political votes to order, and were punished for their sturdy independence. The one lived to see a hospital erected in Shrewsbury out of the large fortune for some two hundred years ago of £30,000 which should have come to his wife, the testator's sister; the other, a baker and corn merchant, son to "the honest juror," saw his supply of fuel required to bake his bread cut off by the local squire, a candidate for Parliament, for whom the worthy baker had dared to refuse to vote. Ovens then were heated by wood, which in this case came from the squire's estate. When next James Hill made the usual application, the faggots were not to be had. He was not discouraged. Wood, he reflected, was dear; coal—much seldomer used then than now—was cheap. He mixed the two, and found the plan succeed, lessened the proportion of wood, and finally dispensed with it altogether. His example was followed by other people: the demand for the squire's firewood languished, and the boycotted voter was presently requested to purchase afresh. "An instance," says Dr Birkbeck Hill, "of a new kind of faggot vote."

Another son of "the honest juror" was the first person to grow potatoes in Kidderminster. Some two centuries earlier "the useful tuber" was brought to England; but even in times much nearer our own, so slowly did information travel, that till about 1750 the only denizen of that town who seems to have known of its existence was this second John Hill. When the seeds he sowed came up, blossomed, and turned to berries, these last were cooked and brought to table. Happily no one could eat them; and so the finger of scorn was pointed at the luckless innovator. The plants withered unheeded; but later, the ground being wanted for other crops, was dug up, when, to the amazement of all beholders and hearers, a plentiful supply of fine potatoes was revealed.

On the spindle side also Rowland Hill's family could boast ancestors of whom none need feel ashamed. Among these was the high-spirited, well-dowered orphan girl who, like Clarissa Harlowe, fled from home to escape wedlock with the detested suitor her guardians sought to force upon her. But, unlike Richardson's hapless heroine, this fugitive lived into middle age, maintained herself by her own handiwork—spinning—never sought even to recover her lost fortune, married, left descendants, and fatally risked her life while preparing for burial the pestilence-smitten neighbour whose poor remains his own craven relatives had abandoned. Though she perished untimely, recollection of her married name was preserved to reappear in that of a great-grandson, Matthew *Davenport* Hill. The husband of Mrs Davenport's only daughter, William Lea, was a man little swayed by the superstitions of his time, as he showed when he broke through a mob of ignorant boors engaged in hounding into a pond a terrified old woman they declared to be a witch, strode into the water, lifted her in his arms, and, heedless of hostile demonstration, bore her to his own home to be nursed back into such strength and sanity as were recoverable. A son of William Lea, during the dreadful cholera visitation of 1832, played, as Provost of Haddington, a part as fearlessly unselfish as that of his grandmother in earlier days, but without losing his life, for his days were long in the land. His sister was Rowland Hill's mother.

On both sides the stocks seem to have been of stern Puritan extraction, theologically narrow, inflexibly honest, terribly in earnest, of healthy life, fine physique—nonagenarians not infrequently. John Symonds, son to him whose wife forfeited succession to her brother, Mr Millington's fortune, because both men were sturdily obstinate in the matter of political creed, was, though a layman, great at extempore prayer and sermon-making. When any young man came a-wooing to one of his bonnie daughters, the father would take the suitor to an inner sanctum, there to be tested as to his ability to get through the like devotional exercises. If the young man failed to come up to the requisite standard he was dismissed, and the damsel reserved for some more proficient rival—James Hill being one of the latter sort. How many suitors of the present day would creditably emerge from that ordeal?

Through this sturdy old Puritan we claim kinship with the Somersetshire family, of whom John Addington Symonds was one, and therefore with the Stracheys; while from other sources comes a collateral descent from "Hudibras" Butler, who seems to have endowed with some of his own genuine wit certain later Hills; as also a relationship with that line of distinguished medical men, the Mackenzies, and with the Rev. Morell Mackenzie, who played a hero's part at the long-ago wreck of the *Pegasus*.

A neighbour of James Hill was a recluse, who, perhaps, not finding the society of a small provincial town so companionable as the books he loved, forbore "to herd with narrow foreheads," but made of James a congenial friend. When this man died, the task fell to his executors, James Hill and another, to divide his modest estate. Among the few bequests were two books to young Tom, James's son, a boy with a passion for reading, but possessed of few books, one being a much-mutilated copy of "Robinson Crusoe," which tantalisingly began with the thrilling words, "more than thirty dancing round a fire." The fellow executor, knowing well the reputation for uncanny ways with which local gossip had endowed the deceased, earnestly advised his colleague to destroy the volumes, and not permit them to sully young Tom's mind. "Oh, let the boy have the books," said James Hill, and straightway the legacy was placed in the youthful hands. It consisted of a "Manual of Geography" and Euclid's "Elements." The effect of their perusal was not to send the reader to perdition, but to call forth an innate love for mathematics, and, through them, a lifelong devotion to astronomy, tastes he was destined to pass on in undiminished ardour to his third son, the postal reformer.

Thomas Wright Hill was brought up in the straitest-laced of Puritan sects, and he has left a graphic description of the mode in which, as a small boy of seven, he passed each Sunday. The windows of the house, darkened by their closed outside shutters, made mirrors in which he saw his melancholy little face reflected; his toys were put away; there were three chapel services, occupying in all some five and a half hours, to which he was taken, and the intervals between each were filled by long extempore prayers and sermon-reading at home, all week-day conversation being rigidly ruled out. The sabbatical observance commenced on Saturday night and terminated on Sunday evening with "a cheerful supper," as though literally "the evening and the morning were the first day"—an arrangement which, coupled with the habit of bestowing not Christian but Hebrew names upon the children, gives colour to the oft-made allegation that our Puritan ancestors drew their inspiration from the Old rather than from the New Testament. The only portion of these Sunday theological exercises which the poor little fellow really understood was the simple Bible teaching that the tenderly-loved mother gave to him and to his younger brother. While as a young man residing in Birmingham, however, he passed under the influence of Priestley, and became one of his most devoted disciples, several of whom, at the time of the disgraceful "Church and King" riots of 1791, volunteered to defend the learned doctor's house.[1] But Priestley declined all defence, and the volunteers retired, leaving only young Tom, who would not desert his beloved master's threatened dwelling. The Priestley family had found refuge elsewhere, but his disciple stayed alone in the twilight of the barred and shuttered house, which speedily fell a prey to its assailants. Our grandfather used often to tell us children of the events of those terrible days when the mob held the town at their mercy, and were seriously opposed only when, having destroyed so much property belonging to Nonconformity, they next turned their tireless energy towards Conformity's possessions. His affianced wife was as courageous as he, for when while driving in a friend's carriage through Birmingham's streets some of the rioters stopped the horses, and bade her utter the cry "Church and King," she refused, and was suffered to pass on unmolested. Was it her bravery or her comeliness, or both, that won for her immunity from harm?

ROWLAND HILL'S BIRTHPLACE, KIDDERMINSTER.
By permission of the Proprietors of the "*Illustrated London News.*"

The third son of this young couple, Rowland, the future postal reformer, first saw the light in a house at Kidderminster wherein his father was born, which had already sheltered some generations of Hills, and whose garden was the scene of the potato story. The child was weakly, and, being threatened with spinal trouble, passed much of his infancy in a recumbent position. But the fragile form held a dauntless little soul, and the almost abnormally large brain behind the too pallid forehead was a very active one. As he lay prone, playing with the toys his mother suspended to a cord stretched within easy reach above him; and, later, working out mental arithmetical problems, in which exercise he found delight, and to the weaving of alluring daydreams, he presently fell to longing for some career—what it should be he knew not—that should leave his country the better for his having lived in it. The thoughts of boys are often, the poet tells us, "long, long thoughts," but it is not given to every one to see those daydreams realised. Though what is boy (or girl) worth who has not at times entertained healthily ambitious longings for a great future?

As he grew stronger he presently came to help his father in the school the latter had established at Birmingham, in which his two elder brothers, aged fifteen and fourteen, were already at work. The family was far from affluent, and its young members were well aware that on their own exertions depended their future success. For them there was no royal road to learning or to anything else; and even as children they learned to be self-reliant. From the age of twelve onwards, my father, indeed, was self-supporting. Like Chaucer's poor parson, the young Hill brothers learned while they taught, even sometimes while on their way to give a lesson, as did my father when on a several miles long walk to teach an equally ignorant boy the art of Navigation; and perhaps because life had to be taken so seriously, they valued the hardly-acquired knowledge all the more highly. Their father early accustomed his children to discuss with him and with each other the questions of the time—a time which must always loom large in the history of our land. Though he mingled in the talk, "it was," my Uncle Matthew said, "a match of mind against mind, in which the rules of fair play were duly observed; and we put forth our little strength without fear. The sword of authority was not thrown into the scale.... We were," added the writer, "born to a burning hatred of tyranny."[2] And no wonder, for in the early years of the last century tyranny was a living, active force.

If, to quote Blackstone, "punishment of unreasonable severity" with a view to "preventing crimes and amending the manners of a people" constitute a specific form of tyranny, the fact that in 1795, the year of Rowland Hill's birth, the pillory, the stocks, and the whipping-post were still in use sufficiently attests this "unreasonable severity." In March 1789, less than seven years before his birth, a yet more terrible punishment was still in force. A woman—the last thus "judicially murdered"—was burnt at the stake; and a writer in *Notes and Queries*, of 21st September 1851, tells its readers that he was present on the occasion. Her offence was coining, and she was mercifully strangled before being executed. Women were burnt at the stake long after that awful death penalty was abolished in the case of the more favoured sex. The savage cruelty of the criminal code at this time and later is also indicated by the fact that over 150 offences were punishable by death. Even in 1822, a date within the recollection of persons still living, and notwithstanding the efforts made by Sir Samuel Romilly and others to humanise that code, capital punishment was still terribly common. In that year, on two consecutive Monday mornings, my father, arriving by coach in London from Birmingham, passed within sight of Newgate. Outside its walls, on the first occasion, the horrified passengers counted nineteen bodies hanging in a row; on the second, twenty-one.

During my father's childhood and youth this country was almost constantly engaged in war. Within half a mile of my grandfather's house the forging of gun barrels went on all but incessantly, the work beginning before dawn and lasting till long after nightfall. The scarcely-ending din of the hammers was varied only by the occasional rattle from the proof shed; and the shocks and jars had disastrous effect upon my grandmother's brewings of beer. Meanwhile "The Great Shadow," graphically depicted by Sir A. Conan Doyle, was an actual dread that darkened our land for years. And the shadow of press-gang raids was a yet greater dread alike to the men who encountered them, sometimes to disappear for ever, and to the women who were frequently bereft of their bread-winners. It is, however, pleasant to remember that sometimes the would-be captors became the captured. A merchant vessel lying in quarantine in Southampton Water, her yellow flag duly displayed, but hanging in the calm weather so limply that it was hardly observable, was boarded by a press-gang who thought to do a clever thing by impressing some of the sailors. These, seeing what was the invaders' errand, let them come peaceably on deck, when the quarantine officer took possession of boat and gang, and detained both for six weeks.

For those whose means were small—a numerous class at that time— there was scant patronage of public conveyances, such as they were. Thus the young Hill brothers had to depend on their own walking powers when minded to visit the world that lay beyond their narrow horizon. And to walking tours, often of great length, they were much given in holiday time, tours which took them to distant places of historic interest, of which Rowland brought back memorials in his sketch book. Beautiful, indeed, were the then green lanes of the Midlands, though here and there they were disfigured by the presence of some lonely gibbet, the chains holding its dismal "fruit" clanking mournfully in windy weather. Whenever it was possible, the wayfarer made a round to avoid passing the gruesome object.

One part of the country, lying between Birmingham and Wolverhampton, a lonely heath long since covered with factories and houses, known as the "Lie Waste," was also not pleasant to traverse, though the lads occasionally had to do so. A small collection of huts of mud-and-wattle construction sheltered some of our native savages—for they were nothing else—whose like has happily long been "improved off the face" of the land. These uncouth beings habitually and literally went "on all fours." Whether the attitude was assumed in consequence of the low roofs of their dwellings, or the outcasts chose that mode of progression in imitation of the animals which were their ordinary companions, history does not say, but they moved with wonderful celerity both in and out of doors. At sight of any passer-by they were apt to "rear," and then oaths, obscene language, and missiles of whatever sort was handy would be their mildest greeting, while more formidable attack was likely to be the lot of those who ventured too near their lairs. Among these people the Hill boys often noticed a remarkably handsome girl, as great a savage as the rest.

As the three elder brothers grew well into their teens, much of the school government fell to their lot, always with the parental sanction, and ere long it was changed in character, and became a miniature republic.[3] Trial by jury for serious offences was instituted, the judge being my grandfather or one of his sons, and the jury the culprit's fellow-pupils. Corporal punishment, then perhaps universal in schools, was abolished, and the lads, being treated as reasonable creatures, early learned to be a self-respecting because a self-governing community. The system, which in this restricted space cannot be described in detail, was pre-eminently a success, since it turned out pupils who did it and themselves credit. "All the good I ever learned was learned at Hazelwood," I once heard say a cheery old clergy-man, probably one of the last surviving "boys." The teaching was efficiently carried on, and the development of individual talent was wisely encouraged, the pupils out of school hours being allowed to exercise the vocation to which each was inclined, or which, owing to this practice, was discovered in each. Thus in boyhood Follet Osler, the inventor of the anemometer and other scientific instruments, was enabled to bring to light those mechanical abilities which, till he exhibited their promise during his hours of voluntary work, were unsuspected even by his nearest of kin. Again, Thomas Creswick, R.A., found an outlet for his love of art in drawing, though, being a very little fellow when he began, some of these studies—of public buildings in Birmingham—were very funny, the perspective generally having the "Anglo-Saxon" peculiarities, and each edifice being afflicted with a "list" out of the perpendicular as pronounced as that of Pisa's leaning tower—or nearly so.

The fame of the "Hazelwood system" spread afar, and many of our then most distinguished fellow-countrymen visited the school. Among the rest, Bentham gave it his hearty approval; and Captain Basil Hall, the writer of once popular books for boys, spoke of the evident existence of friendly terms between masters and pupils, declared the system to be "a curious epitome of real life," and added that the boys were not converted into little men, but remained boys, only with heads and hands fully employed on topics they liked.

Visitors also came from foreign lands. Bernadotte's son, Prince Oscar, afterwards first king of Sweden of that name, travelled to Hazelwood, examined the novel system, and, later, established at Stockholm a "Hillska Scola." From France, among other people, came M. Jullien, once secretary to Robespierre—what thrilling tales of the Great Revolution must he not have been able to tell!—and afterwards a wise philanthropist and eminent writer on education. He sent a son to Hazelwood. President Jefferson, when organising the University of Virginia, asked for a copy of "Public Education,"[4] the work describing the system and the joint production of Rowland, who found the ideas, Matthew, who supplied the composition, and, as regards a few suggestions, of a younger brother, Arthur. Greece, Spain, far-off Mexico even, in course of time sent pupils either to Hazelwood or to Bruce Castle, Tottenham, to which then picturesque and somewhat remote London suburb the school was ultimately transferred. "His Excellency, the Tripolitan Ambassador," wrote my father in his diary of 1823, "has informed us that he has sent to Tripoli for six young Africans; and the Algerine Ambassador, not to be outdone by his piratical brother, has sent for a dozen from Algiers."[5] Happily, neither contingent put in an appearance. In both cases the enthusiasm evoked seems to have been short-lived.

BRUCE CASTLE SCHOOL, TOTTENHAM.
By permission of Messrs. De La Rue.

An old Hazelwood pupil, Mr E. Edwards, in his written sketch of "Sir Rowland Hill," said of the school that no similar establishment "in the world, probably at that time, contained such an array of costly models, instruments, apparatus, and books. There was an observatory upon the top of the house fitted with powerful astronomical instruments. The best microscopes obtainable were at hand. Models of steam and other engines were all over the place. Air-pumps and electrical machines were familiar objects. Maps, then comparatively rare, lined the walls. Drawing and mathematical instruments were provided in profusion. Etching was taught, and a copper press was there for printing the pupils' efforts in that way. A lithographic press and stones of various sizes were provided, so that the young artists might print copies of their drawings to send to their admiring relatives. Finally, a complete printing press with ample founts of type was set up to enable the boys themselves to print a monthly magazine connected with the school and its doings." Other attractions were a well fitted-up carpenter's shop; a band, the musicians being the pupils; the training of the boys in vocal music; a theatre in which the manager, elocution teacher, scene painter, etc., were the young Hill brothers, the *costumière* their sister Caroline, and the actors the pupils; the control of a sum of money for school purposes; and the use of a metallic coinage received as payment for the voluntary work already mentioned, and by which certain privileges could be purchased.[6]

My grandfather inspired his sons and pupils with a longing to acquire knowledge, at the same time so completely winning their hearts by his good comradeship, that they readily joined him in the long and frequent walks of which he was fond, and in the course of which his walking stick was wont to serve to make rough drawings of problems, etc., in road or pathway. "His mathematical explanations," wrote another old pupil in the "Essays of a Birmingham Manufacturer" (W. L. Sargent), "were very clear; and he looked at the bearings of every subject irrespective of its conventionalities. His definition of a straight line has been said to be the best in existence."[7]

THOMAS WRIGHT HILL.
By permission of Messrs. Thos. De La Rue.

In my father's "Life," Dr Birkbeck Hill, when writing of his recollections of our grandfather, said that it seemed "as if the aged man were always seated in perpetual sunshine. How much of the brightness and warmth must have come from his own cheerful temperament?... His Sunday morning breakfasts live in the memory like a landscape of Claude's." At these entertainments the old man would sit in his easy-chair, at the head of the largest table the house could boast, in a circle of small, adoring grandchildren, the intervening, severe generation being absent; and of all the joyous crowd his perhaps was the youngest heart. There were other feasts, those of reason and the flow of soul, with which he also delighted his young descendants: stories of the long struggle in the revolted "American Colonies," of the Great French Revolution, and of other interesting historical dramas which he could well remember, and equally well describe.

His old pupils would come long distances to see him; and on one occasion several of them subscribed to present him with a large telescope, bearing on it a graven tribute of their affectionate regard. This greatly prized gift was in use till within a short time of his last illness.

Young Rowland had a strong bent towards art, as he showed when, at the age of thirteen, he won the prize, a handsome box of water-colour paints, offered by the proprietor of the *London School Magazine* for "the best original landscape drawing by the youth of all England, under the age of sixteen." He painted the scenery for the school theatre, and made many water-colour sketches in different parts of our island, his style much resembling that of David Cox. He was an admirer of Turner long before Ruskin "discovered" that great painter; and, as his diary shows, marvelled at the wondrous rendering of atmospheric effects exhibited in his idol's pictures. Nearly all my father's scenery and sketches perished in a fire which partially burnt down Hazelwood School; and few are now in existence. After the age of seventeen he gave up painting, being far too busy to devote time to art, but he remained a picture-lover to the end of his days. Once during the long war with France he had an adventure which might have proved serious. He was sketching Dover Castle, when a soldier came out of the fortress and told him to cease work. Not liking the man's manner, the youthful artist went on painting unconcernedly. Presently a file of soldiers, headed by a corporal, appeared, and he was peremptorily ordered to withdraw. Then the reason for the interference was revealed: he was taken for a spy. My father at once laid aside his brush; he had no wish to be shot.

In 1835 Rowland Hill resigned to a younger brother, Arthur,[8] the head-mastership of Bruce Castle School, and accepted the post of secretary to the Colonisation Commissioners for South Australia, whose chairman was Colonel Torrens.[9] Another commissioner was John Shaw Lefevre, later a famous speaker of the House of Commons, who, as Lord Eversley, lived to a patriarchal age. But the prime mover in the scheme for colonising this portion of the "Island Continent" was that public-spirited man, Edward Gibbon Wakefield. William IV. took much interest in the project, and stipulated that the chief city should bear the name of his consort—Adelaide.

The Commissioners were capable men, and were ably assisted by the South Australian Company, which much about the same time was started mainly through the exertions of Mr G. F. Angas. Among the many excellent rules laid down by the Commissioners was one which insisted on the making of a regular and efficient survey both of the emigrant ships and of the food they carried. As sailing vessels were then the only transports, the voyage lasted several months, and the comfort of the passengers was of no small importance. "When," said my father in his diary, "defects and blemishes were brought to light by the accuracy of the survey, and the stipulated consequences enforced, an outcry arose as if the connection between promise and performance were an unheard-of and most unwarrantable innovation. After a time, however, as our practice became recognised, evasive attempts grew rare, the first expense being found to be the least." He often visited the port of departure, and witnessed the shipping off of the emigrants—always an interesting occasion, and one which gave opportunities of personal supervision of matters. Being once at Plymouth, my mother and he boarded a vessel about to sail for the new colony. Among the passengers was a bright young Devonian, apparently an agriculturist; and my father, observing him, said to my mother: "I feel sure that man will do well." The remark was overheard, but the Devonian made no sign. He went to Australia poor, and returned wealthy, bought an estate close to his birth-place which was in the market, and there settled. But before sailing hither, he bought at one of the Adelaide banks the finest one of several gold nuggets there displayed, and, armed with this, presented himself at my father's house, placed his gift in my mother's hand, and told how the casual remark made forty years before had helped to spur him on to success.

The story of Rowland Hill and a mysteriously vanished rotatory printing press may be told here.

In 1790 Mr William Nicholson devised a scheme for applying to ordinary type printing the already established process of printing calico by revolving cylinders. The impressions were to be taken from his press upon successive sheets of paper, as no means of producing continuous rolls had as yet been invented; but the machine worked far from satisfactorily, and practically came to nothing. A quarter of a century later Mr Edward Cowper applied Nicholson's idea to stereotype plates bent to a cylindrical surface. But till the advent of "Hill's machine" (described at the Patent Office as "A.D. 1835, No. 6762") all plans for fixing movable types on a cylinder had failed. It is therefore incontestable that the first practical scheme of printing on a continuous roll of paper by revolving cylinders was invented and set to work by Rowland Hill in the year named. The machine was intended mainly for the rapid printing of newspapers, but the refusal of the Treasury to allow an arrangement by which the Government stamp could be affixed by an ingenious mechanical device as the scroll passed through the press—a refusal withdrawn later—deferred for many years the introduction of any rotatory printing machine.

The apparatus was kept at my Uncle Matthew's chambers in Chancery Lane, and was often shown to members of the trade and others. Although driven by hand only, it threw off impressions at the rate of 7,000 or 8,000 an hour, a much higher speed than that hitherto attained by any other machine. But from 1836 onwards my father's attention was almost wholly taken up with his postal reform, and it was only after his retirement from the Post Office in 1864 that his mind reverted to the subject of the printing press. Several years before the latter date his brother had left London; but of the rotatory printing machine, bulky and ponderous as it was, a few small odds and ends—afterwards exhibited at the Caxton Exhibition in 1877—alone remained.

In 1866 the once well-known "Walter Press" was first used in the *Times* office. Of this machine my father has said that "except as regards the apparatus for cutting and distributing the printed sheets, and excepting further that the 'Walter Press' (entered at the Patent Office as "A.D. 1866, No. 3222") is only adapted for printing from stereotype plates, while mine would not only print from stereotype plates, but, what is more difficult, from movable types also, the two machines are almost identical. " He added that "the enormous difficulty of bringing a complex machine into practical use—a difficulty familiar to every inventor—has been most successfully overcome by Messrs Calverley and Macdonald, the patentees."

By whom and through what agency the machine patented in 1835 was apparently transported from Chancery Lane to Printing House Square is a mystery which at this distant date is hardly likely to be made clear.

It has always been a tradition in our family that the courtship between Rowland Hill and Caroline Pearson began when their united ages amounted to eleven years only, the boy being by twelve months the elder. The families on both sides lived at the time at Wolverhampton, and the first kiss is said to have been exchanged inside a large culvert which crossed beneath the Tettenhall Road in the neighbourhood of the Hills' house, and served to conduct a tiny rivulet, apt in wet weather to become a swollen stream, into its chosen channel on the other side the way. The boy delighted to creep within this shelter—often dry in summer—and listen to the rumbling overhead of the passing vehicles. Noisy, ponderous wains some of these were, with wheels of great width and strength, and other timbers in like proportion; but to the small listener the noisier the more enjoyable. These wains have long vanished from the roads they helped to wear out, the railway goods trains having superseded them, although of late years the heavy traction engines, often drawing large trucks after them, seem likely to occupy the place filled by their forgotten predecessors. Little Rowland naturally wished to share the enchanting treat with "Car," as he generally called his new friend, and hand in hand the "wee things" set off one day to the Tettenhall Road. Many years later the elderly husband made a sentimental journey to the spot, and was amazed at the culvert's apparent shrinkage in size. Surely, a most prosaic spot for the beginning of a courtship!

The father of this little girl was Joseph Pearson, a man held in such high esteem by his fellow-citizens that after the passing of the great Reform Bill in 1832 he was asked to become one of Wolverhampton's first two members.[10] He was, however, too old for the wear and tear of Parliamentary life, though when the General Election came on he threw himself with all his accustomed zeal into the struggle, and was, as a consequence, presently laid up with a temporary ailment, which caused one of his political foes to declare that "If Mr Pearson's gout would only last three weeks longer we might get our man in." These words coming to Mr Pearson's ears, he rose from his sick-bed, gout or no gout, and plunged afresh into the fray, with so much energy that "we" did *not* "get our man in," but the other side did.

"He was," once said a many years old friend, "conspicuous for his breadth of mind, kindness of heart, and public spirit." He hated the cruel sports common in his time, and sought unceasingly to put them down. One day, while passing the local bull-ring, he saw a crowd of rough miners and others preparing to bait a bull. He at once strode into their midst, liberated the animal, pulled up or broke off the stake, and carried it away on his shoulder. Was it his pluck, or his widespread popularity that won the forbearance of the semi-savage by-standers? At any rate, not a hostile finger was laid upon him. Meanwhile, he remembered that if brutalising pastimes are put down, it is but right that better things should be set in their place. Thus the local Mechanics' Institute, British Schools, Dispensary, and other beneficent undertakings, including rational sports for every class, owed their origin chiefly to him; and, aided by his friend John Mander, and by the Rev. John Carter, a poor, hard-working Catholic priest, he founded the Wolverhampton Free Library.

Joseph Pearson was one of the most hospitable and genial of men, and, for his time, a person of some culture. He detested cliques and coteries, those paralysing products of small provincial towns, and would have naught to do with them. Men of great variety of views met round his dinner-table, and whenever it seemed necessary he would preface the repast with the request that theology and politics should be avoided. With his Catholic neighbours—Staffordshire was a stronghold of the "Old Religion" —the sturdy Nonconformist was on the happiest of terms, and to listen to the conversation of the often well-travelled, well-educated priests was to him a never-failing pleasure. For Catholic Emancipation he strove heartily and long. With all sects he was friendly, but chiefly his heart went out to those who in any way had suffered for their faith. One effect of this then not too common breadth of view was seen when, after his death, men of all denominations followed him to his grave, and the handsomest of the several journalistic tributes to his memory appeared in the columns of his inveterate political and theological opponent, the local Tory paper. A ward in the Hospital and a street were called after the whilom "king of Wolverhampton."[11]

JOSEPH PEARSON.
From a Photograph by Messrs. Whiteley & Co.
The bust was the last work of Sir Francis Chantry.

He had three daughters, of whom my mother was the eldest. His wife died young, and before her sixteenth year Caroline became mistress of his house, and thus acquired the ease of manner and knowledge of social duties which made of her the charming hostess who, in later years, presided over her husband's London house. She will make a brief reappearance in other pages of this work.

Joseph Pearson's youngest daughter, Clara, was a beautiful girl, a frequent "toast" at social gatherings in the three counties of Stafford, Warwick, and Worcester—for toasts in honour of reigning belles were still drunk at festivities in provincial Assembly Rooms and elsewhere, what time the nineteenth century was in its teens. When very young she became engaged to her cousin, Lieutenant (afterwards Captain) Alexander Pearson, R.N., who at the time of Napoleon's sojourn at St Helena was stationed there, being attached to the man-of-war commanded by Admiral Plampin. One gift which Lieutenant Pearson gave my aunt she kept to the end of her life—a lock of Napoleon's hair. Lieutenant Pearson often saw the ex-Emperor, and, many years after, described him to us children—how, for instance, he would stand, silent and with folded arms, gazing long and fixedly seaward as though waiting for the rescue which never came. The lieutenant was one of the several young naval officers who worshipped at the shrine of the somewhat hoydenish Miss "Betsy" Balcombe, who comes into most stories of St. Helena of that time. Wholly unabashed by consideration of the illustrious captive's former greatness, she made of him a playmate—perhaps a willing one, for life must have been terribly dreary to one whose occupation, like that of Othello, was gone. Occasionally she shocked her hearers by addressing the ex-Emperor as "Boney," though it is possible that the appellation so frequently heard in the mouths of his British enemies had no osseous association in his own ears, but was accepted as an endearing diminutive. One day, in the presence of several witnesses, our cousin being among them, she possessed herself of a sword, flourished it playfully before her, hemmed Napoleon into a corner, and, holding the blade above his head, laughingly exclaimed: "Maintenant j'ai vaincu le vanqueur du monde!" But there was no answering laugh; the superstitious Corsican turned pale, made some short, unintelligible reply, left the room, and was depressed and taciturn for the rest of the day. It was surmised that he took the somewhat tactless jest for an omen that a chief who had been beaten by a woman would never again lead an army of men.

During Rowland Hill's prime, and until the final breakdown of his health, our house was a favourite haunt of the more intimate of his many clever friends. Scientific, medical, legal, artistic, literary, and other prominent men met, exchanged views, indulged in deep talk, bandied repartee, and told good stories at breakfast and dinner parties; the economists mustering in force, and plainly testifying by their bearing and conversation that, whatever ignorant people may say of the science they never study, its professors are often the very reverse of dismal. If Dr Southwood Smith[12] and Mr (later Sir Edwin) Chadwick's talk at times ran gruesomely on details of "intramural interment," the former, at least, had much quaint humour, and was deservedly popular; while Dr Neil Arnott, whose chief hobbies were fabled to be those sadly prosaic things, stoves, water-beds, and ventilation, but who was actually a distinguished physician, natural philosopher, author, and traveller, was even, when long past sixty, one of the gayest and youngest of our guests: a mimic, but never an ill-natured one, a spinner of amusing yarns, and frankly idolised by the juvenile members of the family whose minds he mercifully never attempted to improve.

Charles Wentworth Dilke,[13] founder of the *Athenæum* newspaper, a famous journalist and influential man of letters, at whose house one met every writer, to say nothing of other men and women, worth knowing, was another charming old man, to listen to whose talk was a liberal education. Did we walk with him on Hampstead Heath, where once he had a country house, he became an animated guide-book guiltless of a dull page, telling us of older times than our own, and of dead and gone worthies who had been guests at "Wentworth House." On this much worn, initial-carven, wooden seat used often to sit Keats listening to the nightingales, and, maybe, thinking of Fanny Brawne. At another spot the weakly-framed poet had soundly thrashed a British rough who was beating his wife. Across yonder footpath used to come from Highgate "the archangel a little damaged," as Charles Lamb called Coleridge. At that road corner, in a previous century, were wont to gather the visitors returning from the Well Walk "pump-room," chalybeate spring, and promenade, till they were in sufficient force to be safe from highwaymen or footpads who frequented the then lonely road to London. In a yet earlier century certain gallant Spanish gentlemen attached to Philip and Mary's court, rescued some English ladies from molestation by English ruffians; and memorials of this episode live in the still traceable circle of trees whose predecessors were planted by the grateful ladies, and in the name of the once quaint old hostelry hard by, and of the road known as the Spaniards.

Another wanderer about Hampstead's hills and dales was the great Thackeray, who was often accompanied by some of the family of Mr Crowe, a former editor of the *Daily News*, and father to Eyre Crowe, R.A., and Sir Joseph Archer Crowe. These wanderings seem to have suggested a few of the names bestowed by Thackeray on the characters in his novels, such as "Jack Belsize" and "Lord Highgate," while the title of "Marquess of Steyne" is reminiscent of another Thackerayan haunt—"Dr" Brighton. Hampstead still better knew Dickens, who is mentioned later in these pages. The two writers are often called rivals; yet novels and men were wholly unlike. Each was a peerless genius in his own line, and each adorned any company in which he moved. Yet, while Dickens was the life and soul of every circle, Thackeray—perhaps the only male novelist who could draw a woman absolutely true to life[14]—always struck us as rather silent and self-absorbed, like one who is studying the people around him with a view to their reproduction in as yet unwritten pages. His six feet of height and proportionate breadth, his wealth of grey hair, and the spectacles he was said never to be seen without, made of him a notable figure everywhere. Yet, however outwardly awe-inspiring, he was the kindliest of satirists, the truest of friends, and has been fitly described as "the man who had the heart of a woman."[15] At the Athenæum Club he was often seen writing by the hour together in some quiet corner, evidently unconscious of his surroundings, at times enjoying a voiceless laugh, or again, perhaps when telling of Colonel Newcome's death, with "a moisture upon his cheek which was not dew."

Another literary friend—we had many—was William Henry Wills, also mentioned later: a kind friend to struggling authors, who did not a little to start Miss Mulock on her career as authoress, and who made her known to us. He once told us a curious story about an old uncle with whom as a lad he used to stay in the days before the invasion of the west country by railways with their tendency to modernisation of out-of-the-way places. This ancient man lived in a large ancestral mansion, and literally "dined in hall" with his entire household. There was a sanded floor—formerly, no doubt, rush-strewn—and the family and their "retainers" sat down together at a very long table to the midday repast, the servants taking their place literally "below the salt," which was represented by a large bowl filled with that necessary concomitant. In how many other country houses did this mediæval custom last into the first third of the nineteenth century?[16] Mrs Wills—only sister to the Chambers brothers, William and Robert, who, together with our other publisher friend, Charles Knight, did so much to cheapen the cost and in every way to raise the tone of literature—was, in addition to possessing great charm of manner, an admirable amateur actress, and an unrivalled singer of Scottish songs.

Hampstead, midway in the nineteenth century, was still a picturesque little town, possessed of several stately old houses—one known as Sir Harry Vane's—whose gardens were in some cases entered through tall, wide, iron gates of elaborate design which now would be accounted priceless. It was still the resort of artists, many of whom visited the pleasant house of Edwin Wilkins Field, conspicuous among the public-spirited men who rescued from the builder-fiend the Heath, and made of it a London "lung" and a joy for ever; himself a lawyer, the inspirer of the Limited Liability Act, and an accomplished amateur water-colour painter. His first wife was a niece of Rogers, the banker-poet, famous for his breakfast parties and table talk. At Mr Field's house we came first to know Clarkson Stanfield, R.A., the famous sea-scape painter, and his family, who were musical as well as artistic, and gave delightful parties. It was said that Stanfield was familiar with the build and rig of a ship down to its minutest detail, because he and his lifelong friend and fellow Royal Academician, David Roberts, ran away from school together to sea at a time when life on the ocean wave seemed to most boys the ideal existence. To the last, Stanfield looked like an old sea-dog, and was bluff, hearty and genial. Hampstead still remembers him with pride; and "Stanfield House," wherein the first really good local Free Library was sheltered, is so called because for nearly twenty years it was his dwelling.

At the Fields' house, among other celebrities, artistic, literary and legal, we also met Turner; and it was to "Squire's Mount," and at a crowded evening party there that a characteristic anecdote of this eccentric, gifted painter belongs. The taciturn, gloomy-looking guest had taken an early farewell of host and hostess, and disappeared, only to return some minutes later, wonderfully and fearfully apparelled, and silently commence a search about the drawing-room. Suddenly he seemed to recollect, approached a sofa on which sat three handsomely-attired ladies, whose indignant countenances were a sight for gods and men when the abruptly-mannered artist called on them to rise. He then half dived beneath the seat, drew forth a dreadfully shabby umbrella of the "Gamp" species, and, taking no more notice of the irate three than if they had been so many chairs, withdrew— this time for good. Turner had a hearty contempt for the Claude worship, and was resolved to expose its hollowness. He bequeathed to the nation two of his finest oil paintings on condition that they were placed in the Trafalgar Square Gallery beside two of Claude's which already hung there, and to this day act as foils. A custodian of the Gallery once told me that he was present when Turner visited the room in which were the two Claudes, took a foot-rule from his pocket and measured their frames, doubtless in order that his own should be of like dimensions.

Other artists whom we knew were Mulready, Cooke—as famous for his splendid collection of old Venetian glass as for his pictures—Creswick and Elmore; but much as Rowland Hill loved art, the men of science, such as Airy, the Astronomer Royal; Smyth, the "Astronomical Admiral"; Wheatstone, Lyell; Graham, the Master of the Mint; Sabine, the Herschels, and others were to him the most congenial company. After them were counted in his regard the medical men, philosophers and economists, such as Harley, Coulson, Fergusson, the Clarkes, Sir Henry Thompson—the last to die of his old friends—and Bentham, Robert Owen, James and John Stuart Mill—these last four being among the earliest great men he knew, and counting in some ways as his mentors.

Of his literary friends no two held a higher place in his esteem than Maria Edgeworth and Harriet Martineau. Of the latter and of her able, untiring help in promoting the cause of Penny Postage, mention will appear later. The former, my father, and his brother Arthur, as young men, visited at her Irish home, making the pilgrimage thither which Scott and many other literary adorers had made or were destined to make, one of the most interesting being that of Mrs. Richmond Ritchie, Thackeray's daughter, of which she tells us in her editorial preface to a recent edition of "Castle Rackrent." The two brothers had looked forward to meet a charming woman, but she exceeded their expectations, and the visit remained in the memory of both as a red-letter day.[17]

Among literary men, besides those already mentioned, or to be named later, were Leigh Hunt, De Quincey—who when under the influence of opium did the strangest things, being one day discovered by my father and a friend hiding in some East End slum under the wholly erroneous impression that "enemies" were seeking to molest him—Sir John Bowring, Dr Roget, author of "The Thesaurus," and the Kinglakes. "Eothen," as the writer of that once famous book of travels and of "The Invasion of the Crimea," was habitually called by his friends, was a delightful talker; and his brother, the doctor, was equally gifted, if less fluent, while his sister was declared by Thackeray to be the cleverest woman he ever met.

Dr Roget was a most cultivated man, with the exquisite polish and stately bearing of that now wholly extinct species, the gentlemen of the old school. He was one of the many tourists from England who, happening to be in France after the break-up of the short-lived Peace of Amiens, were detained in that country by Napoleon. Though a foreigner, Dr Roget had lived so long in England, and, as his book proves, knew our language so well, that he could easily have passed for a native of these isles; and thus readily fell a victim to the Corsican's unjustifiable action. Happily for himself, Dr Roget remembered that Napoleon had recently annexed Geneva to France; and he therefore, as a Genevese, protested against his detention on the ground that the annexation had made of him a French subject. The plea was allowed; he returned to England, and finally settled here; but the friend who had accompanied him on the tour, together with the many other *détenus*, remained in France for several years.

Political friends were also numerous, some of whom will be mentioned in later pages. Of others, our most frequent visitors were the brilliant talker Roebuck, once known as "Dog Tear 'Em" of the House of Commons; the two Forsters, father and son, who, in turn and for many years, represented Berwick-upon-Tweed; J. B. Smith (Stockport); and Benjamin Smith (Norwich), at whose house we met some of the arctic explorers of the mid-nineteenth century, congenial friends of a descendant of the discoverer of Smith's Sound, and with whose clever daughters, Madame Bodichon being the eldest, we of the younger generation were intimate. At one time we saw a good deal also of Sir Benjamin Hawes, who, when appointed Under-Secretary to the Colonies in Lord John Russell's Administration of 1846, said to my parents: "Heaven help the Colonies, for I know nothing at all about them!"—an ignorance shared by many other people in those days of seldom distant travel.

My father's legal friends included Denman, Wilde, Mellor, Manning, Brougham, and others; and racy was the talk when some of these gathered round "the mahogany tree," for the extremely small jokes which to-day produce "roars of laughter" in Court were then little in favour, or failed to reach the honour of reproduction in print.

Quite as interesting as any of the other people we mingled with were the foreign political exiles who became honoured guests in many households; and some of these terrible revolutionists were in reality the mildest mannered and most estimable of men. Herr Jansa, the great violinist, was paying a visit to this country in 1849, and out of pure kindness of heart volunteered to play at a concert at Willis's rooms got up for the benefit of the many Hungarian refugees recently landed here. For this "crime" the then young Emperor Francis Joseph caused the old man to be banished; though what was Austria's loss was Britain's gain, as he spent some years among us respected and beloved by all who knew him. We met him oftenest at the house of Sir Joshua Walmsley, where, as Miss Walmsley was an accomplished pianist, very enjoyable musical parties were given. The Hungarian refugees, several of whom were wonderful musicians, were long with us; and some, like Dr Zerffi, remained here altogether. The Italian exiles, Mazzini, Rufini, Gallenga, Panizzi—afterwards Sir Antonio, Principal Librarian at the British Museum, and planner of the Reading Room there— and others came to speak and write English better than many English people. Poerio, Settembrini, and other victims of King "Bomba"—whose sufferings inspired Gladstone to write his famous "Two Letters"—were not here long; Garibaldi was an infrequent bird of passage, as was also Kossuth. Kinkel, the German journalist, a man of fine presence, had been sentenced to lifelong incarceration at Spandau after the Berlin massacre— from which Dr Oswald and his sister with difficulty escaped—but cleverly broke prison and took refuge in England; Louis Blanc, historian and most diminutive of men, made his home for some years among us; and there were many more. Quite a variety of languages was heard in the London drawing-rooms of that time, conversation was anything but commonplace; and what thrillingly interesting days those were!

The story of my father's connection with the London, Brighton, and South Coast Railway, and of that portion of his life which followed his retirement from the Post Office, will be alluded to later in this work.

As it is well not to overburden the narrative with notes, those of mere reference to volume and page of Dr Hill's "Life" of my father are generally omitted from the present story; though if verification of statements made be required, the index to my cousin's book should render the task easy, at least as regards all matter taken from that "Life."

FOOTNOTES:

[1] Another volunteer was a young man named Clark, one of whose sons afterwards married T. W. Hill's elder daughter. An acquaintance of Clark's,

politically a foe, sought to save his friend's house from destruction by writing upon it the shibboleth, "Church and King." But like Millais' Huguenot knight, Clark scorned to shelter himself or property under a false badge, and promptly effaced the kindly-intentioned inscription.

[2] "Remains of T. W. Hill." By M. D. Hill, p. 124.

[3] "Six years have now elapsed," wrote my father in 1823, "since we placed a great part of the government of the school in the hands of the boys themselves; and during the whole of that time the headmaster has never once exercised his right of veto upon their proceedings."

[4] Its full title was "Plans for the Government and Liberal Education of Boys in Large Numbers," and the work speedily went into a second edition.

[5] Algeria was not conquered by France till 1830; and until the beginning of the nineteenth century our shores were still liable to piratical raids. One such (in Norway) is introduced in Miss Martineau's story, "Feats on the Fiords." The pirates, during hundreds of years, periodically swept the European coasts, and carried off people into slavery, penetrating at times even so far north as Iceland. What was the condition of these North African pirate States prior to the French conquest is told by Mr S. L. Poole in "The Barbery Corsairs" ("Story of the Nations" series).

[6] It was a visit paid to Bruce Castle School which caused De Quincey, in that chapter of his "Autobiographic Sketches" entitled "My Brother," to write: "Different, O Rowland Hill, are the laws of thy establishment, for other are the echoes heard amid the ancient halls of Bruce. There it is possible for the timid child to be happy, for the child destined to an early grave to reap his brief harvest in peace. Wherefore were there no such asylums in those days? Man flourished then as now. Wherefore did he not put forth his power upon establishments that might cultivate happiness as well as knowledge." The stories of brutalities inflicted upon weakly boys in some of our large schools of to-day might tempt not a few parents to echo De Quincey's pathetic lament, though perhaps in less archaic language.

[7] It is as follows:—"A straight line is a line in which, if any two points be taken, the part intercepted shall be less than any other line in which these points can be found."

[8] He was an ideal schoolmaster and an enthusiastic Shakespearean, his readings from the bard being much in the same cultured style as those of the late Mr Brandram. Whenever it was bruited about the house that "Uncle Arthur was going 'to do' Shakespeare," there always trooped into the room a crowd of eager nieces, nephews, and others, just as in a larger house members troop in when a favourite orator is "up." At his own request, a monetary testimonial raised by his old pupils to do him honour

was devoted to the purchase of a lifeboat (called by his name) to be stationed at one of our coast resorts.

[9] Colonel Torrens, after whom a river and a lake in South Australia were named, had a distinguished career. For his spirited defence in 1811 of the island of Anholt he was awarded a sword of honour. But he was much more than a soldier, however valorous and able. He was a writer on economics and other important problems of the day; was one of the founders of the Political Economy Club, and of the *Globe* newspaper, then an advocate of somewhat advanced views; and interested himself in several philanthropic movements. His son, Sir Robert Torrens, sometime M.P. for Cambridge, lived for many years in South Australia, and was its first Premier. While there he drew up the plan of "The Transfer of Land by Registration," which became an Act bearing his name, and is one of the measures sometimes cited as proof that the Daughter States are in sundry ways well ahead of their Mother. In consequence of the good work the plan has accomplished in the land of its origin, it has been adopted by other colonies, and is a standard work on the list of Cobden Club publications. Colonel Torrens's eldest granddaughter married Rowland Hill's only son.

[10] The candidates ultimately chosen were the Hon. Charles Pelham Villiers, who represented the constituency for sixty-three years—from January 1835 till his death in January 1898—and Mr Thomas Thornley of Liverpool. Both men, as we shall see, served on that select Committee on Postage which sat to enquire as to the merits of my father's plan of postal reform, and helped to cause its adoption. The two men were long known locally as "Mr Pearson's members." Mr Villiers will be remembered as the man who, for several years in succession, brought in an Annual Motion on behalf of Free Trade, and as being for a longer while, perhaps, than any other Parliamentarian, "the Father of the House"; but the fact is not so well known that he came near to not representing Wolverhampton at all. The election agent who "discovered" him in London described him in a letter to my grandfather (who was chairman of the local Liberal Association) as "a young gentleman named Villiers, a thorough free-trader, of good connexions, and good address." Thus his advent was eagerly looked for. Always given to procrastination, the candidate, however, was so long in making his appearance or communicating with the constituents, that his place was about to be taken by a more energetic person who went so far as to issue his address and begin his canvass. Only just in time for nomination did Mr Villiers drive into Wolverhampton. Whereupon Mr Throckmorton gracefully retired.

[11] He died in July 1838, in the midst of the agitation for the postal reform, in which he took an enthusiastic interest.

[12] Grandfather to Miss Octavia Hill.

[13] His son was one of the Commissioners who aided Prince Albert to inaugurate the Great Exhibition of 1851, and was created a baronet in recognition of his services.

[14] What other man ever depicted a Becky Sharpe, a Beatrix Esmond, a Mrs Bute Crawley, or a Lady Kew—to say nothing of minor characters?

[15] "Thackeray's London." By W. H. Rideing.

[16] Less than half a century before the time described by Mr Wills, the mother of Sir Humphrey Davy left the fact on record that in Penzance, a town of 2,000 inhabitants, there were but one cart, one carpet, no such thing as a silver fork, no merchandise brought to the place save that carried by pack-horses, and every one who travelled went on horseback. On this state of things Palmer's mail coaches had a most rousing effect.

[17] When Miss Edgeworth's father in 1804 wrote the preface to her "Popular Tales," he quoted Burke as saying that in the United Kingdom one person in every hundred could read, and added that he hoped his daughter's works would attract the attention of a good many "thousands." Millions of readers were probably undreamed of. The schoolmaster has made some progress since those days.

CHAPTER I

THE OLD POSTAL SYSTEM

"POSTAGE is one of the worst of our taxes. Few taxes, if any, have so injurious a tendency as the tax upon the communication by letters. I cannot doubt that a taxation upon communication by letters must bear heavily upon commerce; it is, in fact, taxing the conversation of people who live at a distance from each other. The communication of letters by persons living at a distance is the same as a communication by word of mouth between persons living in the same town. You might as well tax words spoken upon the Royal Exchange as the communications of various persons living in Manchester, Liverpool, and London."—Lord ASHBURTON, a conservative peer.

"We build National Galleries, and furnish them with pictures; we propose to create public walks for the air and health and exercise of the community at the general cost of the country. I do not think that either of these, useful and valuable as they are to the community, and fit as they are for Government to sanction, are more conducive to the moral and social advancement of the community than the facility of intercourse by post."—SAMUEL JONES LOYD (Lord OVERSTONE), banker and financier.

"It is commercial suicide to restrict the free transmission of letters."—(Sir) WILLIAM BROWN, a Liverpool merchant.

"We are cut off from our relatives by the high rates of postage."—G. HENSON, a working hosier of Nottingham.

In a short sketch of the postal reform written by my brother,[18] in the year of the late Queen's first jubilee— which was also the jubilee of the publication of our father's "Post Office Reform," the pamphlet that swept away the old system—the following passage from Miss Martineau's "History of the Thirty Years' Peace, 1815-1845" is quoted with excellent effect. From a novel point of view, and in somewhat startling colours, it presents us with a picture of the state of things which, under that old system, existed in our country through four-tenths (less one year) of the nineteenth century, and is therefore within the recollection of people still living.

We look back now, Miss Martineau says,[19] with a sort of amazed compassion to the old crusading days when warrior husbands and their wives, grey-headed parents and their brave sons parted, with the knowledge that it must be months or years before they could hear even of one another's existence. We wonder how they bore the depth of silence, and we feel the same now about the families of polar voyagers;[20] but till the commencement of Her Majesty's reign it did not occur to many of us how like to this was the fate of the largest classes in our own country. The fact is that there was no full and free epistolary intercourse in the country except for those who, like Members of Parliament, had the command of franks. There were few families in the wide middle class who did not feel the cost of postage to be a heavy item in their expenditure; and if the young people sent letters home only once a fortnight, the amount at the year's end was a rather serious matter. But it was the vast multitude of the poorer classes who suffered, like the crusading families of old, and the geographical discoverers of all time. When the young people went out into the world the separation between them and those left behind was almost like that of death. The hundreds of thousands of apprentices, of shopmen, of governesses, of domestic servants, were cut off from family relations as effectually as if seas or deserts divided them (vol. iv. p. 11).

Yet it was not so much the number of miles of severance or the paucity of means of communication that raised walls of oblivion between members of those poorer families which form the large majority of our race; for by 1840—the year when the postal reform was established—communication between even distant places was becoming comparatively easy. Separation was mainly caused by dear postal charges. Fourpence carried a letter 15 miles only; the average rate, even taking into account the many penny letters circulated by the local town-posts—which, it is said, numbered some two hundred, the greater part being very profitable undertakings—was 6-¼d.[21] Mr Brewin of Cirencester, in his evidence before the Parliamentary Committee of 1838 (Third Report), put the case with startling effect when he said: "Sixpence is a third of a poor man's daily income. If a gentleman whose fortune is a thousand a year, or £3 a day, had to pay one-third of his daily income—a sovereign—for a letter, how often would he write letters of friendship?"

But Mr Brewin's illustration, admirable as it is, did not cover the entire case. And, first, it is worth pointing out that the "poor man's daily income" was not only actually smaller, but, generally speaking, it had also smaller purchasing power in the 'thirties than it came to have later in the century when freer trade and lighter taxation prevailed. The real hardship, however, was that too often the man "whose fortune is a thousand a year"—and sometimes much more—was, unlike his poorer brother on 1s. 6d. a day, exempt altogether from postal charges.

For the franking system is a hoary iniquity. It dates back considerably more than two hundred years. To such an extent was the practice, legally or illegally, carried, that, as Mr Joyce, in his "History of the Post Office," tells us: "In Great Britain alone the postage represented by the franked letters, excluding those which were, or which purported to be, 'On His Majesty's Service,' amounted in 1716 to what was, for that time relatively to the total Post Office revenue, the enormous sum of £17,500 a year" (p. 142). By 1838 the number of franked missives was some 7,000,000 a year. Of these, rather less that 5,000,000 were "double" letters, about 2,000,000 eight-fold letters, and some 77,000 thirteen-fold letters, free carriage of which caused a loss to the revenue during the twelvemonths of about £1,065,000.

The franking privilege—which enabled its possessor to write his name outside a letter, thereby rendering it exempt from postal charge—was in vogue long before it received formal recognition by Parliament, and is indeed said to have been given by way of bribe to the Commons what time the Post Office became a Crown monopoly. The first intention was that franking should be enjoyed only by Members during each session; but later it was practised in and out of session. When the measure came before the House, a few Members condemned it as "shabby," "a poor mendicant proviso," etc. But the Bill was passed. The Upper House rejected it. Then the Commons, with a knowledge of human nature creditable to their understanding if to nothing else, inserted a clause providing that the Lords' letters should also be franked; whereupon the Bill became an Act.

The old system worked with great tenderness towards the "haves," and with corresponding harshness towards the "have nots." It enabled some members of the favoured classes to send by post free of charge such things as fifteen couples of hounds, two maid servants, a cow, two bales of stockings, a deal case containing flitches of bacon, a huge feather-bed, and other bulky products, animate and inanimate. "The 'Ambassador's bag,'" said Mr Roebuck one night in the House of Commons, "was often unduly weighted. Coats, lace, boots, and other articles were sent by it; even a pianoforte, and a horse!"[22]

On the other hand, the unfavoured many were heavily taxed for the transmission of missives often smaller, easier of carriage, and lighter of weight; and were so taxed to make up for the immunity enjoyed by the favoured few, since the revenue, at all costs, must be maintained. Thus to Rowland Hill's parents, and to many thousands more, in those days of slender income and heavy taxation, the postman's knock was a sound of dread. The accepted letter might prove to be a worthless circular or other useless sheet, on which the too-trusting recipient had thrown away the money needed for necessary things whose purchase must be deferred.

Incredibly high the postal rates sometimes were. A packet weighing 32 oz. was once sent from Deal to London. The postage was over £6, being, as Rowland Hill's informant remarked, four times as much as the charge for an inside place by the coach.[23] Again, a parcel of official papers, small enough to slip inside an ordinary pocket, was sent from Dublin to another Irish town addressed to Sir John Burgogne. By mistake it was charged as a letter instead of as a parcel, and cost £11! For that amount the whole mail-coach plying between the two towns, with places for seven passengers and their luggage, might have been hired. Extreme cases these perhaps, but that they could and did happen argued something rotten in the state of—the old system.

The peers of the realm and the Members of Parliament could not only frank their own letters, but those also of their friends, who, perhaps, in nine cases out of ten could well afford to do without such help. The number of franks which privileged people could write was limited by law,[24] but was frequently exceeded if a donor hated to say "No," or found that compliance with requests enhanced his popularity, or was to his advantage. Members of Parliament sometimes signed franks by the packet, and gave them to constituents and friends. It was an easy, inexpensive way of making a present, or of practising a little bribery and corruption. The chief offenders were said to be the banker Members, who, in one day (of 1794), sent 103,000 franked letters through the London Post Office alone. No wonder a "banker's frank" came to be a byword. Franks were also sometimes given to servants instead of, or to eke out, their wages; and the servants, being then as a rule illiterate, sold the franks again.

Forgery of franks was extensively practised, since to imitate a man's writing is not difficult. Mr Joyce tells us that, under the old system, the proportion of counterfeit to genuine franks varied from half to three-quarters of the entire number. Why forgery should be resorted to is easy to understand. The *un*privileged nursed a natural grudge against the privileged, and saw no harm in occasionally enjoying a like immunity from postal charges. Prosecutions availed little as deterrents. Even the fate of the Rev. Dr Dodd, hanged at Tyburn in 1771 for the offence, could not check the practice.

The strictness of the rules against forging the frank on a letter, so long a capital offence, contrasted strangely with the extraordinary laxity of those relating to the franking of newspapers. To pass freely through the post, a newspaper, like a letter, had to be franked by a peer or a Member of Parliament. But no pretence was ever made that the signatures were genuine; and not only was anybody at liberty to write the name of peer or Member, but the publishers themselves were accustomed to issue the newspapers with their customer's name and address, and the franking signature already *printed* on each cover! Indeed, were this useless form to be disregarded, the paper was counted as an unpaid letter, and became liable to a charge of perhaps several shillings.

The cost of conveying newspapers by post was practically covered by the duty stamp. Yet "No newspaper could be posted in any provincial town for delivery within the same, nor anywhere within the London District (a circle of 12 miles radius from the General Post Office) for delivery within the same circle, unless a postage of 1d., in addition to the impressed newspaper stamp, were paid upon it—a regulation which, however, was constantly evaded by large numbers of newspapers intended for delivery in London being sent by newsagents down the river to be posted at Gravesend, the Post Office then having the trouble of bringing them back, and of delivering them without charge."[25]

The newspaper duty at its lowest charge was 1d., and at its highest 4d., and varied with the varying burden of taxation. Thus during the long period of George III.'s almost incessant wars it rose from the lower to the higher figure. Before a word could be printed on any newspaper the blank sheet had to be taken to the Stamp Office to receive the impress of the duty stamp, and therefore prepayment of newspaper postage was secured. It may be that when the stamp duty rose to 3d. and 4d., the official conscience was satisfied that sufficient payment had been made; and thus the franking signature became an unnecessary survival, a mere process of lily-painting and refined gold-gilding, which at some future time might be quietly got rid of. If so, the reason becomes evident why the forgery of franks on newspapers was viewed with leniency, the authorities having, by means of the stamp, secured their "pound of flesh." But no duty stamp was ever impressed on letters which were treated altogether differently, prepayment in their case being, if not actually out of the question, so rare as to be practically non-existent.

The duty on newspapers was an odious "tax on knowledge," and rendered a cheap Press impossible. Only the well-to-do could indulge in the luxury of a daily paper; and recollection of childish days brings back a vision of the sheet passing through a succession of households till its contents had become "ancient history," and it ended its existence in tatters. The repeal of the stamp duty and of that other "tax unwise," the paper duty, changed all this, and gave rise to the penny and halfpenny Press of modern times and the cheap and good books that are now within the reach of all. The fact is worth recording that yet another—perhaps more than one other—article of daily use did duty in a plurality of households during those far-off days of general dearness. This was tea, then so costly that it was a common practice for poor people to call at the houses of the well-to-do, and ask for the used leaves, though not to cleanse carpets and glassware as we do at the present day, but to infuse afresh.

The making of exemptions is a huge mistake; and, according to the cynic, a mistake is more reprehensible than a crime. Exemptions create discontent, and justly so. Peel, inimical as he was to the postal reform, was well aware of the evils of the franking system, and said that "were each Government Department required to pay its own postage, much would be done towards checking the abuse."[26]

It was Rowland Hill's wish that franking should be totally abolished. But vested interests—that worst bar to all social progress—proved stronger than the reformer; and his plan, in that and some other details, was not carried out in its entirety. Franking was enormously curtailed, but it was a scotching rather than a killing process; and after his retirement the evil thing slowly but steadily increased. Nor does the tendency at the present day give sign of abatement.

Yours very affectionately Rowland Hill
From a Photograph by the London Stereoscopic Co.

As some of that increasingly large portion of the public which knows nothing of the old postal system are under the erroneous impression that others than Rowland Hill suggested the use of postage stamps for letters, it is well to point out that the employment of such stamps before 1840, so far from cheapening or rendering easier the payment of postal charges, must have made them considerably dearer, and have yet further complicated the process of letter-"taxing."[27]

Postage stamps, like railway tickets, are mere tokens of prepayment, and, however mentally hazy on the subject of the origin of postage stamps some of us may be, we can all easily understand how absurd, indeed impossible, introduction of the tickets would have been in the dark ages before railway trains began to run. Equally impossible would have been the employment, or even the suggestion, of stamps when letters were posted unpaid. Under the old system the letters of the unprivileged classes were rated, primarily, according to the distance travelled, though not necessarily the distance actually separating writer and recipient, because, although before 1840 railways existed, no close network of lines covered our land, providing, as it does to-day, direct and plentiful means of inter-communication; and therefore the Post Office, to suit its own convenience, often obliged some of its mail matter to perform very circuitous routes, thereby not only retarding delivery, but rendering still greater the already great variability of rates. "Thus, for example, letters from Loughton to Epping (places only 2 or 3 miles apart) were carried into London and out again, and charged a postage of 7d.—that being the rate under the old system for letters between post towns ranging from 30 to 50 miles apart."[128] That this circumambulatory practice was responsible for waste of time as well as increase of cost is shown by the fact that of two letters, the one addressed to Highgate, and the other to Wolverhampton (120 miles further along the same coach road), and both posted in London at the same hour, the Highgate letter would be delivered last. As regards cost, an anomaly quite as absurd as the two foregoing existed in the case of letters between Wolverhampton and Brierley Hill which were carried by a cross-post passing through Dudley. If a letter went the whole way, the postage was 1d.; but if it stopped short at Dudley, 4d. was charged. Of the letters which performed circuitous routes, Scott, in the fortieth chapter of "Guy Mannering," humorously remarks that, "There was a custom, not yet wholly obsolete, of causing a letter from one town to another, perhaps within the distance of 30 miles, to perform a circuit of 200 miles before delivery; which had the combined advantage of airing the epistle thoroughly, of adding some pence to the revenue of the Post Office, and of exercising the patience of the correspondents."

The question of charge was still further complicated, because, secondarily, there existed "single," "double," "treble," and yet heavier rates of postage; as when the treble rate was passed, further increase was reckoned by weight, the charge being quadrupled when the letter weighed an ounce, rising afterwards by a "single" postage for every additional quarter ounce. It was as well, perhaps, that the people who lived before the 'forties did not lead the feverish life of to-day. Otherwise, how would the post officials, to say nothing of the public, have remembered these positively bewildering details?

A "single" letter had to be written on a single sheet of paper, whose use probably gave rise to the practice of that now obsolete "cross" writing which often made an epistle all but illegible, but to which in those days of dear postage recourse was unavoidable when much matter had to be crammed into the limited compass of that single sheet. If a second sheet, or even the smallest piece of paper, were added to the first, the postage was doubled. The effect of fastening an adhesive stamp on to a single letter would therefore have been to subject the missive to a double charge; while to have affixed a stamp to an envelope containing a letter would have trebled the postage. In other words, a man living, say, 400 miles from his correspondent, would have to pay something like 4s. for the privilege of receiving from him a single sheet of paper carried in a wholly unnecessary cover bearing an equally unnecessary, because entirely useless, adornment in the shape of an adhesive stamp. For obvious reasons, therefore neither "the little bags called envelopes," as in his pamphlet Rowland Hill quaintly described these novel adjuncts, nor the stamps, were, or could be, in use.[29]

One veracious anecdote will suffice to show what came of evasion, wilful or unintentional, of a hard and fast postal rule. A letter was once sent from London to Wolverhampton, containing an enclosure to which a small piece of paper had been fastened. The process called "candling" showed that the letter consisted of three parts; and the single postage being 10d., a charge was made of 2s. 6d.[30]

It will thus be seen that in reckoning the postage on a letter, distance, the number of enclosures (if any), and, finally, weight had to be taken into consideration. Nor should it be forgotten that of single inland letters the variations of charge amounted to over forty. Under so complicated a system, it was, save in very exceptional circumstances, far easier to collect the postage at the end of the letter's journey than at its beginning; and, in the absence of prepayment, of what possible use could stamps have been, or what man in his senses would have proposed them?[31] Had later-day ignorance of the actual state of things under the old postal system been less widespread than it is, any claim to authorship of postage stamps before reform of that system was attempted or achieved would, for lack of the credulous element among the public, scarcely have been hazarded.

The "candling" of letters was practised to ascertain whether single, double, treble, or still heavier postage should be charged. The missive was carried into a darkened room, and held up against a strong artificial light. This process not only gave the examining official some idea of the number of enclosures, if any, but often revealed their character. It was to defeat temptation to dishonesty caused by this scrutiny that the practice, not yet obsolete, was adopted of cutting a banknote in two before posting it, and keeping back the second half till receipt of the first had been acknowledged.

Single letter postage between London and Edinburgh or Glasgow cost 1s. 3-½d., between London and Aberdeen 1s. 4-½d., and between London and Thurso 1s. 5-½d., the odd halfpenny being the duty exacted in protectionist days to enable the epistle to cross the Scottish border. A letter to Ireland *via* Holyhead paid, in addition to ordinary postage, steamer rates and toll for using the Menai and Conway bridges. Or, if a letter took the southerly route to Ireland, the extra charge was levied at Milford. Single letter postage to Londonderry was 1s. 5d. To the many other more distant Irish towns it was still heavier.

These single charges—enforced, too, at a time when the nation, wearied out with many years of almost incessant war, was poorer far than it is now—seem to us exorbitant. When, therefore, we think of them as doubled, trebled, quadrupled, and so forth, it is easy to understand why to all but the rich letter-writing became an almost lost art; and we realise more clearly the truth of Miss Martineau's word-picture which a superficial reader might be inclined to pronounce overdrawn.

The rates had been oppressive enough in 1801 when, in order to swell the war-tax, a further contribution to the Exchequer of £150,000 was enforced. But in 1812 a yet further contribution of £200,000 was required; and these higher rates—the highest ever reached—were maintained for a quarter of a century after the peace of 1815: that is, till Rowland Hill's reform swept the old system away.

In order to increase the postal revenue, the screw had been tightened in a variety of ways, even to the arresting of further progress in Ralph Allen's much-needed "cross-posts" reform.[132] As Mr Joyce puts it: "In 1695 a circuitous post would be converted into a direct one, even though the shorter distance carried less postage; in 1813 a direct post in place of a circuitous one was constantly being refused on the plea that a loss of postage would result."[133] In the latter year all sorts of oppressive and even bewildering new regulations were enforced whose tendency was to make of the Post Office a yet harsher tax-raising machine. One new charge was of "an additional penny on each letter for the privilege of the mail-coach passing through"[134] certain towns; and other rules were equally vexatious.

The lowest single postage to Paris was 1s. 8d.; and in the case of foreign letters partial prepayment was the rule. For instance, when a letter travelled from London to Paris, the writer paid 10d., which freed it as far as Calais only, its recipient paying the other 10d. on its delivery in the French capital. Collection of postage at the end of the entire journey would have been contrary to regulation.

The lowest single postage to Gibraltar was 2s. 10d.; and to Egypt, 3s. 2d. When a letter crossed the Atlantic to Canada or the United States an inland rate at each end of the transit was charged in addition to the heavy ocean postage. A packet of manuscript to either of those countries cost £5 under the old system. But at this "reduced" (!) rate only a 3-lb. packet could be sent. Did one weigh the merest fraction of a pound over the permitted three, it could not go except as a letter, the postage upon which would have been £22, 0s. 8d.[135] One can hardly expect the public of to-day to believe that rates such as these were ever in force. They sufficiently explain why it was that the ill-to-do relatives of equally ill-to-do people who emigrated to the Colonies or foreign countries often lost all trace of them.

In the *Morning Chronicle* of 22nd August 1837, appeared an announcement that, "Henceforth postage on letters to the Mediterranean will be at the rate of only 10s. an ounce"—showing that even as regards countries nearer home than America postal charges rendered letter-writing an expensive occupation even to the well-to-do if they had a large foreign correspondence. To-day "a letter can be sent from London westward to San Francisco or eastward to Constantinople or Siberia for a less amount of postage than was charged in 1836 on one going from Charing Cross to Brompton."[36] And in the future the cost is likely to become less.

The old postal rates being so burdensome, it was inevitable that tricks and evasions of many sorts should be practised, notwithstanding the merciless penalties that were inflicted on delinquents detected in the act.

It is probably no exaggeration to say that hundreds, if not thousands, of newspapers were annually posted which no one particularly cared to read. Yet it is certain that many a recipient eagerly welcomed the paper sent him even though he might rarely unfold its pages. As newspapers went free—or nominally did so, for after all the postage was indirectly taken out of the pocket of the man who invested 5d. in every copy of his "daily"—and letters, except those which passed between members of the privileged classes, did not, the newspaper came to be a frequent bearer of well-disguised messages from one member of the unprivileged classes to another. The employment of inks of different colours, of variations in modes of writing names, callings, and addresses, and even peculiar flourishes executed by the pen, conveyed valuable information to him who received the paper, and enabled many tradesmen to keep up a brisk correspondence without contributing a farthing to the revenue.

How, for example, should the uninitiated postal authorities know that the innocent-looking superscription on a newspaper sent from London to "Mr John Smith, Grocer, Tea-dealer, etc, No. 1 High Street Edinburgh," conveyed to Mr Smith the assurance that on Tuesday the price of sugar was falling, and that the remittances he had sent in discharge of his indebtedness had been received? Yet so it was, for however fictitious the name and address, the case is genuine, the conspiring pair of correspondents having come forward during the agitation for penny postage as voluntary witnesses to the necessity for the reform, their evidence being the revelation of their fraud made on condition that they should be held exempt from prosecution. There were six different modes of writing Mr Smith's name, one for each working day of the week; and the wording of his trade varied still oftener, and served to give him the latest news of the market. If Mr

Smith's fellow-tradesman (and fellow-conspirator) in London wrote the address immediately after the name, omitting all mention of Mr Smith's calling, the latter knew that the goods he had sent had reached their destination. Variations rung upon the locality name, such as High Street (without the number), High St., 1 High Street, 1 High St., No. 1 High Street, or No. 1 High St., related to pecuniary matters. For while we have seen how satisfactory was the news conveyed in "No. 1 High Street," "High St.," on the contrary, told Mr Smith that the bills he sent had been dishonoured.

But Mr Smith and colleague were by no means the only correspondents who deliberately plotted to defraud the revenue; for, under the old system, it seemed to be each person's aim to extract the cost of postage on his own letters out of the pocket of some other person. In this achievement, however, there can be little doubt that, as a rule, the well-to-do made the most successful score.

The story told by Mr Bertram in "Some Memories of Books" about the apprentice to a printing firm is another instance of evasion. The young man was frequently in want of clothing, and made known his need to those at home with as little outlay as though he had been a member of Parliament or peer of the realm. He printed small slips of paper bearing such legends as "want trousers," "send new coat," etc., pasted them into newspapers, and sent these to his parents.

At the present day indulgence in a practice of this sort would seem contemptible, a fraud to which only the meanest of mankind would resort. But had we too lived when postage was charged on a fourth part only of the entire mail, and when the writers of the letters forming that fourth part, and we among them, were taxed to make up the loss on the franked three-quarters, perhaps even we, immaculate as we believe ourselves to be, might have been tempted to put our scruples into our pocket to keep company with our slender purse, and have taken to "ways that are dark," though, if less astute than Mr John Smith and his London correspondent, possibly also to "tricks that are vain"—with unpleasant consequences to ourselves.

There is an oft-quoted story about Coleridge, who, one day while wandering through the Lake District, saw a poor woman refuse a letter which the postman offered her. The kindly poet, in spite of the woman's evident reluctance to accept the gift, paid the money she could not raise; but when the letter was opened, it was seen to be a blank sheet of paper not intended for acceptance, but sent by her son according to preconcerted agreement as a sign that he was well.[37] This, then, is not only yet another illustration of the frauds to which the "have nots" were driven to resort, but, further, shows how profitless, even costly, was the labour imposed upon the Post Office by the system to which the authorities clung with so unaccountable an affection. For an unaccepted sheet of paper does not travel from London to the Lake District for nothing; and when we multiply one unaccepted letter by many thousands, one may form some idea of the amount of fruitless trouble as well as fruitless outlay which was incurred by the Department.

The enforced silence between severed relations and friends was therefore rendered yet more painful when the letters—genuine letters too, not dummies—got as far as the post office nearest to their intended destination, or even to the door of the poor dwellings to which they were addressed, yet failed to cross the threshold because their should-be recipients were too poverty-stricken to "take them up." In many instances mothers yearning to hear from absent children would pawn clothing or household necessaries rather than be deprived of the letters which, but for that sacrifice, must be carried back to the nearest post office to await payment. One poor woman, after striving for several weeks to make up the money to redeem a longed-for letter from her granddaughter in London, went at last to the local office with the shilling which a pitying lady gave her, only to find that the letter had been returned to town. She never received it. Another poor woman begged a local postmaster's daughter to accept a spoon by way of pledge till the ninepence charged upon a letter awaiting payment at the office could be raised. A labouring man declined an eightpenny letter though it came from a far-off daughter because the price meant one loaf the less for his other children. It was much harder for the poorest classes to find pence enough to lavish on postage in those yet earlier and often hungrier nineteenth century decades than even the "Hungry Forties"; during which years a man had sometimes to spend more than eightpence—more occasionally than double that sum—on his children's loaf.

The refused missives, after waiting a while at the local office for the chance of redemption, went back to the chief office, were consigned to the "dead" department, and were there destroyed, thus costing the Service—meaning, of course, the public—the useless double journey and the wasted labour of not a few officials.

Sometimes a kind-hearted postmaster would advance the sum due for a letter out of his own pocket, taking his chance of being repaid. But not every postmaster could afford to take such risks, nor was it desirable that they should be laid upon the wrong shoulders.

In 1837 the Finance Account showed a profitless expenditure of £122,000 for letters "refused, mis-sent, re-directed, and so forth." This loss of revenue was, of course, quite distinct from that already mentioned as caused by the use of franks fictitious and genuine. Truly, the unprivileged paid somewhat dearly for the advantages enjoyed by the privileged, since it lay with the former both to make good the loss and to provide the required profit.

Under the old system the postman would often be detained, sometimes as much as five minutes, at each house at which he called while he handed in his letters, and received the money due upon them. In business quarters this sort of thing had long been found intolerable, and therefore, by private arrangement with the merchants, the postman, on the first, and by far the heaviest, delivery of the day, did not wait for his money. But after the second delivery he had to call at every house where he had left letters earlier in the day and collect the postage: a process which often made the second delivery lengthy and wearisome. A test case showed that while it took a man an hour and a half to deliver 67 letters for which he waited to receive payment, half an hour sufficed for the delivery of 570 letters for which he did not wait to be paid.[38]

Another evil of the old system was the temptation to fraud which it put in the way of the letter-carriers. When a weak or unscrupulous man found a supply of loose cash in his pocket at the end of his delivery, his fingers would itch—and not always in vain—to keep it there. Again, an honest man, on his way back to the office with the proceeds of his round upon him, was not safe from attack if his road was lonely or the streets ill-lighted or deserted. The old foot and horse posts were often robbed. Murders even, Mr Joyce reminds us, were not infrequent, and executions failed to check them.

The system of account-keeping was "an exceedingly tedious, inconvenient, and, consequently, expensive process."[39] The money which the recipient of a letter paid to the postman passed to the local postmaster, who sent it on to the head office. It went through many hands, and peculation was rife. "The deputy postmasters could not be held to effectual responsibility as regards the amounts due from them to the General Office; and as many instances of deficit came at times to light, sometimes following each other week after week in the same office, there can be no doubt that the total annual loss must have reached a serious amount."[40]

On the arrival of the mails at the General Post Office, the clerks were required to see that the charge entered upon every letter had been correctly made, and that each deputy postmaster had debited himself with the correct amount of postage; to stamp the letters—that is, to impress on them the date when they were posted; to assort them for delivery, in which work the letter-carriers assisted; to ascertain the amount of postage to be collected by each letter-carrier, and to charge him therewith. In addition to all this, another detail must not be forgotten—that in the London Office alone there were daily many thousands of letters which had to undergo the "candling" process.

For the outgoing mails the duties were somewhat similar, and quite as complicated, and some seven hundred accounts had to be made out against as many deputy postmasters.

Simplification of account-keeping under the old system, however much needed, seemed hopeless of attainment.

Even in England, the most prosperous "partner" of the United Kingdom, there were at the time of the late Queen's accession, districts larger than Middlesex, within whose borders the postman never set foot. Of the 2,100 Registrar's districts into which England and Wales were divided, 400 districts, each containing on the average about 20 square miles and some 4,000 inhabitants—making in all a population of about a million and a half—had no post office whatever. The chief places in these districts, containing about 1,400 inhabitants each, were on the average some 5 miles, and in several instances as much as 16 miles, from the nearest post office.[41]

The 50,000 Irish, or immediate descendants of Irish in Manchester, said Cobden in his evidence before the Parliamentary Committee of 1838, were almost as completely cut off from communication with their relatives in Ireland as though they were in New South Wales.[42] And when he drew this comparison, it counted for much more than it would do to-day. Great Britain and Australia were then practically much further asunder than they are now, sailing vessels at that time taking from four to six months to do the single, and sometimes nearly twelve the double voyage. A good many years had yet to elapse before the Indian Ocean was bridged by the fast steamships which have reduced that several months' journey to one of a few weeks only.

The great free-trader's calico printing works were situated at a little town or village, of some 1,200 inhabitants, called Sabden, 28 miles from Manchester. Although a manufacturing centre, it had no post office, and nothing that did duty for one.

In the opening paragraph of the twenty-seventh chapter of "The Heart of Midlothian," Scott says that in 1737 "So slight and infrequent was the intercourse betwixt London and Edinburgh, that upon one occasion the mail from the former city arrived at the General Post Office in Scotland with only one letter in it. The fact is certain. The single epistle was addressed to the principal director of the British Linen Company."

In "Her Majesty's Mails" Mr Lewins says that: "About the same time the Edinburgh mail is said to have arrived in London containing but one letter addressed to Sir William Pulteney, the banker" (p. 85).

The old system being at once clumsy, irrational, irritating, and unjust, little wonder need be felt that when Queen Victoria's reign began, each inhabitant of England and Wales received on an average one letter in three months, of Scotland one in four months, and of Ireland one a year.[43]

Until 1748 there were but three posts a week between London and Birmingham. In that year the number was doubled. The notice making known this improvement contains denunciations of the people who were in "any way concerned in the illegal collecting or delivery of Letters or Packets of Letters." The fines for the offence were "£5 for every letter, and £100 for every week this practice is continued." But fines could not arrest the smuggling, because the practice was remunerative to the smugglers, and popular among those who employed them, and who thus enjoyed cheap rates of postage. Therefore the illegal traffic went on growing, till by the time the old system came to an end it had assumed vast proportions.

Publishers and other business men wrote letters on one large sheet of paper for different people living in the same district. On reaching its destination the sheet was divided into its separate parts, each of which being then delivered by hand or local post. A similar practice in respect of money payments prevailed.[44] One publisher and bookseller said he was "not caught" till he had thus distributed some 20,000 letters. Several carriers made the collection and distribution of letters their only business, and in the collecting process women and children were employed. In one district the illegal practice was more than fifty years old, and in at least another, as we see by the notice quoted in the preceding paragraph, its age must have exceeded a century. In one then small town the daily average of smuggled letters amounted to more than 50, and on one occasion rose above 150. The Mr Brewin of Cirencester already mentioned said he knew two carriers who conveyed four times as many letters as did the mail.[45] One carrier confessed to having smuggled about 60 letters a day. On another carrier's premises a bag was seized containing 1,100 letters. Twelve walking carriers between Birmingham and Walsall were employed exclusively in conveying letters at a charge of a penny apiece. Five Glasgow merchants illegally transmitted letters at the rate severally of three, eighteen, sixteen, eight, and fifteen to one that went legally. Five-sixths of the Manchester letters contributed nothing whatever to the postal revenue.[46] Nor does the list of delinquencies end here.

Letters were also smuggled in warehousemen's bales and parcels; among manufacturers' patterns and other things which coach proprietors, on payment of a trifle for booking, carried free of charge; in weavers' bags, in farmers' "family boxes," and in other ways.[1]

Even the mail-coach drivers and guards engaged in the unlawful traffic, though in many instances letters were sent in coach parcels not so much to save postage as to facilitate transmission and ensure early delivery.

Mr Maury, of the American Chamber of Commerce, assured the Select Committee that when regular steam communication between Liverpool and New York was established, the first steamer carried *five* letters in the large bag provided in expectation of a heavy dispatch. Ten thousand letters were, however, placed in another bag sent to the care of the consignee of the same vessel; and Mr Maury himself contributed some 200 free letters to this second bag. Every ten days a steamer left this country for America each carrying some 4,000 smuggled letters—a fact of which the postal authorities were well aware; and almost every shipbroker hung a bag in his office for the convenience of those who sent letters otherwise than through the post. Letters so collected by one broker for different ships in which he was interested were said to be sometimes "enough to load a cab." In 111 packages containing 822 newspapers sent in the course of five months to America, 648 letters were found concealed. The postmaster of Margate reported that in the visitors' season the increase of population there made no proportionate increase of postage, a fact which he attributed to the illegal conveyance of letters by steamers. The growing facilities for travel caused a corresponding growth of letter-smuggling. At the same time, the more general establishment of local penny posts tended to secure to the Post Office the conveyance of letters between neighbouring towns and villages;[47] and undoubtedly did much to recoup that extensively swindled Department for its loss of revenue caused by franking, evasions like those of Mr John Smith and others, and letter-smuggling.

As usual, the people who practised the deception were scarcely so much to blame as those who, spite of every effort at reform, persisted in maintaining a system which created favouritism, hampered trade, severed family ties, and practically created the smuggling offence which scandalised the official conscience. Had the rates been less exorbitant, and had they fallen impartially on rich and poor, these dishonest practices might have had little or no existence. They ceased only when at last the old order changed, and, happily, gave place to new.

FOOTNOTES:

[18] "The Post Office of Fifty Years Ago." By Pearson Hill. Cassell & Co. (1887).

[19] As the passage is slightly condensed, quotation marks are not employed. The words generally—whole sentences sometimes—are, however, Miss Martineau's own.

[20] Written while yet the fate of the Franklin Expedition was an unsolved mystery.

[21] The two sorts of post were kept quite distinct, the business of the general post and that of the local posts being carried on in separate buildings and by different staffs. It was not till the postal reform had been established some years that Rowland Hill was able to persuade the authorities of the wisdom of that amalgamation of the two which formed an important feature of his plan.

[22] "Hansard," cxlvi. 189.

[23] Travelling as well as postage has cheapened. A fourth part of £6 is 30s.—the price of each "inside place." To-day a first-class railway *return* ticket between Deal and London costs less than half 30s.

[24] Fourteen franks a day was the number each M.P. could issue.

[25] "The Post Office of Fifty Years Ago," p. 6.

[26] "Life," i. 135. Peel voted against the Penny Postage Bill; and even that kindly friend to the poorer classes, the "good" Lord Shaftesbury—then Lord Ashley—followed Sir Robert's example.

[27] That is, of calculating the amount of postage to be levied on each letter.

[28] "The Origin of Postage Stamps," p. 17. By Pearson Hill.

[29] A recent discussion in *Notes and Queries* (Tenth Series, vol. i.) has shown that envelopes are mentioned by Swift and later writers of the eighteenth and early nineteenth centuries. They are sometimes called "envelopes" and sometimes "covers." Their use must have been exceedingly limited, and still more limited, perhaps, is the number of people who have actually seen them. They were probably square sheets of paper used to enclose a number of missives addressed to one person or several persons living in the same neighbourhood; and were, most likely, better known to the race of letter smugglers (about whom see further) than to any one else. An obituary notice in the *Liverpool Daily Post and Mercury* of 23rd May, 1906, on the late

Mr J. D. Tyson, "a notable Liverpool insurance broker," shows how new the use of envelopes as we now understand them was more than half a century ago. The writer says: "Even the introduction of the envelope was greatly opposed by most of the old firms; and for fear the envelope would be thrown away and all traces of posting be lost, the juniors were instructed to pin the envelope to the letter. This had soon to give way when the usefulness of the envelope became so pronounced."

[30] The neat and rapid folding of the large sheets of paper on which single letters were written was regarded as one of the fine arts; and lessons in it were sometimes given to boys at school. I have a distinct recollection of seeing a number of people seated round a table and practising letter-folding, and of my begging to be allowed to join the circle and try my diminutive 'prentice hand at the game. A dignified and elaborate process was the sealing of the folded letter, impressing much the juniors of the family, who looked on admiringly, while the head thereof performed the ceremony, the only drawback being the odious smell of the unnecessarily large, old-fashioned "lucifer" match employed to light the candle. When one of the seals hanging to the broad silken strap showing below the paternal or grand-paternal waistcoat was pressed upon the bountifully spread, hot wax till a perfect impression was left, the letter thus completed would be held up for all to see. What would those stately, leisurely-mannered gentlemen of the olden time, who, perhaps, took five or more minutes over the fastening of a letter, have said to our present style of doing things—especially to the far from elegant mode of moistening the gummed envelope flap which has superseded the cleanly spreading of the scented wax and application of the handsome seal of armorial bearings carved on a precious stone and set in a golden shield?

[31] According to an extract taken from the "New Annual Directory for 1800," in the Guildhall Library, prepayment might be made in the case of the local "penny" (afterwards "twopenny") post. That this fact should need an advertisement seems to argue that, even as regards the local posts, prepayment was not a common practice.

[32] This was he who did "good by stealth, and blush[ed] to find it fame." Out of his contract with the Post Office he made the large income, for that time, of £12,000 a year, and spent the greater part of it in those acts of beneficence which, aided by Pope's famous lines, have preserved for him well-deserved, lasting fame.

[33] "History of the Post Office," p. 357.

[34] "History of the Post Office," p. 357.

[35] "The Post Office of Fifty Years Ago," p. 13.

[36] "The Jubilee of the Uniform Penny Postage," p. 22. By Pearson Hill.

[37] "Letters, Conversations, and Recollections of S. T. Coleridge," ii. 114. In different versions of the story the absent relative is described as father, husband, or brother; and in not a few cases the hero's action, through a mistake made by Miss Martineau when writing the History already alluded to, has been claimed for Rowland Hill, who is further supposed—quite erroneously—to have been then and there inspired with the resolve to undertake postal reformation.

[38] "Eighteenth Report of the Commissioners of Revenue Inquiry," pp. 621, 622. Now, if 570 letters, payment for which had not to be waited for, could be delivered in half an hour, it follows that in the hour and half consumed in delivering those 67 other letters, three times 570, or 1710, *prepaid* letters might have been distributed. This one small fact alone furnishes proof of the necessity for prepayment, for this test delivery was made in the heart of the city of London, where prompt delivery and common-sense postal regulations are of paramount importance to business men.

[39] "Post Office Reform," p. 29.

[40] "Post Office Reform," p. 29.

[41] "The Post Office of Fifty Years Ago," p. 12.

[42] "Third Report of the Select Committee on Postage," p. 22.

[43] "The Post Office of Fifty Years Ago," p. 14.

[44] "Third Report of the Select Committee on Postage," p. 12.

[45] *Ibid.* pp. 13, 14.

[46] "Third Report of the Select Committee on Postage," pp. 13, 14.

[47] "Third Report of the Select Committee on Postage," pp. 15-30.

CHAPTER II

SOME EARLY POSTAL REFORMERS

In Mr Joyce's already quoted and exhaustive work upon the Post Office as it existed before 1840 an interesting account is given of the reformers who, long before Rowland Hill's time, did so much to render the service efficient, and therefore to benefit the nation. As pioneers in a good cause, they deserve mention in another volume dealing with the same public Department; and their story is perhaps the better worth repeating because it shows how curiously similar is the treatment meted out to those who are rash enough to meddle with a long-established monopoly, no matter how greatly it may stand in need of reform. In every instance the reformer struggled hard for recognition of the soundness of his views, toiled manfully when once he had acquired the position he deserved to hold, was more or less thwarted and harassed while he filled it, and, precisely as if he had been a mischievous innovator instead of a public benefactor, was eventually got rid of.

As regards the Post Office, each of the best-known reformers was handicapped by the fact that, with one notable exception, he was that unwelcome thing, an outsider. Murray was an upholsterer, or, according to another account, a clerk in the Assize Office; Dockwra was a sub-searcher at the Custom House; and Palmer was the proprietor of the Bath theatre. My father, as has been shown, had been a schoolmaster, a rotatory printing press inventor, and a member of the South Australian Commission. Even when his plan was accepted by the Government, he had yet to set foot within the Post Office, though not for want of trying to enter, because while collecting material for his pamphlet in 1836 he had applied to the authorities for permission to inspect the working of the Department, only to meet with a refusal.

The one notable exception was Ralph Allen, Pope's "humble Allen," and, as mentioned in the previous chapter, the author of the cross-posts. The original of Fielding's "Squire Allworthy" had, Mr Joyce tells us, "been cradled and nursed in the Post Office," and his grandmother was postmistress at St Columb, Cornwall. Here he kept the official accounts in so neat and regular a manner that he attracted the attention of the district surveyor, and, later, was given a situation in the Bath Post Office, eventually becoming its chief official.[48]

Mr Joyce's narrative, as we have seen, is brought down only to the end of the old postal system. To that which superseded it he makes but brief allusion, because the subject had already been dealt with in the two volumes edited and added to by Dr Birkbeck Hill.

In the present work the story will be carried less than thirty years beyond the time at which Mr Joyce's narrative ends—that is, so far as postal reform is concerned. The later history of the Post Office, which would easily make a volume as large as Mr Joyce's, has yet to find an author, and to rank worthily beside his should be written with a corresponding care and accuracy of detail.

One chapter only need be devoted here to the most prominent early postal reformers, and their story shall begin with Witherings (1635). Speaking of his work, Mr Joyce says, "This was the introduction of postage."[49] To Witherings, therefore, must be awarded the merit of having furnished cause for a new meaning of the word "post," whose earlier usage still survives in some provincial hotel notices announcing "posting in all its branches."[50]

In Witherings' time the postal rates were, for single letters, "under 80 miles, 2d.; under 140 miles, 4d.; over 140 miles, 6d.—for until 1840 the charges were calculated according to distance. For double letters double rates were, of course, exacted. If "bigger" than double, the postage became 6d., 9d. and 1s. Single postage to and from Scotland was 8d., to and from Ireland 9d. These were heavy rates at a time when the country was far less wealthy and the relative value of money higher than is now the case. But at least service was rendered for the heavy rates, as "Henceforth the posts were to be equally open to all; all would be at liberty to use them; all would be welcome."[51]

Witherings especially distinguished himself in the management of the foreign postal service, which he accelerated and made more efficient. In 1637 he was appointed "Master of the Posts," and was thus the only reformer from outside who, withinside, rose to become supreme head of the Department. The office was given to enable him to undertake, unhindered, the improvements he proposed to make in the inland posts. Three years later he was dismissed, and an end put to "the career of one who had the sagacity to project and the energy to carry out a system, the main features of which endure to the present day."[52]

In 1643 the postal revenue amounted to some £5,000 a year only. By 1677 the Department's profits were farmed at £43,000 a year, and the officials consisted of one Postmaster-General and seventy-five employees. A writer of the day tells us that "the number of letter missives is now prodigiously great."

In 1658 John Hill, a Yorkshire attorney, did good work, and tried to accomplish more. He already supplied post horses between York and London, undertook the conveyance, at cheap rates, of parcels and letters, and established agencies about the country for the furtherance of a scheme to greatly reduce the postal charges throughout the kingdom; his proposal being a penny rate for England and Wales, a twopenny rate for Scotland, and a fourpenny rate for Ireland. But the Government declined to consider the merits of the plan.

When Dockwra—who gave practical shape to the scheme which Murray had assigned to him—established his reform of a penny post, London had no other post office than the general one in Lombard Street,[53] and there was no such thing as a delivery of letters between one part of London and another. Thus, if any Londoner wished to write to any other Londoner, he was obliged to employ a messenger to convey his missive to its destination; and as the houses then had no numbers, but were distinguished only by signs, the amateur letter-carrier must have been often puzzled at which door to knock.

Dockwra soon put his great scheme into working order. He divided city and suburbs into districts—in that respect forestalling a feature of Rowland Hill's plan—seven in number, each with a sorting office; and in one day opened over four hundred receiving offices. In the city letters were delivered for 1d., in the suburbs for 2d. It must have been quite as epoch-making a reform to the Londoners of the seventeenth century, as was the far wider-reaching, completer scheme established a hundred and sixty years later to the entire nation. For Dockwra's, though for its time a wonderful advance, was but a local institution, the area served being "from Hackney in the north to Lambeth in the south, and from Blackwall in the east to Westminster in the west."[54] He also introduced a parcel post.

The local penny posts—for they were afterwards extended to many other towns—have given some people the erroneous impression that Rowland Hill's plan of penny postage was simply an elaboration and a widening of Dockwra's older system. Things called by a similar name are not necessarily identical. Indeed, as we have seen, the word "postage" had formerly quite a different meaning from that it now has; and, although Dockwra's "penny post" and Rowland Hill's "penny postage" related equally to postage in its modern interpretation of the word, that the system established in 1840 materially differed from preceding systems will be shown in the succeeding chapter.[55]

Dockwra's reform was inaugurated in 1680, proved of immense benefit to the public, was intended to last for ever, and did last for a hundred and twenty-one years. In 1801 the charges on the local—to say nothing of those on the general—post were raised from 1d. and 2d. to 2d. and 3d., while its area, which in Queen Anne's reign had been extended to from 18 to 20 miles beyond London, shrank into much narrower limits.[56] The increase of charge was due to that augmented contribution, on the part of the Post Office, to the war-tax which has been already mentioned. During the last twenty-five of the years 1801-1840 the country was at peace, but the tendency of "temporary" war-taxes is to become permanent, or to die a very lingering death; and, as has been shown, no diminution was made in postal rates; and letter-writing in thousands of homes practically ceased to be.

In 1663 the entire profits of the Post Office had been settled on James, Duke of York; and Dockwra's reform, like other large measures, being costly to establish, he had to seek financial help outside the Department, the requisite money being furnished by a few public-spirited citizens of London. The undertaking was a losing speculation at first, but presently began to prosper; and the Duke's jealousy was at once roused. "So long," says Mr Joyce, "as the outgoings exceeded the receipts, Dockwra remained unmolested; but no sooner had the balance turned than the Duke complained of his monopoly being infringed, and the Courts of Law decided in his favour. Not only was Dockwra cast in damages, but the undertaking was wrested out of his hands."[57]

During James's reign this eminent public servant met with no recognition of his valuable work; but under William and Mary he was granted a pension, and after some delay was reinstated as comptroller of the penny post. But in 1700 both situation and pension came to an end; and the man who had conferred so signal a benefit upon his fellow-citizens was finally dismissed.

In the seventeenth and eighteenth centuries the posts in Ireland were few and far between. Carrick-on-Shannon was the only town in County Leitrim which received a mail, and that not oftener than twice a week. Several districts in Ireland were served only at the cost of their inhabitants.

Besides London, Bath alone—favoured by its two distinguished citizens, Ralph Allen and John Palmer—had, before 1792, more than one letter-carrier; and many important centres of population, such as Norwich, York, Derby, Newcastle-on-Tyne, and Plymouth, had none at all—the postmaster, and in some instances a single assistant, constituting the entire staff, no sort of duty outside the official walls being undertaken. The Channel Islands were treated as though they had been in another planet. Before 1794 they had no postal communication with the rest of the United Kingdom, though for some years local enterprise had provided them with an inter-insular service. When Palmer appeared on the scene, the number of towns in the British Isles which received mails increased rapidly, while those already served two or three times a week began to receive a post daily.

In no respect, perhaps, has greater progress been made than in the matter of mail conveyance, both as regards acceleration and safety, and in other ways. In Witherings' time about two months were required for a letter and its answer to pass between London and Scotland or London and Ireland. Exchange of correspondence between the three kingdoms was, strange to say, far less expeditiously carried on than that between London and Madrid. But when it is remembered how direful was the condition of our thoroughfares in the seventeenth and eighteenth centuries, the impossibility of anything like swift progress becomes evident. Ruts there were, says Arthur Young, which measured 3 feet in depth, and in wet weather were filled to the brim with water; while in "Guy Mannering" Scott speaks of districts "only accessible through a succession of tremendous morasses." In "Waverley" (*temp.* 1745) is described the "Northern Diligence, a huge, old-fashioned tub drawn by three horses, which completed the journey from Edinburgh to London ('God willing,' as the advertisement expressed it) in three weeks." Twenty years later, even, the coaches spent from twelve to fourteen days upon the journey, and went once a month only. In some places the roads were so bad that it was necessary to erect beacons alongside them to keep the travelling public after dark from falling into the ponds and bogs which lined the highways and sometimes encroached upon them. Elsewhere, the ponderous "machines" groaned or clattered over rocky and precipitous ways, rolling and pitching like a vessel on an angry sea. Not even by the more lightly-freighted men on foot and boys mounted on the wretched steeds provided for the Post Office service could swifter progress be made. No wonder that letter and answer should travel but slowly.

In 1784, when Palmer proposed the abolition of these slow-moving and far from trustworthy mail-carriers,[58] and the substitution in their place of the existing stage-coaches,[59] great were the scorn and indignation of the postal authorities. Seven miles an hour instead of three and a half! And coaches instead of post-boys! Were ever such mad proposals heard of! The officials were "amazed that any dissatisfaction, any desire for change should exist." Not so very long before, they had plumed themselves on the gratifying fact that "in five days an answer to a letter might be had from a place distant 200 miles from the writer." And now, even in face of that notable advance, the public wanted further concessions! One prominent official "could not see why the post should be the swiftest conveyance in England." Another was sure that if travelling were made quicker, the correspondence of the country would be thrown into the utmost confusion. But he thought—and perhaps the parentage of the thought was not far to seek—that to expedite the mails was simply impossible. The officials, indeed, were "unanimously of opinion that the thing is totally impracticable."[60] And, doubtless, Palmer was set down as "a visionary" and "a revolutionist"—names to be bestowed, some fifty-three years later, upon another persistent reformer. A second Committee, formed to consider Palmer's proposals, reported that it had "examined the oldest and ablest officers of the Post Office, and they had no confidence whatever in the plan." "It is always," said Brougham, when, in the Upper House, he was advocating adoption of the later reform, "the oldest and ablest, for the Committee considered the terms synonymous."[61]

Thus does history repeat itself. As it was with Palmer, so, before him, it was with Witherings and Dockwra; and, after him, with Rowland Hill. The unforgivable offence is to be wiser than one's opponents, and to achieve success when failure has been predicted.

But worse things than prophecy of failure accompany reforms, attempted or accomplished, and act like a discordant chorus striving to drown sweet music. Prophecy of dire results, such as ruin of society, disruption of the Empire, etc., are sometimes raised, and carry dismay into the hearts of the timid. My father, who was born less than forty-three years after "the change of style," as a child often heard old people, in all seriousness, lament the loss of "our eleven days," and declare that since it was made everything in this country had gone wrong.[62] I too, when young, have heard aged lips attribute the awful cholera visitation of 1832 to our sinfulness in passing the Catholic Emancipation Bill; and the potato disease and consequent Irish famine in the mid 'forties to interference with the sacred Corn Laws. We laugh at this sort of thing to-day, but are we much wiser than our forebears?

Although these great reforms differ widely in character, the gloomy predictions concerning them are substantially alike. The terrible things prophesied never come to pass; and of the reforms when once established no sane person wishes to get rid.

When at last Palmer had borne down opposition and been placed in authority, he set to work in a far-reaching, statesmanlike manner. The old, worthless vehicles which, owing to their frequent habit of breaking down on the road, had become a constant source of complaint, were gradually got rid of; and by 1792 all his mail-coaches were new. He was a born organiser, and insisted on the introduction and maintenance of business-like methods. Unnecessary stoppages along the road were put an end to, and necessary stoppages shortened; the mail-bags to be taken on were made up before the coaches appeared, the mail-bags to be taken off were ready to the guard's hand; and strict punctuality was enforced. The guards and coachmen were armed, and no one unskilled in the use of firearms was employed in either capacity. The harness and other accoutrements were kept in good repair, the coaches were well-horsed, and the relays were made with reasonable frequency.[63]

Palmer had calculated that sixteen hours ought to suffice for the London and Bath coach when covering the distance between the two cities. The time usually spent on the road was thirty-eight hours. The first mail-coach which started from Bath to London under his auspices in 1784 performed the journey in seventeen hours, proving with what nearness to absolute accuracy he had made his calculations. For a while seventeen hours became the customary time-limit. Not long after this date mail-coaches were plying on all the principal roads.

Before the first of Palmer's coaches went to Liverpool, that seaport was served by one letter-carrier. Ten years later, six were needed. One postman had sufficed for Edinburgh; now four were required. Manchester till 1792 had but one letter-carrier, and its postal staff consisted of an aged widow and her daughter. Previous to 1794 the Isle of Wight was served by one postmaster and one letter-carrier only.

Before Palmer took over the management of the coaches they were robbed, along one road or another, at least once a week. It was not till his rule was ten years old that a coach was stopped or robbed; and then it was not a highwayman, but a passenger who did the looting. Before 1784 the annual expenditure incurred through prosecution of the thieves had been a heavy charge on the service, one trial alone—that of the brothers Weston, who figure in Thackeray's "Denis Duval"—having cost £4,000. This burden on the Post Office revenue henceforth shrank into comparatively insignificant dimensions.

Palmer traversed the entire kingdom along its coach routes, making notes of the length of time consumed on each journey, calculating in how much less time it could be performed by the newer vehicles, and always keeping an observant eye on other possible improvements.

Before the end of the eighteenth century Dockwra's London penny post[64] had fallen upon evil days. Neglect and mismanagement had been its lot for many years; there was a steady diminution of its area, and no accounts were kept of its gains. Palmer looked into the condition of the local post, as, in addition to the mail conveyance, he had already looked into the condition of the newspaper post and other things which stood in need of rectification; and, later, the old penny post, now transformed into a twopenny post, was taken in hand by Johnson, who, from the position of letter-carrier, rose, by sheer ability, to the office of "Deputy Comptroller of the Penny Post."

As a rule, Palmer was fortunate in choosing subordinates, of whom several not only accomplished useful work long after their chief had been dismissed, but who introduced reforms on their own account. Hasker, the head superintendent of the mail-coaches, kept the vehicles, horses, accoutrements, etc., to say nothing of the officials, quite up to Palmer's level. But in another chosen man the great reformer was fatally deceived, for Bonner intrigued against his benefactor, and helped to bring about his downfall.

One reform paves the way for succeeding reforms. Palmer's improved coaches caused a marked increase of travelling; and the establishment of yet better and more numerous vehicles led to the making of better roads. By this time people were beginning to get over the ground at such a rate that the late Lord Campbell, when a young man, was once, in all seriousness, advised to avoid using Palmer's coaches, which, it was said, owing to the speed at which they travelled between London and Edinburgh, and elsewhere, had caused the death of several passengers from apoplexy! "The pace that killed" was 8 miles an hour. By the time the iron horse had beaten the flesh-and-blood quadruped out of the field, or rather road, the coaches were running at the rate of 12 miles an hour.

Everywhere the mails were being accelerated and increased in number. For now the science of engineering was making giant strides; and Telford and his contemporary MacAdam—whose name has enriched our language with a verb, while the man himself endowed our thoroughfares with a solid foundation—were covering Great Britain with highways the like of which had not been seen since the days of the Roman Conquest.

And then arrived the late 'twenties of the nineteenth century, bringing with them talk of railways and of steam-propelled locomotives whose speed, it was prophesied by sanguine enthusiasts, might some day even rival that of a horse at full gallop. The threatened mail-coaches lived on for many a year, but from each long country highway they disappeared one after another, some of them, it is said, carrying, on their last journey, the Union Jack at half-mast; and, ere long, the once busy roadside inn-keepers put up their shutters, and closed the doors of their empty stables. More than half a century had to elapse before the hostelries opened again to the cyclists and motorists who have given to them fresh life and energy.

And thus passed away the outward and visible witnesses to Palmer's great reform, not as many things pass because they have reached the period of senile decay, but when his work was at the high water-mark of efficiency and fame. Perhaps that singular fact is suggestive of the reason why the disappearance of the once familiar pageant gave rise to a widespread regret that was far from being mere sentimentality.

When they were in their prime, the "royal mail-coaches" made a brave display. Ruddy were they with paint and varnish, and golden with Majesty's coat-of-arms, initials, etc. The driver and guard were clad in scarlet uniforms, and the four fine horses—often increased in a "difficult" country to six or more—were harnessed two abreast, and went at a good, swinging pace. Once upon a time a little child was taken for a stroll along a suburban highroad to watch for the passing of the mail-coaches on their way from London to the north—a literally everyday pageant, but one unstaled by custom. In the growing dusk could be distinguished a rapidly-moving procession of dark crimson and gold vehicles in single file, each with its load of comfortably wrapped-up passengers sitting outside, and each drawn by four galloping steeds, whose quick footfalls made a pleasant, rhythmic sound. One heard the long, silvern horns of the guards, every now and then, give notice in peremptory tones to the drivers of ordinary conveyances to scatter to right and left, and one noted the heavy cloud of dust which rolled with and after the striking picture. A spectacle it was beside which the modern railway train is ugly, the motor-car hideous: which rarely failed to draw onlookers to doorways and windows, and to give pedestrians pause; and which always swept out of sight much too quickly. The elderly cousin accompanying the child drew her attention to the passing procession, and said that her father was doing something in connection with those coaches—meaning, of course, their mails— something that would make his country more prosperous and his own name long remembered. The child listened in perplexity, not understanding. In many noble arts—above all, in the fashioning of large, square kites warranted, unlike those bought at shops, to fly and not to come to pieces— she knew him to be the first of men. Yet how even he could improve upon the gorgeous moving picture that had just flashed past it was not easy to understand.

In the days when railways and telegraphs were not, the coach was the most frequent, because the fastest, medium of communication. It was therefore the chief purveyor of news. On the occurrence of any event of absorbing interest, such as the most stirring episodes of the twenty-years-long war with France, or the trial of Queen-Consort Caroline, people lined the roads in crowds, and as the coach swept past, the passengers shouted out the latest intelligence. Even from afar the waiting throngs in war time could always tell when the news was of victories gained, or, better still, of peace, such as the short-lived pact of Amiens, and the one of long duration after June 1815. On these occasions the vehicle was made gay with flags, ribbons, green boughs, and floral trophies; and the passengers shouted and cheered madly, the roadside public speedily becoming equally excited. It fell one day to Rowland Hill's lot, as a lad of nineteen, to meet near Birmingham an especially gaily-decked coach, and to hurry home with the joyful intelligence of the "crowning mercy"—at one stage of the battle, 'tis said, not far from becoming a defeat—of Waterloo.

The once celebrated Bianconi was known as "the Palmer of Ireland." Early in the nineteenth century he covered the roads of his adopted country with an admirably managed service of swift cars carrying mails and passengers; and thus did much to remedy postal deficiencies there, and to render imperative the maintenance in good order of the public highways. Once, if not oftener, during his useful career, he came to the Post Office on official business, and "interviewed" Rowland Hill, who found him an interesting and original-minded man, his fluent English, naturally, being redolent of the Hibernian brogue. Bianconi's daughter, who married a son of the great O'Connell, wrote her father's "Life"; and, among other experiences, told how on one occasion he was amazed to see a Catholic gentleman, while driving a pair of horses along the main street of an Irish town, stopped by a Protestant who coolly detached the animals from the carriage, and walked off with them. No resistance could be offered, and redress there was none. The horses were each clearly of higher value than the permitted £5 apiece, and could therefore legally become the property of any Protestant mean enough, as this one was, to tender that price, and (mis)appropriate them. When Catholic Emancipation—long promised and long deferred—was at last conceded, this iniquitous law, together with other laws as bad or worse, was swept away.[65]

With the advent of railways the "bians" gradually disappeared, doing so when, like the mail-coaches, they had reached a high level of excellence, and had been of almost incalculable public benefit.

The mail-coach, leisurely and tedious as it seems in these days of hurry, had a charm of its own in that it enabled its passengers to enjoy the fresh air—since most of them, by preference, travelled outside—and the beauties of our then comparatively unspoiled country and of our then picturesque old towns, mostly sleepy or only slowly awakening, it is true, and, doubtless, deplorably dull to live in. The journey was at least never varied by interludes of damp and evil-smelling tunnels, and the travelling ruffian of the day had less opportunity for outrage on his fellowman or woman. The coach also, perhaps, lent itself more kindly to romance than does the modern, noisy railway train; at any rate, a rather pretty story, long current in our family, and strictly authentic, belongs to the ante-railway portion of the nineteenth century. One of my mother's girl-friends, pretty, lively, clever, and frankly coquettish, was once returning alone by coach to London after a visit to the country. She was the only inside passenger, but was assured that the other three places would be filled on arrival at the next stage. When, therefore, the coach halted again, she looked with some curiosity to see who were to be her travelling companions. But the expected three resolved themselves into the person of one smiling young man whose face she recognised, and who at once sat down on the seat opposite to hers, ere long confessing that, hearing she was to come to town by that coach, he had taken all the vacant places in order to make sure of a *tête-à-tête*. He was one of several swains with whom she was accustomed to flirt, but whom she systematically kept at arm's-length until she could make up her mind whether to say "yes" or "no." But he had come resolved to be played with no longer, and to win from her a definite answer. Whether his eloquent pleading left her no heart to falter "no," or whether, woman-like, she said "yes" by way of getting rid of him, is not recorded. But that they were married is certain; and it may as well be taken for granted that, in accordance with the time-honoured ending of all romantic love stories, "they lived happy ever after."

No eminent postal reformer rose during the first thirty-seven years of the nineteenth century unless we except that doughty Parliamentary free lance, Robert Wallace of Kelly, of whom more anon. But the chilling treatment meted out by officials within the postal sanctuary to those reform-loving persons sojourning outside it, or even to those who, sooner or later, penetrated to its inner walls, was scarcely likely to tempt sane men to make excursions into so inhospitable a field.

Yet it was high time that a new reformer appeared, for the Department was lagging far behind the Post Offices of other countries—especially, perhaps, that of France—and the wonderful nineteenth "century of progress" had now reached maturity.

FOOTNOTES:

[48] "History of the Post Office," p. 146.

[49] "History of the Post Office," p. 18.

[50] The word "postage," we are told, was originally applied to the hire of a horse for "posting," and was extended to letters in comparatively recent times only. It is therefore well when meeting with the word in other than modern documents not to conclude too hastily that it relates to epistolary correspondence. An Act of 1764 is said to be the first in which was used "postage" in the sense of a charge upon letters. But in 1659 the item, "By postage of letters in farm, £14,000," appears in a "Report on the Public Revenue in the Journals of the House of Commons," vii. 627. The fact likewise seems well worth recalling that in the translation of the Bible of

1611 the words "post" and "letters" are connected, notably in "2 Chronicles," xxx. 6, and in "Esther." Chapter xvii. of Marco Polo's travels, by the by, contains an interesting description of the horse and foot posts in the dominions of Kubla Khan, which were so admirably organised that the journeys over which ordinary travellers spent ten days were accomplished by the posts in two.

[51] "History of the Post Office," p. 18.

[52] *Ibid.* p. 21.

[53] In George I.'s reign, besides London, Chester is said to have been the only town in England which possessed two post offices.

[54] "History of the Post Office," p. 37.

[55] "The ancient penny post resembled the modern penny post only in name," says Justin M'Carthy in "A History of Our Own Times," chap. iv. p. 99.

[56] The "New Annual Directory for 1800" (see Guildhall Library), speaking of the "Penny Post," defines its area as "the cities of London [and] Westminster, the borough of Southwark and their suburbs."

[57] "History of the Post Office," pp. 37-40.

[58] Or, in his own words, mails trusted to "some idle boy without a character, mounted on a worn-out hack, who, so far from being able to defend himself against a robber, was more likely to be in league with one." Apparently, the people of this class had no better name in France, and probably other countries, to judge by a fragment of conversation taken from Augier, and chronicled in Larousse's "*Dictionnaire du XIXe Siècle,*" xii. 1497:—"La poste est en retard." "Oui, d'une heure à peu près. Le piéton prend courage à tous les cabarets."

[59] As a contemporary of Palmer, Scott was never guilty of an anachronism not unknown to present-day authors who sometimes cause the puppet men and women of their romances to travel before 1784 in *mail* when they really mean *stage* coaches. The terms are too often taken to be synonymous.

[60] "Report of the Committee of Inquiry (1788)."

[61] "Hansard," xxxix. 1201, etc.

[62] For nearly two centuries the change was opposed here, partly perhaps chiefly, because it was inaugurated on the Continent by a Pope, Gregory XIII. Common-sense and the noblest of all sciences were on the side of His Holiness; but religious bigotry was too strong even for that

combination; and for those many years religious bigotry held the field. Opposition did not cease even when the correction was made; and grave divines preached against the wickedness of an Act which, they said, brought many millions of sinners eleven days nearer to their graves; and in one of Hogarth's series of Election Pictures, a man is seen bearing a placard on which is inscribed the words, "Give us back our eleven days." Most of us, too, are familiar with the cruel story of the witch mania which was shared by men as excellent as Sir Matthew Hale and John Wesley. To-day, we are glad that old, friendless men and women, to say nothing of their harmless, necessary cats, are permitted to die peacefully. Are there any now among us who would restore the Act, *De Comburendo Heretico*, expunged from the Statute Book in William's III.'s reign—a removal which doubtless scandalised not a few sincerely devout persons?

[63] In the oldest days of coaching, the horses which started with the vehicle drew it to the journey's end. Relays of horses were a happy afterthought.

[64] Dublin became possessed of a local penny post before 1793; but not until that date, or a hundred and thirteen years after the establishment of Dockwra's reform in London, was it considered worth while to extend the boon to Manchester—which had now displaced Bristol as the second town in the kingdom—or to the last-named city and to Birmingham. At this time, too, it was still customary to address letters bound for the centre of the cutlery industry to "Sheffield, near Rotherham", the latter being the more important town.

[65] For a graphically described contrast between the treatment meted out in those "good old times" to Catholics and that to Protestants, see Sydney Smith's too-seldom read "Peter Plymley's Letters."

CHAPTER III

THE PLAN

"IF in 1834 only a moderate reduction had been made in the extortionate rates of postage which were then in force, Rowland Hill might not have embarked upon his plan; and, even if he had done so, that plan might have failed to evoke from the public sufficient force to overcome opposition in high quarters. In proportion to the extent of the evil did men welcome the remedy."—JOYCE'S "History of the Post Office," p. 420.

The postal reform "perhaps represents the greatest social improvement brought about by legislation in modern times."—JUSTIN M'CARTHY in "A History of Our Own Times," chap. iv. p. 89.

For many years my father's attention had been turned towards the question of postal reform; although in that respect he was far from standing alone. The defects of the old system were so obvious that with many people they formed a common subject of conversation; and plans of improvement were repeatedly discussed. So far back as 1826 Rowland Hill's thoughts had outgrown the first stage on the road to "betterment"—that of mere fault-finding with the things that are. He had drawn up a scheme for a travelling post office. The fact that, whereas the mails from all parts as a rule reached London at 6 A.M., while the distribution of letters only began three hours later, struck him as a defect in need of urgent remedy. If, he argued, the inside of the mail-coach, or "an additional body thereto, were to be fitted with shelves and other appliances, the guard might sort and [date] stamp the letters, etc., on the journey. By so doing, time would be saved: the mails would either leave the provincial towns three hours later, giving more time for correspondence, or the letters could be delivered in London three hours earlier." In January 1830 he suggested the dispatch of mail matter by means of pneumatic tubes. But neither project went beyond the stage of written memoranda; nor, in face of the never-failing hostility manifested by the post officials towards all reforms, especially those emanating from outsiders, was likely to do more.

Early in the 'thirties reductions in certain departments of taxation had been made; and my father's mind being still turned towards the Post Office, he fell into the habit of discussing with his family and others the advisability of extending similar reductions to postal rates.

And this seems a fitting place to mention that while from every member of his family he received the heartiest sympathy and help throughout the long struggle to introduce his reform, it was his eldest brother, Matthew, who, more than any other, did him yeoman service; and, after Matthew, the second brother, Edwin.[66] Of the five Hill brothers who reached old age, it has been claimed for the eldest that, intellectually, he was the greatest. He had not, perhaps, the special ability which enabled my father to plan the postal reform, a measure which probably none of his brothers, gifted as in various ways all were, could have thought out, and brought to concrete form; neither had the eldest the mathematical power which distinguished Rowland. But in all other respects Matthew stood first; and that he was one of the wittiest, wisest, most cultivated, and, at the same time, most tender-hearted of men in an age especially rich in the type there can be no doubt. He was the first Birmingham man to go to the Bar, and for twenty-eight years was his native city's first recorder.

The second brother, Edwin, was also an unusually clever man, and had a genius for mechanics which placed him head and shoulders above his brethren. His help in furthering the postal reform, as well as in other ways, was given "constantly and ably," said my father. Out of a very busy brain Edwin could evolve any machine or other contrivance required to meet the exigencies of the hour, as when, to make life less hard to one who was lame and rheumatic, he devised certain easily-swinging doors; and when in 1840 he was appointed Supervisor of stamps at Somerset House he was quite in his element. Among other things, he invented an ingenious method, said the First Report of the Commissioners of Inland Revenue, by which the unwieldy, blank newspaper sheets which, as we have seen, were obliged, before being printed, to go to Somerset House to receive the impress of the duty stamp, were separated, turned over, and stamped with a speed and accuracy which had previously been considered unattainable.[67] He was also the inventor of the envelope-folding machine known as De La Rue's, and shown at the Great Exhibition of 1851. The process of embossing the Queen's head on the postal envelopes was likewise his invention; and, further, he published two once well-known works—the one on "Principles of Currency," the other on "Criminal Capitalists." He applied the latter title to those proprietors of houses and shops who knowingly let them out as shelters for criminals or depots for the sale of stolen goods; and he proposed that, in order to check crime, these landlords should first be struck at.[68]

Matthew it was who, after many conversations with Rowland on the subject so frequently in the latter's thoughts, advised him to draw up his plan in pamphlet form. The advice was followed, and the detailed scheme laid before the adviser, who approved of it so highly that he suggested its publication by their mutual friend, Charles Knight. This was done, with what far-reaching effect we know. But my uncle's help did not end here. For him, who, self-aided, had won an influential position both at the Bar and in the brilliant, intellectual society of his day, it was easier than for his lesser known junior to have access to men likely to prove powerful advocates of the scheme and good friends to its author. Henceforth, as his biographers remind us, the eldest brother devoted to the proposed reform all the time and labour he could spare from his own work.[69] He introduced Rowland to men of influence in both Houses of Parliament, to several of the chief journalists, and other leaders of public opinion. Their sympathy was soon enlisted, as was also that of many of my father's own friends, and, ere long, that of the great majority of the nation when once the merits of the plan came to be understood.

Facsimile of Manuscript Page (in Sir ROWLAND HILL'S handwriting) of the Draft of his Pamphlet on Post Office Reform. See 3rd Edition (1837) page 49.

When, in 1834, Rowland Hill joined the Association formed for the total abolition of the odious "taxes on knowledge" there was a duty of 1s. 6d. on every advertisement; a paper duty at 1-½d. the lb.; and the newspaper stamp duty was at its highest—4d. This last burden—undoubtedly a war-tax—was reduced once more to 1d. only in 1835, when we had been at peace for twenty years. So easy is it to lay a war-tax on the nation: so difficult to take it off again. Weighted after this fashion, how could journalistic enterprise prosper? The Association was of opinion that if the Press could be cheapened newspapers would increase, and advertisements multiply, while the fiscal produce of journalism would be as large as ever. In estimating this probable expansion Rowland Hill applied a principle on which he subsequently relied in reference to postal reform, namely, that the increased consumption of a cheapened article in general use makes up for the diminished price.

The Revenue for the financial year which ended with March 1836 had yielded a large surplus; and a reduction of taxation was confidently looked for. Thus the time seemed ripe for the publication of my father's views upon the postal question; and he set to work to write that slighter, briefer edition of his pamphlet which was intended for private circulation only.

It was in this year also that he made the acquaintance of one of the greatest of all those—many in number—who helped to carry his proposed scheme into accomplished fact—Robert Wallace of Kelly, Greenock's first Member of Parliament and the pioneer postal reformer of the nineteenth century. From the time Mr Wallace entered Parliament, at the General Election which followed the passing of the great Reform Bill of 1832, he took the deepest interest in postal matters, and strove to reform the Department with a persistency which neither ridicule could weary nor opposition defeat. He was in the field two years before Rowland Hill; and while thus unconsciously preparing the way for another man, was able to accomplish several useful reforms on his own account.

In 1833 Mr Wallace proposed that postage should be charged by weight instead of by number of enclosures, thereby anticipating my father as regards that one suggestion. But nothing came of the proposal. He was more fortunate when moving for leave to throw open to public competition the contract for the construction of mail-coaches, which, when adopted, led to an annual saving of over £17,000. He also secured the appointment of a Commission of Inquiry into the management of the Post Office. The Commission was established in 1835, continued to work till 1838, issued ten Reports,[70] and by its untiring efforts was, as my father always maintained, justly entitled to much of the credit of his own later success. Mr Wallace was, of course, to the fore in the Commission, and gave valuable evidence in favour of the establishment of day mails, which subsequently formed a feature of Rowland Hill's plan, and was eventually carried into effect with great advantage to the public and to the Revenue. To Mr Wallace we also owe the boon of registration of letters. He likewise pleaded for a reduction of postal rates, and of more frequent communication between different centres of population. In Parliament, during the session of 1836, and in the last speech he made there before the publication of Rowland Hill's pamphlet, he urged the abandonment of the manifestly unjust rule of charging postage not according to the geographical distance between one place and another, but according to the length of the course a letter was compelled to take.[71] As regards the question of reduced postal rates, he said: "It would be proper not to charge more than 3d. for any letter sent a distance of 50 miles; for 100 miles, 4d.; 200 miles, 6d.; and the highest rate of postage ought not to be more than 8d. or 9d. at most."[72]

A detailed plan of wholesale reform (as was my father's) Mr Wallace never had, and he no more dreamed of postage stamps—though the suggestion of these has been sometimes attributed to him as well as to other men—or of prepayment than he did of uniformity of rate. He was an older man than Rowland Hill, and of higher social standing; yet was he so incapable of jealousy or other petty meanness, that when the younger man, on completion of his scheme, laid it before the veteran Scotsman, the latter threw aside all other plans and suggestions, took up the only practicable reform, and worked for it as heartily as if it had been his own.

To Mr Wallace every would-be postal reformer turned with unerring instinct as to his best friend; and it was through the instrumentality of this public benefactor that Rowland Hill had been furnished with sundry Parliamentary Blue Books containing those statistics and other valuable facts, mastery of which was essential to the completion of his pamphlet, since it was necessary to understand the old system thoroughly before destroying it.

"As I had never yet been within the walls of any post office," wrote my father of Mr Wallace's friendly act, "my only sources of information for the time consisted of those heavy Blue Books, in which invaluable matter too often lies hidden amidst heaps of rubbish. Into some of these [books] I had already dipped; but Mr Wallace, having supplied me by post with an additional half-hundred-weight of raw material,[73] I now commenced that systematic study, analysis, and comparison which the difficulty of my self-imposed task rendered necessary."

Basing his calculations on the information drawn from these and other volumes, Rowland Hill found that, after the reduction of taxation in 1823, the price of soap fell by an eighth, tea by a sixth, silk goods by a fifth, and coffee by a fourth. The reduction in price was followed by a great increase of consumption, the sale of soap rising by a third, and that of tea by almost half. Of silk goods the sale had more than doubled, and of coffee more than tripled. Cotton goods had declined in cost during the previous twenty years by nearly a half, and their sale was quadrupled.[74]

In his pamphlet Rowland Hill dwelt upon this fact of increased consumption following on decreased price. It was clear, then, that the taxes for remission should be those affording the greatest relief to the public accompanied with the least loss to the Revenue; and that scrutiny should be made into the subject in order to discover which tax, or taxes, had failed to grow in productiveness with increase of population and prosperity. The test showed that, whereas between 1815 and 1835 the nation had added six millions to its numbers, and that trade had largely increased, the postal revenue was rather smaller in the later than in the earlier year. During the same period the revenue from the stage-coaches had grown by 128 per cent. In France, where the postal charges were more reasonable, the revenue of the Department had, in the same twenty years, increased by 80 per cent.

Reform in our own postal system was obviously a necessity.

But the fiscal loss to the country, as shown in the state of our postal revenue, serious as it was, seemed to Rowland Hill a lesser evil than the bar, artificial and harmful, raised by the high charges on correspondence, to the moral and intellectual progress of the people. If put upon a sound basis, the Post Office, instead of being an engine for the imposition of an unbearable tax, would become a powerful stimulus to civilisation.

Still delving among the Parliamentary Blue Books, he further gathered that the cost of the service rendered—that is, of the receipt, conveyance, and distribution of each ordinary missive sent from post town to post town within the United Kingdom—averaged 84/100ths of a penny only; 28/100ths going to conveyance, and 56/100ths to the receipt and delivery, collection of postage, etc. Also that the cost of conveyance for a given distance being generally in direct proportion to the weight carried, and a newspaper or franked letter weighing about as much as several ordinary letters, the average expense of conveying a letter chargeable with postage must be still lower, probably some 9/100ths of a penny: a conclusion supported by the well-known fact, already alluded to,[75] that the chargeable letters weighed, on an average, one fourth only of the entire mail.

He also found that the whole cost of the mail-coach service for one journey between London and Edinburgh was only £5 a day.[76] The average load of the mail diurnally carried being some six hundred-weight, the cost of each hundred-weight was therefore 16s. 8d. Taking the average weight of a letter at a quarter of an ounce, its cost of carriage for the 400 miles was but 1/36th part of a penny—in the light of Rowland Hill's amended estimate actually less. Yet the postage exacted for even the lightest "single" letter was 1s. 3-½d. The ninth part of a farthing—the approximate cost of conveyance—is a sum too small to be appreciable, and impossible to collect. Therefore, "if the charge for postage be made proportionate to the whole expense incurred in the receipt, transit, and delivery of the letter, and in the collection of its postage, it must be made uniformly the same from every post town to every other post town in the United Kingdom."[1] In other words, "As it would take a ninefold weight to make the expense of transit amount to one farthing, it follows that, taxation apart, the charge ought to be precisely the same for every packet of moderate weight, without reference to the number of its enclosures."[177]

The custom of charge by distance seemed self-condemned when a simpler mode was not only practicable but actually fairer. Now, with increase of the number of letters the cost of each was bound to diminish; and with reduction of postage, especially the great reduction which seemed easy of attainment, increase of number could not fail to follow.

The simple incident of the falling apple is said to have suggested to Newton the theory of gravitation. So also the discovery that the length of a letter's journey makes no appreciable difference to the cost of that journey led Rowland Hill to think of uniformity of rate; and in that portion of his "Life" which is autobiographic he said that the "discovery" that such a rate would approach nearer to absolute justice than any other that could be fixed upon was "as startling to myself as it could be to any one else, and was the basis of the plan which has made so great a change in postal affairs" (i. 250).

Mention has already been made of the time-wasting and costly mode in which, during or after delivery of the letters, the postage had to be collected, necessarily in coin of the realm. In rural districts the postman's journey, when twofold, doubled the cost of its delivery, its distance, and its time-duration. The accounts, as we have seen, were most complicated, and complication is only too apt to spell mismanagement, waste, and fraud. Simplicity of arrangement was imperative. But simplicity could only be attained by getting rid of the complications. The work must be *changed*. Time must be saved, and unprofitable labour be done away with. But how? By abolishing the tiresome operations of "candling" and of making the "calculations" (of postal charge) now inscribed on every letter; by expediting the deliveries, and by other devices. Above all, the public should learn to undertake its due share of work, the share non-performance of which necessitated the complications, and swelled the expenses. That is, the *sender* of the letter should pay for its transit before the Post Office incurred any cost in connection with it, only, as under the existing system and in numberless cases, to meet with a refusal on the part of the should-be receiver to accept it.

In other words, prepayment must be made the rule. Prepayment would have the effect of "simplifying and accelerating the proceedings of the Post Office throughout the kingdom, and rendering them less liable to error and fraud. In the central Metropolitan Office there would be no letters to be taxed, no examination of those taxed by others; no accounts to be made out against the deputy postmasters for letters transmitted to them, nor against the letter-carriers. There would be no need of checks, no necessity to submit to frauds and numberless errors for want of means to prevent or correct them. In short, the whole of the financial proceedings would be reduced to a single, accurate, and satisfactory account, consisting of a single item per day, with each receiver and each deputy postmaster."[78]

Distribution would thenceforth be the letter-carriers' only function; and thus the first step towards the acceleration of postal deliveries would be secured. And while considering this last point, there came into Rowland Hill's mind the idea of that now common adjunct to everybody's hall-door—the letter-box. If the postman could slip his letters through a slit in the woodwork, he need not wait while the bell or knocker summoned the dilatory man or maid; and his round being accomplished more expeditiously, the letters would be received earlier.[79] The shortening of the time consumed on the round would unquestionably facilitate the introduction of those hourly deliveries in thickly populated and business districts which formed part of the plan of postal reform.

How best to collect the prepaid postage had next to be decided; and among other things, Rowland Hill bethought him of the stamped cover for newspapers proposed by his friend Charles Knight three years before, but never adopted; and, finally, of the loose adhesive stamp which was his own device. The description he gave of this now familiar object reads quaintly at the present day. "Perhaps this difficulty"—of making coin payments at a post office—"might be obviated by using a bit of paper just large enough to bear the stamp, and covered at the back with a glutinous wash which, by applying a little moisture, might be attached to the letter."[80]

The disuse of franks and the abandonment of illicit conveyance, the breaking up of one long letter into several shorter ones, and the certain future use to be made of the post for the distribution of those circulars and other documents which either went by different channels or were altogether withheld,[81] should cause the number of missives to increase enormously. Although, were the public, in accordance with its practice in other cases, to expend no more in postage than before, the loss to the nett Revenue should be but small. Even were it to be large, the powerful stimulus given by easy communication and low-priced postage to the productive power of the country, and the consequent increase of revenue in other departments, would more than make up for the deficiency. On all these grounds, then, the adoption of the plan must be of incalculable benefit.

The uniform rate of a penny the half-ounce ought to defray the cost of letter-carriage, and produce some 200 per cent. profit. My father originally proposed a penny the ounce; and thirty-three years later, being then in retirement, he privately advised the Government of the day to revert to the ounce limit. His suggestion was adopted; but the limit has since been brought up to four ounces—a reduction which, had it been proposed in 1837, must inevitably have ensured the defeat of the postal reform.

As regards the speedy recovery of the nett Revenue appearances seem to indicate that he was over-sanguine; the gross Revenue not reaching its former amount till 1851, the nett till 1862.[82] The reasons were several, but among them can hardly be counted faulty calculations on Rowland Hill's part. We shall read more about this matter in a later chapter. Meanwhile, one cause, and that a main one, shall be mentioned. As railways multiplied, and mail-coaches ceased to ply, the expenses of conveyance grew apace.[83]

No. 2, BURTON CRESCENT,
Where "Post Office Reform" was written. A group of people stand opposite the house.
From a Photograph by Messrs. Whiteley & Co.

Under the increased burden the old system, had it endured much longer, must have collapsed. The railway charges for carrying the mails, unlike the charges for carrying passengers and goods, have been higher, weight for weight, than the charges by the mail-coaches, and the tendency in later years has by no means made towards decrease.

The pamphlet was entitled "Post Office Reform: Its Importance and Practicability."[84] Use of the words "Penny Postage" was carefully avoided, because a reformer, when seeking to convert to his own way of thinking a too-often slow-witted public, is forced to employ the wisdom of the serpent in conjunction, not only with the gentleness of the dove, but also with something of the cunning of the fox or weasel. Thus canny George Stephenson, when pleading for railways, forbore to talk of locomotives running at the tremendous rate of 12 miles an hour lest his hearers should think he was qualifying for admission to a lunatic asylum. He therefore modestly hinted at a lower speed, the quicker being supposed to be exceptional. So also Rowland Hill, by stating the arguments for his case clearly, yet cautiously, sought to lead his readers on, step by step, till the seeming midsummer madness of a uniform postal rate irrespective of distance should cease to startle, and, instead, be accepted as absolutely sane.

In this way he engaged the attention, among others, of the once famous Francis Place, tailor and politician, to whom he sent a copy of "Post Office Reform." Mr Place began its perusal with an audible running accompaniment of "Pish!" and "Pshaw!" varied by an occasional remark that the "hitch" which must inevitably destroy the case would presently appear. But as he read, the audible monosyllabic marginal notes ceased, and when he turned the last page, he exclaimed in the needlessly strong language of the day: "I'll be damned if there *is* a hitch after all!" and forthwith became a convert. Leigh Hunt expressed his own sentiments in happier form when he declared that the pamphlet's reasoning "carries us all along with it as smoothly as wheel on railroad."

Through the kindness of Mr Villiers, the long-time senior Member for Wolverhampton, the pamphlet, while still in manuscript, was confidentially submitted to the Government. The author, through his friend, expressed his willingness to let them have the entire credit of introducing the plan if they would accept it. Otherwise he reserved the right to lay it before the public. Many years after, Mr Villiers wrote of the satisfaction he felt that the measure was left to the unbiassed judgment of the people, for, after all, the Government had not the courage to accept the offer, and the only outcome of a rather pleasant interview, in January 1837, with the Chancellor of the Exchequer, Mr Spring Rice, was the suggestion made by him and adopted by Rowland Hill, that the penny rate should be charged not on an ounce, but on half an ounce—to the cautious keeper of the national purse seemingly a less startling innovation.

That the plan should be treated, not as a party question, but strictly on its merits, was its author's earnest, oft-repeated desire. Nor could it be properly regarded from a political aspect, since it counted among its advocates in the two Houses, and outside them, members of both parties. Yet, notwithstanding this support, and the fact that the friends of the proposed reform daily grew more numerous, the best part of three years was consumed in converting to recognition of its merits not only a fairly large portion of the official world, but the Prime Minister himself. However, the same Prime Minister, Lord Melbourne, it was who declared that it was madness to contemplate as possible the abolition of the Corn Laws.

"Post Office Reform" made no small sensation. It was widely read and discussed, as indeed was but natural, seeing how thoroughly dissatisfied with the old system nearly every one outside the official circle was. The proposed reform was, as a rule, heartily approved, although by some would-be clever people it was mercilessly ridiculed; and a writer in the *Quarterly Review* assailed it, declaring, among other things, that "prepayment by means of a stamp or stamped cover is universally admitted to be quite the reverse of convenient, foreign to the habits of the people," etc.—yet another illustration of the folly of indulging in prophecy unaccompanied by knowledge. He further professed to see in the proposal "only a means of making sedition easy."![85]

To this attack Matthew Hill made a scathing reply in the *Edinburgh Review*, using, to flagelate the foe, the ready wit and unanswerable logic of which he was a master. Then passing to the financial side of the question, he pointed out that the temporary diminution of income ought to be regarded as an outlay. The loss, he argued, would be slight in comparison with the object in view. Even if the annual deficit were one million during ten years, that would be but half what the country had paid for the abolition of slavery; and *that* payment was made with no prospect of *money* return. Should hope of ultimate profit fail, a substituted tax might be imposed; and were it asked, what tax? the answer should be, *any*—certain that none could operate so fatally on all other sources of revenue as the present postal tax.

Time was on the side of the reformer, and before long the public, having digested both the pamphlet and the debates thereon, took up the question with enthusiasm. In the largest city in the kingdom as in the smallest hamlet, meetings were convened in support and furtherance of the proposed reform. Within twelve months two thousand petitions were presented to Parliament, causing, on one occasion, a curious scene. Mr Scholefield, having laid on the table a petition from Birmingham, praying for adoption of the penny postage plan, the Speaker called on all members who had charge of similar petitions to bring them up. At once a "crowd" rose to present them amid cheering on all sides.

The number of signatures reached a quarter of a million; and as many of the petitions proceeded from Town Councils, Chambers of Commerce, and other such Corporations, a single signature in many instances represented a considerable number of persons.

Grote, the historian of Greece, and an earnest worker for the reform, presented a petition. One from the city contained over 12,500 signatures, bore the names of the Lord Mayor and many London merchants, and was filled in twelve hours. In the Upper House, the Lord Radnor of the time, an earnest friend to reforms of many sorts, presented no fewer than forty petitions. The signatures were of many classes, all sects, and both political parties.

In the City, on the proposal of Mr Moffatt, afterwards Member for Southampton, the "Mercantile Committee" was formed. Its founder, whom Rowland Hill has described as "one of my most zealous, steady, and efficient supporters," threw himself with great earnestness into the formation of this Committee, raising funds, and gathering together the able men, London merchants and others, who became its members. Its principal aim was to collect evidence in favour of the plan; and to its ceaseless energy much of the success of the movement was due. Mr Ashurst, father to a late Solicitor to the Post Office, was requested to become Solicitor to the Committee. He accepted the invitation, declined to receive remuneration for his services, and worked with unflagging industry.[86] Mr Bates, of the house of Baring Brothers, acted as Chairman; Mr Cole as Secretary. In addition to the above, and to Mr Moffatt, may be mentioned the names of Messrs William Ellis, James Pattison, L. P. Wilson, John Dillon,[87] John Travers, J. H. Gladstanes, and W. A. Wilkinson—all warm supporters of the plan from the beginning.

Mr Cole excelled in the invention of pictorial devices of the sort which are far more likely to convert the average citizen to faith in a newly propounded reform than all the arguments, however able, that were ever spoken or written; and are therefore most valuable. He drew, for instance, a mail-coach with a large amount of postal matter piled, by artistic licence, on the roof instead of inside "the boot." Six huge sacks contained between them 2,296 newspapers weighing 273 lbs.; a seventh sack, as large as any of its fellows, held 484 franked letters, and weighed 47 lbs.; while a moderate-sized parcel was filled with Stamp Office documents. They were all labelled "go free." A bag of insignificant dimensions leant up against one of the sacks. It held 1,565 ordinary letters, weighed 34 lbs., and was marked "pay £93." This tiny packet paid for all the rest! Cole was too sensible a man to make use of an illustration which, if untrue, could only have inspired ridicule. His figures were absolutely correct, and represented the actual proportions of the mail matter carried from London to Edinburgh on 2nd March 1838. His Brobdingnagian "single" and Lilliputian "double" letters, whose names are indicative of their relative size, were one evening handed round the House of Commons with telling effect. They were, of course, designed to satirise the old system practice of "taxing" letters according to number of enclosures. Both had passed through the post that day, the giant having been charged just half what was paid on the dwarf.

In all the large centres of population the great mercantile houses were foremost among those who took up the good cause, and the Press also threw itself into the struggle with much heartiness except in those cases where the cue given was—attack! Happily these dissentients were soon outnumbered and outvoiced. A few journals, indeed, achieved marvellously sudden conversions—behaviour which even in the present more enlightened days is not absolutely unknown. Twenty-five London and eighty-seven provincial papers—there were far fewer papers then than there are now—supported the proposed reform, and their championship found an echo in some of the foreign Press. In London the *Times* (after a while), the now defunct *Morning Chronicle*, and the *Spectator* were pre-eminent. Mr Rintoul, founder and first editor of the *Spectator*, not only championed the reform long before its establishment, but continued to give the reformer constant support through trials and triumphs till 1858, when, to the great loss of journalism and of all good causes, death severed Mr Rintoul's connection with that paper.[88]

Outside London, the *Scotsman*—then renowned for its advanced views—the *Manchester Guardian*, the *Liverpool Mercury*, and the *Leeds Mercury*—then in the hands of the well-known Baines family—were, perhaps, especially active. Their support and that of other ably conducted provincial papers never varied, and to the end of his life Rowland Hill spoke gratefully of the enlightened and powerful aid thus given.

FOOTNOTES:

[66] "All the members of his family," says Mr John C. Francis in *Notes and Queries*, 10th Series, No. 141, 8th September 1906, "were proud of Rowland and his scheme. There was no jealousy: each worked in harmony. The brothers looked at all times to each other for counsel; it was a perfect home, with the good old father as its head. Truly have his words been verified: 'The union of my children has proved their strength.'" ... "Never did a family so unite in working for the common good."

[67] "By his inventive mechanical skill," says Mr Francis, "he greatly improved the machinery [at Somerset House]. My father frequently had occasion to see him, and always found him ready to consider any suggestion made. Especially was this the case when he obtained permission for a stamp to be made with the sender's name round the rim. This was designed for him by Edwin Hill."

[68] Of Edwin's kindness of heart many instances are remembered. Of these, two, characteristic of the man, shall be selected. The head gardener at Bruce Castle lived in the (then) village of Tottenham down a narrow entry at a corner of which stood one of the inevitable drink-traps which in this civilised country are permitted to be set up wherever the poor most do congregate. John simply could not pass that public-house. He was too good a man to be allowed to sink into a sot; and eventually my uncle bethought him of building a gardener's cottage in a corner of the Castle grounds. The

plan succeeded: John lived to a hale old age, and some of his children did well in the world. One afternoon, when my uncle was walking along the Strand on his way home from Somerset House after an arduous day's work, he saw a shabbily-dressed child sobbing bitterly. Now, Edwin Hill could never pass a little one in distress, and therefore stopped to ask what was the matter. The child had wandered from home, and was lost. The address it gave was at some distance, and in quite an opposite direction from that in which my uncle was bound. Most men would have made over the small waif to the first policeman who came in sight. But not this man. He took the wearied mite in his arms, carried it home, and placed it in its anxious mother's arm.

[69] "Matthew Davenport Hill," p. 142. By his daughters, R. and F. Hill.

[70] In the Ninth of which was embodied the Commissioners' examination of Rowland Hill made in February 1837. It is curious that even these able men, when discussing the plan with its author, spoke with most hesitation of that detail of whose wisdom so many officials were more than doubtful, yet which, from the first, never presented any real difficulty—the practicability of prepayment—"Life," i. 274.

[71] As we have seen, in the chapter on "The Old Postal System," Sir Walter Scott has made a somewhat biting remark upon the "few pence" which the Post Office added to its revenue on letters which were sent a long round in order to meet Departmental convenience.

[72] "Hansard," xxxv. (2nd Series), 422.

[73] "Raw material by the half-hundred-weight" and "by post" in non-prepayment days is suggestive of heavy demands upon my father's purse. But no demand was made. Mr Wallace's frank as an M.P. would cause the packages he sent to be carried free of charge. It was literally a *cabful* of books which arrived, thus adding yet another item to the oft-quoted list of huge things which could "go free" when sent by a member of the privileged classes. One trembles to think what would have been the charge to one of the *un*privileged.

[74] After the adoption of free trade the prices of foreign produce fell still further, and their consumption since Rowland Hill drew up his estimates has grown enormously. With increase of business following on increase of consumption, came necessarily increase of employment and of national prosperity. So also when the old postal system was abolished, and the business of the Department advanced by leaps and bounds, a very large addition had to be made to the number of employees. That fact is obvious, but another, perhaps because it is less obvious, is but little known. "The introduction of penny postage," wrote my father in 1869, "was really

followed by a reduction in the hours, and an increase in the remuneration to nearly every man in the Department, save only the Postmaster-General and the Secretary"—himself. In some quarters the reverse was erroneously believed to be the case.—"Life," ii. 345.

[75] Chap. i. p. 50.

[76] "When at length I obtained precise information, I found that in taking care not to make my estimate too low, I had made it considerably too high; and I think the history of this rectification too curious and characteristic to be omitted. Two years later, the Parliamentary Committee appointed to consider my plan ordered, at my suggestion, a Return on the subject, when, to my surprise and amusement, the Report of the Post Office gave as the cost of the mail the exact sum estimated by me—viz., £5. Struck with this coincidence, the more so as I had intentionally allowed for possible omission, I suggested the call for a Return in detail, and, this being given, brought down the cost to £4, 8s. 7-¾d. In the Return, however, I discovered an error, viz., that the charge for guards' wages was that for the double journey instead of the single; and when this point was adjusted in a third Return, the cost sank to £3, 19s. 7-¾d. When explanation of the anomaly was asked for, it was acknowledged by the Post Office authorities that my estimate had been adopted wholesale." (Rowland Hill in the "Appendix to the Second Report of the Select Committee on Postage, 1838," pp. 257-259.) In estimating the real cost of a letter between London and Edinburgh we must therefore seek for a fraction still smaller than the one indicated by my father's calculations.

[77] "Post Office Reform," p. 19.

[78] "Post Office Reform," pp. 24, 25.

[79] This proposal was by no means received at the outset with universal favour. When the public was notified, after Government's acceptance of the plan of postal reform, of the advisability of setting up letter-boxes, many people—the majority, no doubt—adopted the suggestion as a matter of course. But others objected, some of them strongly; and one noble lord wrote in high indignation to the Postmaster-General to ask if he actually expected him, Lord Blank, "to cut a hole in his mahogany door."

[80] "Post Office Reform," pp. 45, 94-96.

[81] Among these he included small orders, letters of advice, remittances, policies of insurance, letters enclosing patterns, letters between country attorneys and their London agents, documents connected with magisterial and county jurisdiction, and with local trusts and commissions for the management of sewers, harbours, roads, schools, charities, etc., notices of meetings, of elections, etc., prices current, catalogues of sales, prospectuses,

and other things which, at the present time, are sent by post as a matter of course.

[82] Cobden was even more optimistic. In a letter to Rowland Hill he said: "I am prepared to find that the revenue from the penny postage *exceeds*, the first year, any former income of the Post Office."

[83] It was in 1838 that the mails began to go by rail.

[84] This was not my father's first pamphlet. In 1832 he published "Home Colonies: Sketch of a Plan for the Gradual Extinction of Pauperism and for the Diminution of Crime." The pamphlet advocated the settlement of able-bodied paupers on waste lands—a proposal frequently revived by different writers—by the cultivation of which the men would be made self-supporting, and the State be saved their charge. The successful working of similar experiments in Belgium and Holland was instanced as proof that the theory was not mere Utopianism.

[85] No. 128, p. 531. The author of the diatribe was John Wilson Croker, whose name is preserved from oblivion by Macaulay's fierce criticism in one of his famous "Essays," that on Croker's edition of Boswell's "Life of Johnson"—criticism which in severity rivals that on the poet Montgomery in the same series. Many years later Gladstone said to Dr Hill: "You have succeeded in doing what Macaulay attempted to do, and failed—you have suppressed Croker."—(Mrs Lucy Crump's "Letters of George Birkbeck Hill.")

[86] Mr Ashurst, as we are reminded in Mr Bolton King's "Mazzini" (pp. 88 and 104), was a solicitor who had been a friend of Robert Owen, and who made Mazzini's acquaintance at the time of the once famous Governmental letter-opening scandal which agitated the far-off 'forties, and caused Carlyle, Duncombe, Shiel, Macaulay, and many more people both in the House of Commons and out of it to denounce a practice which, as was only too truly said, through sending "a warning to the Bourbons, helped to entrap hapless patriots," meaning the brothers Bandiera. The agitation led to the abolition of the custom of opening private letters entrusted for conveyance to the Post Office; or did so for a while. It is a custom that is very old, and has not lacked for apologists, as what evil custom ever did? During Bishop Atterbury's trial in 1723, a Post Office clerk deposed on oath that some letters which were offered in evidence were facsimiles made of actual documents stopped, opened, and copied in the office "by direction"; and on Atterbury's asking if the witness had received warrant for the act, the Lords put in the plea of public expediency, and the enquiry came to an end.

[87] Mr John Dillon, of the once famous old firm of Morrison, Dillon, & Co., was probably one of the last wealthy London merchants who lived

above their place of business. The Dillons were hospitable people, and their dwelling was commodious and beautifully furnished; but not many merchant princes of the present day would choose as a residential quarter—Fore Street, E.C.

[88] Mr Rintoul was fortunate in being father to a devoted daughter who, from an early age, gave him valuable assistance in his editorial work. While still a young girl, and for the space of some few weeks when he was suffering from severe illness, she filled the editorial chair herself, and did so with ability. At the present day we are frequently assured by people who did not live in the times they criticise so freely that the "early Victorian" women were inferior to those of the present day. The assertion is devoid of truth. The women of half a century and more ago were bright, witty, unaffected, better mannered and perhaps better read than their descendants, often highly cultivated. They dressed simply, not extravagantly—happily for the bread-winning members of their family— did not gamble, were self-reliant, original-minded, and *not*, as has been asserted, absurdly deferential to their male relations. Indeed, it is probable that there were, proportionately, quite as many henpecked husbands in the land as there are now. If in some ways the Victorian women had less liberty than have the women of to-day and travelled less, may it not, as regards the former case, have been partly because the community was not so rich as it is at the present time, and because the facilities for travel were fewer and the conditions harder? In intellectual power and noble aims the women of half a century ago were not inferior to those of to-day. Certain it is that the former gave less time to pleasure and more to self-culture, etc. There are to-day many women who lead noble, useful lives, but their generation does not enjoy a monopoly of all the virtues. To take but a few instances from the past: has any woman of the present time excelled in true nobility of character or usefulness of career Elizabeth Fry, first among female prison reformers; Florence Nightingale, pioneer of the nursing sisterhood, and indefatigable setter to rights of muddle in Crimean War hospitals and stores; Caroline Herschel, distinguished astronomer; Mary Somerville, author and scientist—though three of these belong to a yet earlier generation—and Barbara L. S. Bodichon, artist, foundress of Girton College, and originator of the Married Women's Property Act? The modern woman is in many ways delightful, and is, as a rule, deservedly independent; but it is not necessary to accompany insistence on that fact by cheap and unmerited sneers at former generations of the sex. It is also not amiss to ask if it was not the women of the past age who won for the women of the present the liberties these latter enjoy.

CHAPTER IV

EXIT THE OLD SYSTEM

BY the early summer of 1837 the agitation in favour of the postal reform was in full movement, and in the midst of it the old king, William IV., died. His youthful successor was speedily deluged with petitions in favour of penny postage. One of the first acts of her first Parliament was to appoint the Select Committee for which Mr Wallace had asked—"To enquire into the present rates and mode of charging postage, with a view to such a reduction thereof as may be made without injury to the revenue; and for this purpose to examine especially into the mode recommended for charging and collecting postage in a pamphlet published by Mr Rowland Hill." Of this Committee, which did so much to help forward the postal reform, the doughty Member for Greenock was, of course, chosen as Chairman. The Committee sat for sixty-three days; and in addition to the postal officials and those of the Board of Stamps and Taxes (Inland Revenue), examined Rowland Hill and over eighty other witnesses of various occupations and from different parts of the country.

The story of their arduous labours is told at great length in Dr Birkbeck Hill's edition of my father's Autobiography. There is therefore no need to elaborate it here. The evidence told heavily against the existing postal system—whose anomalies, absurdities, and gross injustice have been described in the first chapter of this work—and, with corresponding force, demonstrated the necessity for its reform.[89]

It might have been supposed that the Committee's careful and elaborate examination of Rowland Hill's plan, supported as it was by an unanswerable array of facts, would have sufficed to ensure its adoption. "He had yet to learn the vast amount of *vis inertia* existing in some Government Departments. The minds of those who sit in high places are sometimes wonderfully and fearfully made, and 'outsiders,' as he was destined to find, must be prepared to knock long and loudly at the outer door before they can obtain much attention."[90]

That the Post Office authorities would oppose the plan was a foregone conclusion. They fought against it in the strenuous fashion known metaphorically as "tooth and nail." The Postmaster-General of the day—he who said that "of all the wild and visionary schemes which he had ever heard or read of it was the most extraordinary"[91] —gave it as his opinion that if twelve times the number of letters were carried, the expenses of conveyance would become twelve times heavier—a strange argument for an educated man to use. He also declared that with increase of correspondence the walls of the Post Office would burst—a premonition which, not unnaturally, provoked Rowland Hill into asking whether the size of the building should be regulated by the amount of correspondence, or the amount of correspondence by the size of the building.

The Secretary to the Post Office, Colonel Maberly, was apparently free from the dread of the possible effect of increased correspondence which exercised the minds of other post officials besides the Postmaster-General. The Secretary told the Committee he was sure that even if no charge were made people would not write more frequently than they did under the existing system; and he predicted that the public would object to prepayment. He approved of a uniform rate, but apparently in theory only, as he added that he thought it quite impracticable. He doubted whether letter-smuggling—to which practice Mr Peacock, Solicitor to the Post Office, and other officials made allusion as an evil on a very large scale— would be much affected by the proposed reduction of postage, since "it cannot be reduced to that price that smugglers will not compete with the Post Office at an immense profit." He pronounced the scheme to be "fallacious, preposterous, utterly unsupported by facts, and resting entirely on assumption"; prophesied its certain failure, if adopted, and said the revenue would not recover for forty or fifty years.[92]

Some of the officials made the rather humiliating confession that they should not know how to deal with the multitude of letters likely to follow a change of system, and a "breakdown" was so frequently predicted, that it was hard to avoid the suspicion that the wish was father to the thought. The dread expressed of this increase of correspondence is, in the light of these later days, unaccountable. "Has any one," pertinently asked my father, "ever heard of a commercial company *afraid* of an expected growth in its business?"

It was maintained that a fivefold increase of letters would necessitate a fivefold number of mail-coaches, and Rowland Hill was accused of having omitted this "fact" in his calculations. The objection was absurd. The coaches were by no means fully laden, many having very little to carry, and the chargeable letters, as we have seen, formed only a small portion of the entire mail. Twenty-four coaches left London every evening, each bearing its share of that small portion; but had the whole of it been conveyed in one coach, its bulk would not have displaced a single passenger.

Colonel (afterwards General) Colby,[93] indeed, told the Committee that his attention was first drawn to the desirability of cheapening postage while travelling all over the kingdom, when he had "observed that the mails and carriages which contained the letters formed a very stupendous machinery for the conveyance of a very small weight; that, in fact, if the correspondence had been doubled, trebled, or quadrupled, it could not have affected the expense of conveyance."[94]

To determine this question of the weight of the mails, the Committee caused a return to be made in the case of the coaches leaving London. The average was found to be only 463 lbs.—a little over a quarter of the weight which, according to Post Official estimates, a mail-coach would be capable of carrying.[95]

In the chapter on the old system we have seen the straits to which the poor were reduced when having to "take up" a letter which had come from distant relative or friend. Yet how eager was this class to enjoy the privilege possessed by those better off than themselves, was shown during the examination of Mr Emery, Deputy-Lieutenant for Somerset, and a Commissioner of Taxes, when he told the Committee that the poor people near Bristol had signed a petition for the reduction of postage, and that he "never saw greater enthusiasm." Testimony to a similar effect abounds in the Committee's Reports.

That some, at least, of the public were not so alarmed at the prospect of prepayment as were the officials generally, is seen by the evidence of several witnesses who advised that it should be made compulsory. The public were also quick to appreciate the advantage of payment by stamps instead of money. Sir (then Mr) William Brown of Liverpool, said he had seen the demoralising effect arising from entrusting young men with money to pay for postage, which, under the existing arrangement, his house [of business] was frequently obliged to do. His view was corroborated by other witnesses.[96]

Mr Samuel Jones Loyd (afterwards Lord Overstone) greatly regretted "that the post was ever taken as a field for taxation, and should be very glad to find that, consistently with the general interests of the revenue, which the Government has to watch over, they can effect any reduction in the total amount so received, or any reduction in the charges without diminishing the total amount."[97]

Lord Ashburton was of much the same opinion.

Rowland Hill himself dissented from the view generally—and indeed still—held that so long as the Department as a whole thrives, its funds may justly be applied to maintain special services which do not repay their own costs. On the contrary, he thought that every division of the service should be at least self-supporting, though he allowed that, for the sake of simplicity, extensions might be made where there was no immediate expectation of absolute profit. All beyond this he regarded as contrary to the true principles of free trade—of the "Liberation of Intercourse," to use the later-day, and in this case more appropriate, phrase. Whenever, therefore, the nett revenue from the Post Office is too high for the interests of the public, the surplus, he maintained, should be applied to the multiplication of facilities in those districts in which, through the extent of their correspondence, such revenue is produced.[98]

Most of the Post Office chiefs examined by the Committee viewed with disfavour the proposal to "tax" letters by weight. An experiment had been made at the Office from which it was inferred that a greater number could be taxed in a given time on the plan in use than by charging them in proportion to the weight of each letter. The test, however, was of little value because the weighing had not been made by the proposed half-ounce, but by the quarter-ounce scale; and, further, because it was already the custom to put nearly every letter into the balance unless its weight was palpable to the hand.[99]

While some of the officials objected to uniformity of rate as "unfair in principle," others thought well of it on the score that uniformity "would very much facilitate all the operations of the Post Office."[100]

But, admissions apart, the hostility to the plan was, on the part of the Post Office, unmistakable. This opposition rendered Rowland Hill's work all the harder. "My own examination," he says, "occupied a considerable portion of six days, my task being not only to state and enforce my own views, but to reply to objections raised by such of the Post Office authorities as were against the proposed reform. This list comprised—with the exception of Mr Peacock, the Solicitor—all the highest officials in the chief office; and, however unfortunate their opposition, and however galling I felt it at the time, I must admit on retrospect that, passing over the question of means employed, their resistance to my bold innovation was very natural. Its adoption must have been dreaded by men of routine, as involving, or seeming to involve, a total derangement of proceeding—an overthrow of established order; while the immediate loss of revenue—inevitable from the manner in which alone the change could then be introduced (all gradual or limited reform having by that time been condemned by the public voice)—a loss, moreover, greatly exaggerated in the minds of those who could not, of did not, see the means direct and indirect of its recuperation, must naturally have alarmed the appointed guardians of this branch of the national income."[101]

Some members even of the Committee were opposed to essential features of the reform, so that it barely escaped, if not actual wreckage, serious maiming at their hands. "The divisions on the two most important of the divisions submitted to the Committee," wrote Rowland Hill, "and, indeed, the ultimate result of their deliberations, show that the efforts that had been made had all been needed."[102]

A resolution moved by Mr Warburton recommending the establishment of a uniform rate of inland postage between one post town and another resulted in a tie, and was only carried by the casting vote of the chairman, Mr Wallace. Mr Warburton further moving that in view of "any large reduction being made in the rates of inland postage, it would be expedient to adopt a uniform rate of one penny per half-ounce without regard to distance," the motion was rejected by six to three, the "aye" stalwarts being the mover, and Messrs Raikes Currie[103] and M. J. O'Connell. Then Mr Warburton, still manfully striving, moved to recommend a uniform rate of three halfpence: the motion being again lost. The following day Mr Warburton returned to the charge, and urged the adoption of a twopenny uniform rate, rising by a penny for each additional half-ounce. This motion was not directly negatived like its predecessors, but was met by an amendment which was tantamount to a negative. Again the votes were equal; and again the motion was carried by the casting vote of the chairman.

The rejected amendment was moved by Mr Thomson, who proposed that a draft report originating with Lord Seymour should be adopted, the chief recommendations of which were the maintenance of the charge by distance, such rate to vary from 1d. (for under 15 miles) to 1s. (for above 200 miles), or of some similar scale. Had the Seymour amendment been adopted, "not only the recommendations for uniformity and decided reduction of postage would have been set aside, but also those for increased facilities, for the general use of stamps, and for charge by weight instead of by the number of enclosures."[104] In fact, the old postal system would have been simply scotched, not killed—and very mildly scotched, many of its worst features being retained. Yet this amendment would have gone forth as the recommendation of the Committee but for the casting vote of Mr Wallace.

It is but fair to Lord Seymour to say that, however "erroneous in its reasonings on many points," the amendment yet contained passages justifying the reformer's views, "particularly as regards the evils which high rates of postage brought upon the poor, the vast extent of illicit conveyance, the evils of the frank system, and even many of the advantages of a uniform charge." Had the recommendations in the Seymour Report been prepared "two years before, almost every one of them would have been received as a grace; but it was now too late, their sum total being altogether too slight to make any approach towards satisfying the expectations which had subsequently arisen."[105]

The adoption of a twopenny rate was not only contrary to Rowland Hill's plan, but actually rendered "strict uniformity impracticable, since reservation would have to be made in favour of the local penny rates then in existence which could not be raised without exciting overpowering dissatisfaction."[106]

"Seldom, I believe, has any committee worked harder," wrote my father, in after years. "Mr Wallace's exertions were unsparing, his toil incessant, and his zeal unflagging." The *Times* spoke but the truth when in its issue of 31st May 1839, it said that the Post Office Inquiry was "one conducted with more honesty and more industry than any ever brought before a Committee of the House of Commons."[107]

Yet how near it came to destroying the reform outright.

The third and concluding Report of the proceedings of this memorable Committee was entrusted for revision to the competent hands of Mr Warburton, who made of it a model Blue Book. "On all important points," wrote Rowland Hill, "it gave to my statements and conclusions the sanction of its powerful authority. Nevertheless, as the Committee had determined on the recommendation of a twopenny rate, the Report had to be framed in at least formal accordance with this fact; though both Mr Wallace, in whose name it went to the Committee, and Mr Warburton, its author, were strongly in favour of the penny rate. A careful perusal of the document, however, will show that, though the twopenny rate is formally recommended, the penny rate is the one really suggested for adoption. In this sense it was understood by the public; and, to my knowledge, it was wished that it should be so understood."[108]

Outside the official circle, opinion, though mainly favourable, was still a good deal divided; and the dismal prophecies which always precede the passing into law of any great reform had by no means ceased to be heard. It is therefore not altogether surprising that even so clear-sighted a man as Sydney Smith—whose wisdom is too seldom remembered by those who think of him only as a wit—should have laughed at "this nonsense of a penny post." But when the "nonsense" had had three years of trial he wrote to its author, uninvited, a letter of generous appreciation.

Miss Martineau, as an able journalist and political economist, gave valuable assistance to the postal reform. To read her statesmanlike letters to my father, even after the lapse of over half a century, is indeed a "liberal education." In these, when writing of the old system, she employed several notable phrases, of which, perhaps, one of the finest was that describing the barrier raised by heavy postal rates between severed relatives as "the infliction which makes the listening parent deaf and the full-hearted daughter dumb." In a letter, written shortly before penny postage became a reality, to him whom in her Autobiography she calls "the most signal social benefactor of our time," she told how "we are all putting up our letter-boxes on our hall doors with great glee." In the same letter she described the joy of the many poor "who can at last write to one another as if they were all M.P.s!" *As if they were all M.P.s!* What a comment, what a, may be, unconsciously satirical reflection on the previous state of things![109]

The great O'Connell gave to the postal reform the aid of his powerful influence both within and without Parliament. He was a friend of Matthew Davenport Hill, and at an early stage of the agitation assured my uncle of his hearty appreciation of the plan. O'Connell himself would have proposed the Parliamentary Committee on Postage, of which, as we have seen, one of his sons was made a member, had not Mr Wallace already taken the initiative; and, later, when the Bill was before the House, four of the O'Connells, headed by their chieftain, went into the "Ayes" lobby, together with other members from the Green Isle. The proposed reform naturally and strongly appealed to the sympathies of the inhabitants of the poorer of the two islands. In May 1839, on the occasion of a public deputation to the Prime Minister, Lord Melbourne, to urge adoption of the reform, O'Connell spoke in moving terms of its necessity. One passage of his speech recalls the remark made, many years after, by Gladstone when, at the final interview between himself and a later Irish leader, the aged statesman, in answer to a question put by the historian of "Our Own Times," said that, in his opinion, O'Connell's principal characteristic was "a passion of philanthropy."[110] "My poor countrymen," said O'Connell in 1839, "do not smuggle [letters], for the high postage works a total prohibition to them. They are too poor to find out secondary conveyances; and if you shut the Post Office to them, which you do now, you shut out warm hearts and generous affections from home, kindred, and friends."[111]

Hume, one of the great economists, a member of that "Manchester School" which the shallow wits of the present time deride, and present at this deputation, was a man who never advocated any course likely to be improvident. Yet, undismayed by possible loss of revenue, he gave the postal reform his heartiest support;[112] while Mr Moffatt, bolder still, volunteered, should the Government shrink from the undertaking, to start a City Company to work the Post Office, meanwhile guaranteeing to the State the same annual income that it was accustomed to receive.

Mr Warburton, who headed the deputation, said, with telling emphasis, that the proposed reform was a measure which a Liberal party had a just right to expect from a Liberal Administration. The deputation, a very important one, numbering, among others, 150 Members of Parliament, was unmistakably in earnest, and the Government hesitated no longer. Mr

Warburton's hint was perfectly well understood; and Lord Melbourne's reply was cautious but favourable.[113]

Some three weeks later Mr Warburton wrote to tell my father that "penny postage is to be granted."[114] Three days later still, Mr Warburton wrote again that the very date was now settled on which public announcement of that fact would be made. A few days later still, Mr Warburton rose in the House to ask the Home Secretary, Lord John Russell, whether the Government intended to proceed with a twopenny or a penny rate. Lord John replied that the Government would propose a resolution in favour of a uniform penny postage.

By Mr Warburton's advice, Rowland Hill was present when this announcement was made, and deep was the gratification he felt.

Still somewhat fearful lest the Government should hesitate to adopt prepayment and the postage stamps—details of vital necessity to the success of the plan—its author, about this time and at the request of the Mercantile Committee, drew up a paper, which they published and widely circulated, entitled "On the Collection of Postage by Means of Stamps."

In the Upper House, Lord Radnor, a little later, repeated Mr Warburton's question; and Lord Melbourne replied that the Chancellor of the Exchequer would shortly bring the matter forward.

My father drew up yet another paper, entitled "Facts and Estimates as to the Increase of Letters," which was also printed by the Mercantile Committee, and a copy sent to every member of Parliament in the hope that its perusal might secure support of the measure when introduced to the Commons.

On 5th July, the Chancellor of the Exchequer, Mr Spring Rice, brought in his Budget, the adoption of uniform penny postage being proposed in it.

During the debate, Rowland Hill sat underneath the gallery, but when the division came on he had, of course, to withdraw. The two door-keepers however, who took a lively interest in the progress of affairs, and were zealous friends to the reform, advised its author to keep within hail; and at intervals one or other of them gave a hurried whisper through the grating in the door. "All right!" "Going on capitally!" "Sure of a majority!" came in succession; and when the anxious listener was laughingly informed that Colonel Sibthorpe—a Tory of Tories, and at one time beloved of *Punch's* caricaturists—had gone into the "Ayes" lobby, the cause indeed seemed won. In a House of only 328 members there were 215 "ayes," and 113 "noes," being a majority of 102, or nearly 2 to 1.

But the House of Lords had still to be reckoned with; and towards it the untiring Mercantile Committee next directed its attention. Some of its members were formed into a deputation to interview the more influential peers, the Duke of Wellington for one.[115] Mr Moffatt thereupon put himself into communication with the old soldier, and received from him a characteristic and crushing reply. "F. M. the Duke of Wellington presents his compliments to Mr Moffatt. The Duke does not fill any political office. He is not in the habit of discussing public affairs in private, and he declines to receive the visits of deputations or individuals for the purpose of such discussions," etc.

Nothing daunted, Rowland Hill resolved to try direct appeal, and wrote to the Duke, setting forth briefly "a few facts in support of the Bill," etc. No answer was received, but the letter had a scarcely looked-for effect.

The second reading of the Bill in the Commons took place on the 22nd July, Mr Goulburn, Sir Robert Inglis, and Sir Robert Peel attacked the measure; and Mr Baring, Lord Seymour, the Chancellor of the Exchequer, Mr Wallace, and Mr Warburton defended it. The House did not divide. The Bill was read a third time on 29th July, and passed.

My paternal grandfather was in the House on the occasion, and was probably the happiest and proudest man there, the author of the plan not even excepted.

A few days later, my father, through Lord Duncannon,[116] received a summons to confer with Lord Melbourne at the latter's house the following Sunday. Lord Duncannon was present at the interview; and the three soon went to work in the most friendly fashion.

The subject in hand having, after a while, been thoroughly mastered, Lord Melbourne began to walk up and down the room, his lips moving as if rehearsing his speech for the House of Lords, but uttering no word. While thus employed, a servant entered, and made an all but inaudible announcement to his master. "Show him into the other room," said Lord Melbourne; and presently passed through the folding doors into the adjoining apartment. A hum of conversation at once began, one of the voices rising at last to angry tones, and the postal reformer's name being once audibly pronounced by the irate speaker. "It is Lord Lichfield," quietly observed Lord Duncannon. Gradually, peace seemed to be restored; the visitor departed, and Lord Melbourne, re-entering, said: "Lichfield has been here. Why a man cannot talk of penny postage without getting into a passion passes my understanding."

The following day, 5th August, the Prime Minister, in a long speech, moved the second reading of the Penny Postage Bill in the Upper House.

The Postmaster-General supported the measure, but did not conceal his distrust of it from a financial point of view.

To Lord Brougham's speech allusion has already been made.[117]

The Duke of Wellington did not believe that reduced rates of postage would encourage the soldiers on foreign or colonial service to write home oftener than before;[118] and in the earlier part of his speech drew so doleful a picture of the state of our national finances and of the danger likely to accrue to them through the lowering of any duty, that the anxious listener—who, by Lord Melbourne's wish, was in the House—seated on the steps of the throne, feared he was about to witness the slaughter of the scheme for which he and others had worked so strenuously. But Lord Duncannon, observing the downcast countenance, came up and kindly whispered: "Don't be alarmed; he is not going to oppose us."

Nor did he; for, after alluding to the evils of high postal rates, the Duke went on to say that, in his opinion, the plan most likely to remedy these was that known as Mr Rowland Hill's. "Therefore," he concluded, "I shall, although with great reluctance, vote for the Bill, and I earnestly recommend you to do the same."[119]

The Bill passed.[120] It received the Royal assent on the 17th August; and at once Mr Wallace wrote to congratulate Mrs Hill on the success of her husband's efforts, "a success to which your unremitting exertions have greatly contributed."

CAROLINE PEARSON, LADY HILL.

Mr Wallace's tribute was well deserved. My mother was a devoted wife, a true helpmate, therein resembling the late Lady Salisbury, Mrs Gladstone, Lady Campbell-Bannerman, and many lesser known women. During the long postal reform agitation, her buoyant hopefulness and abiding faith in her husband's plan never failed to cheer and encourage him to persevere.

Years after, when their children were old enough to understand the position, their father would tell them how much he owed to her, and bade them never to forget the debt. She was, moreover, a pattern scribe, sitting, hour after hour, untiring, unshirking, giving her opinion when asked for it, and in a handwriting both legible and beautifully formed, covering page after page with the sentences he dictated. More than one pamphlet, his journal, and letters innumerable were thus written by her; and she also helped in the arduous preparation for his examination before the Commissioners of Post Office Inquiry in 1837, the Select Committee on Postage of 1838, and the still later Committee of 1843. Years of useful work did she thus devote to the reform, and many a time was she seated already busy at her task when the first hour of the long day's vigil struck four. From her own lips little was ever heard of this; but what other members of the family thought of it is shown by the remark made by an old kinswoman of my father. Some one having spoken in her presence of her cousin as "the father of penny postage," she emphatically exclaimed: "Then I know who was its mother!"

The free-traders naturally hailed the postal reform with enthusiasm. It was an economic measure entirely after their own hearts, being, like their own effort for emancipation, directed against monopoly and class favouritism. Moreover, it gave an immense impetus to their crusade, since it enabled the League's literature to be disseminated with an ease and to an extent which, under the old system, would have been impossible. Thus one reform helps on another. "The men of the League are your devoted servants," wrote Cobden in one of his cheery letters. "Colonel Thompson,[121] Bright, and I have blessed you not a few times in the course of our agitating tour."

Cobden was one of the earliest and heartiest of Rowland Hill's supporters. He thought so highly of "Post Office Reform" that he urgently advised its republication in a cheaper form, offering to defray half the cost.[122] Of the plan, when it had been some time established, he wrote that "it is a terrible engine for upsetting monopoly and corruption: witness our League operations, *the spawn of your penny postage.*"

When Sir Robert Peel—more enlightened or more independent in 1846 than in 1839 and later—repealed the Corn Tax, Cobden again wrote to Rowland Hill. "The League," he said, "will be virtually dissolved by the passing of Peel's measure. I shall feel like an emancipated negro—having fulfilled my seven years' apprenticeship to an agitation which has known no respite. I feel that *you* have done not a little to strike the fetters from my limbs, for without the penny postage we might have had more years of agitation and anxiety."[123]

The Post Office, as we have seen, had hitherto existed chiefly for the benefit of the aristocratic and moneyed classes—those of the latter, at least, who were Members of Parliament, then rich men only—the general public having to pay dearly for the privilege of using the Department for conveyance of their correspondence. But with the advent of the new system, the Post Office straightway became the paid servant—and a far more faithful and efficient one than it is sometimes given credit for being—of the entire nation, since upon every man, woman, and child in the United Kingdom were henceforth conferred equal rights to postal intercourse.

Strange to say, the passing of the Penny Postage Bill had, to some extent, depended upon the successful making of a bargain. In April 1839 Lord Melbourne's Government brought in what was known as the Jamaica Bill, which proposed to suspend for five years that Colony's Constitution. The measure was strenuously opposed by the Conservatives led by Peel and by some of the Liberals. On the second reading of the Bill, the Government escaped defeat by the narrow majority of five, and at once resigned. Peel was sent for by the Queen, but, owing to the famous "Bedchamber Difficulty," failed to form a Ministry. Lord Melbourne returned to office, and the Radical members agreed to give his Administration their support on condition that penny postage should be granted. "Thus," says my brother, "one of the greatest social reforms ever introduced was actually given as a bribe by a tottering Government to secure political support."[124] A party move not altogether without precedent.

When the new postal system became a legalised institution both Mr Wallace and Mr Warburton, independently of one another, wrote to Lord Melbourne, and urged him to give Rowland Hill a position in which he would be enabled to work out his plan. Of Mr Wallace's letter my father said that it was but a specimen of that tried friend's general course. "He makes no reference to his own valuable labours, but only urges claim for me." Mr Warburton's letter was equally generous and self-oblivious.

Lord Melbourne turned no deaf ear to these appeals. In the autumn of 1839 the reformer was appointed for a term of two years—afterwards extended to three—to the Treasury to superintend the working of his plan. Obviously, his proper place, and that to which the public expected him to be raised, was the Post Office; but the hostile element there was probably too formidable to be withstood. The new Chancellor of the Exchequer— Mr Spring Rice had gone to the Upper House as Lord Monteagle—was Mr (afterwards Sir) Francis Baring, whom Rowland Hill found an able, zealous, high-minded chief, and whose friendship he valued to the last.

Of what can only be correctly described as the fanatical opposition of the Post Office authorities to the reform, it is easy, and customary, to point the finger of scorn or of derision. This is unjust. Honourable men occupying responsible positions as heads of an important branch of the Civil Service, and bound, therefore, to safeguard what they believe to be its truest interests, have a difficult task to carry out when they are confronted with the forcible acceptance of an untried scheme in whose soundness they have little or no faith. That the policy the postal officials pursued was a mistaken one time has abundantly proved; but if their opposition argued lack of understanding, they merely acted as the generality of men similarly situated would have done. Even Rowland Hill, who, as an outsider, battered so long at the official gates, was wont to confess, when, later, he found shelter within the citadel they defended, that he was not a little apt to feel towards other outsiders a hostility similar to that which his old enemies had felt towards him. The sentiment is not inspired by the oft-alleged tendency to somnolence that comes of the well-upholstered official armchair and assured salary, but from the heart-weariness born of the daily importunity of persons who deluge a long-suffering Department with crude and impracticable suggestions, or with complaints that have little or no foundation.[125]

By the time the postal reform had come to be an established institution, not a few former adversaries loyally aided the reformer to carry out its details, by their action tacitly confessing, even when they made no verbal acknowledgment, that their earlier attitude had been a mistake. Now that all are dead their opposition may rightly be regarded with the tenderness that is, or should be, always extended to the partisans of a lost cause.

A great deal of the opposition was, however, far from honest, and unfortunately had very mischievous effects. On this subject something will be said in the course of the ensuing chapter.

FOOTNOTES:

[89] The members in addition to Mr Wallace were Viscount Lowther, Lord Seymour, Sir Thomas Fremantle, and Messrs Warburton, Poulett Thomson, Raikes Currie, Morgan John O'Connell, Thornley, Chalmers, Pease, Mahony, Parker (Sheffield), George William Wood, and Villiers. Three of these—Lord Seymour, Mr Parker, and Mr Thomson (afterwards Lord Sydenham)—were opponents of the plan, but that their opposition was mainly official was evidenced when, the Government having adopted the plan of reform, all three became its advocates.—"Life," i. 287.

[90] "The Jubilee of the Uniform Penny Postage," p. 18. By Pearson Hill, 1890. Cassell & Co. Ltd.

[91] "Hansard," xxxviii. 1462, 1464.

[92] "Third Report of the Select Committee on Postage," pp. 29, 34, etc. The gross revenue which rather more than recovered in 1851, was achieved on a four-and-three-quarters-fold increase of letters only, whereas the Postmaster-General said that recovery would require a twelvefold increase. Rowland Hill calculated that recovery would ensue on a five-and-three-quarters increase.

[93] Director of the Ordnance Survey, a distinguished geologist, and an earnest worker in the cause of postal reform from quite an early date. He had lost his hands during the Napoleonic wars; and when he dined at our house always brought his knife, fork, etc., and his manservant, who screwed them into place, and changed them when needful, a process which deeply interested us children. He did not, however, permit this serious loss to stand in the way of his leading an active and useful public career.

[94] "Third Report," p. 48.

[95] Ibid. p. 49. The Superintendent of the Mail-coaches considered that each coach could carry 15 hundred-weight or 1680 pounds.

[96] "Third Report," p. 42.

[97] Ibid. p. 27.

[98] "Post Office Reform," p. 55.

[99] "First Report," questions 1369, 1372.

[100] "Third Report," p. 34, etc.

[101] "Life," i. 325-327.

[102] "Life," i. 325-327.

[103] Father to a later Postmaster-General.

[104] "Life," i. 328.

[105] "Life," i. 329.

[106] Ibid. i. 330.

[107] The Times was now a hearty champion of the reform, and wrote frequently and ably in support of it.

[108] "Life," i. 337. During the writing of this Report my father had frequent occasion to call upon its author in order to check elaborate calculations and to put important questions in the clearest light—on the principle, apparently, that two heads, when each is mathematical, are better than one. "Philosopher Warburton," as he was sometimes called, was one

of the best friends the postal reform had. He was a man of wide influence, and an indefatigable worker. Originally a timber merchant, he abandoned commerce for science his favourite pursuits being mathematics and astronomy. He was a member of the Political Economy Club from its foundation in 1821 till his death in 1858; he was one of the founders of the London University, and served on its first council; and he represented Bridport, Dorset, in successive Parliaments from 1825 to 1841. It is often asserted that a recluse, bookworm, or scientist cares for nothing outside his own four walls or lower than the starry heavens. In this case never was saying more completely falsified. Mr Warburton was unusually public-spirited, a prominent Parliamentarian, and a lucid writer. When my father visited him, he was always received in his friend's sanctum, the dining-room, whose appearance never altered. Dining there would have been impossible, although the table was always set out at full length. It was entirely covered with piles of volumes, most of them Blue Books. The sideboard, save for one small space reserved for astronomical instruments, was similarly loaded, as were also all the chairs but one in addition to that reserved for Mr Warburton's use. The floor was likewise piled with books, very narrow passages only being left to enable people to move about; and the whole place bore a look upon it as of "the repose of years." When, after talking a while, Mr Warburton resumed his pen, my father had time, during his several visits, to read the whole of one of Macaulay's brilliant and then newly-published Essays in a volume which always occupied a particular spot on a table.

[109] Many years after the establishment of the postal reform, on the occasion of a tour to the English Lakes, our parents took my younger sister and me to visit Miss Martineau at her prettily-situated Ambleside house. We two girls were charmed with her bright, sensible talk, and her kindly, winning personality. We found her also much better-looking than from her portraits we had expected to see her. *They* missed the wonderful lighting up of the clever face which, when animated, looked far younger than when in repose. Among other interesting items of information, she told us of her, I fear, useless efforts to rescue the local rural population, then mostly illiterates, from the curse of intemperance. She contemplated giving a lecture on the subject, and showed us some horrifying coloured drawings representing the ravages effected by alcohol on the human system which she had prepared for it; but, as she knew that no one would come if the lecture were announced as about Drink, she said she should call it a "Discourse on Our Digestive Organs," or something of the sort. We never heard the fate of that proposed lecture.

[110] "The Story of Gladstone's Life," p. 38. By Justin M'Carthy.

[111] "Life," i. 342. How well the great orator understood his poorer countrymen's need was shown when, for a few weeks before the 10th of January 1840, a tentative reduction to a uniform fourpenny rate outside London was introduced. The increase of letters during those few weeks stood at, for England and Wales, 33; Scotland, 51; and Ireland, 52 per cent. When my father and his brothers—as told in the Introductory Chapter— used to wander about the "green borderland" outside the smaller Birmingham and Wolverhampton of the early nineteenth century, they sometimes, in the summer and autumn seasons, fell in with the Irish haymakers and harvesters, and were struck with the frugal manner in which they lived, their sobriety and their unwillingness to break into the little hoard of money—their wages—which they aimed to take back intact to their families in Ireland at the end of their few months' service here. The postal reform enabled these men to write letters and to send their money home cheaply, frequently, and without waiting for the season's close.

[112] Writing of penny postage, eight years later, to the American historian Bancroft, Hume said: "I am not aware of any reform amongst the many I have promoted during the past forty years that has had, and will have, better results towards the improvement of the country, socially, morally, and politically."

[113] In Earl Russell's "Recollections," at p. 231, a quotation is made from an entry in his journal for 1839, which says: "The Cabinet"—of which he was a member—"was unanimous in favour of the ingenious and popular plan of a penny postage."

[114] "Life," i. 343.

[115] Only those who remember any of the generation which lived through the long and anxious years of the terrible war with France can form an adequate idea of the veneration—adoration even—felt by the nation for the great Duke—*the* Duke as he was generally called. My father, at no time addicted to the "scarlet fever," was nevertheless one of the heartiest devotees; and one day during our three years' sojourn at Brighton he took some of us children to the railway station to see the veteran, then about to return to town after a visit to the seaside. There he sat alone under the sheltering hood of his open carriage which, with its back turned towards the locomotive, was mounted on an ordinary truck at the rear end of the train. He wore a dark, military cloak and close-fitting cloth cap, and with his thin face, hooked nose, and piercing eyes looked like an ancient eagle. His unwandering gaze was bent sea-wards as though he descried a foreign fleet making with hostile intentions for our shores. He was so used to being stared at that but for his at once giving the military salute in acknowledgment of our father's respectful bow and bared head, we might

have thought him unconscious of the presence of strangers. He seemed so to be even when our father took us close to the train, and bade us look well at the greatest of living Englishmen because he was so old that we might not see him again. It would, however, have been difficult to forget a face so striking. After all, that was not our only sight of him. We often afterwards saw him riding in Hyde Park, where the crowd saluted him as if he were Royalty itself; and, later still, we looked on at his never-to-be-forgotten funeral. Mention of the "Iron Duke" and of the Brighton railway brings back to memory another old soldier who figured in the same wars and, as Earl of March, achieved distinction. This was the then Duke of Richmond, on whom we children looked with awesome curiosity, because rumour, for once a truth-teller, declared that ever since 1815 he had carried somewhere within his corporeal frame a bullet which defied all attempts at extraction, and, indeed, did not prevent his attaining to a hale old age. While my father was on the directorate of the London and Brighton railway, and lived at that seaside resort, he often travelled to town with some distinguished man whom he invited to share his *coupé*. (Why, I wonder, is this pleasant sort of compartment rarely or never seen nowadays?) More than once the Duke of Richmond was his companion. The time was the mid 'forties, when railway locomotives were far less powerfully built than they are now, and when, London Bridge Terminus being up a rather long incline, it was customary, on the departure of a train from the ticket-taking platform, to employ a second engine to aid the one in front by pushing from behind. The travellers were seated in an end *coupé*, and opposite their seats were, of course, only the usual glass windows. When, therefore, the Duke for the first time saw the auxiliary engine coming close up against the carriage, he did not know what it meant, turned pale, and showed considerable uneasiness. My father soon assured him that all was right, and then asked why he, a veteran campaigner, was unnerved by a mere railway engine. Whereupon the old soldier laughingly replied that he would far sooner face the foe on the battlefield than sit quietly right in face of the "iron horse."

[116] Lord Duncannon had been a member of the Commission of Post Office Inquiry of 1835-1838 (already mentioned) which examined Rowland Hill in February 1837. He was at first a strong opponent of the Reform, but during the examination became one of its heartiest supporters. The other two Commissioners were Lord Seymour—who, later, served on Mr Wallace's Select Committee, was afterwards Duke of Somerset, and gave to the world an unorthodox little volume—and Mr Labouchere, afterwards Lord Taunton, and uncle to the better-known proprietor of *Truth*.

[117] Chap. ii. p. 80. With Lord Brougham and others, my father, some years before, had been associated in the movement for the "Diffusion of Useful Knowledge," a Society which, in England and Wales acted as

pioneers in the good work of publishing cheap and wholesome literature, just as in Scotland did the Chambers Brothers. Unfortunately, Brougham believed himself to be scientific, and contributed to the series an article so full of mistakes that some wag immediately dubbed the Society that for the "*Con*fusion of Useful," etc. Brougham was a supporter of the postal reform, and my father found in him more kindliness than the world gave him credit for possessing. The great lawyer was a very eccentric man, and *Punch* caricatured him unmercifully, invariably representing him as clad in the large-checked "inexpressibles" which he is said to have always worn because, in a moment of weakness, he had purchased as a bargain so huge a roll of cloth of that pattern that it supplied him with those garments for the rest of his days. The story is pretty generally known of his causing to be published the news of his death, and of his sitting, very much alive, in a back room of his darkened house, and reading, with quite pardonable interest, the obituary notices which appeared in the different newspapers. He wrote an execrable hand, which varied in degrees of illegibility. The least illegible he and his secretary alone could read; a worse he only; the very worst, not even he could decipher, especially if he had forgotten the matter of which it treated. This story has, of course, been fathered on many bad writers; but any one possessed of a Brougham autograph must feel convinced that to none but him could possibly belong its authorship.

[118] How much mistaken the old warrior was as regards the soldiers' letters has been abundantly proved. During the first eight months of postal communication between the United Kingdom and our comparatively small army in the Crimea—and long, therefore, before the Board School era—more than 350,000 letters passed each way; while when the Money Order system, for the first time in history, was extended to the seat of war, in one year over £100,000 was sent home for wives and families.

[119] "Life," i. 352-360.

[120] When it passed the Lords, Cobden is said to have exclaimed: "There go the Corn Laws!"

[121] Colonel Perronet Thompson was the author of the once famous "Anti-Corn-Law Catechism," which might, with great advantage, be reprinted now. He was a public-spirited man, one of the foremost among the free-traders, and deserves to be better remembered than he is.

[122] The pamphlet was published at a shilling; in those days of paper taxation, when books were necessarily dear and correspondingly scarce, a by no means exorbitant price.

[123] During a part of Cobden's Parliamentary career and that of his and our friends, J. B. Smith and Sir Joshua Walmsley, all three men were next-

door neighbours, living in London in three adjoining houses. Hence Nos. 101, 103, and 105 Westbourne Terrace came to be known as "Radical Row."

[124] "The Post Office of Fifty Years Ago," p. 24.

[125] Losses, for example, are often imputed to the Post Office for which it is entirely blameless. Did space allow, scores of instances might be cited. One of the most absurd was the case of a London merchant, who, in the course of very many months, wrote at intervals angry letters to the Postmaster-General asking why such or such a letter had not reached its destination. No amount of enquiries could trace the errant missives; and the luckless Department was, at corresponding intervals, denounced for its stupidity in equally angry letters to the Press. One day, while certain city improvements were being carried out, an ancient pump, near the merchant's office, which had long refused to yield any water was taken down, when its interior presented an unusual appearance. An errand-boy had, at odd times, been sent to post the Firm's letters, and had slipped them into the narrow slit where once the vanished pump-handle used to work. The introduction of street letter-boxes was then recent, and their aspect still unfamiliar. The boy had therefore taken the venerable relic for one of those novel structures, and all the missing letters lay therein.

CHAPTER V

AT THE TREASURY

TO any one disposed to belief in omens it would seem that the beginning of Rowland Hill's connection with the Treasury augured ill for its continuance. Even the letter which invited him to office went near to miss reaching its destination.

He had left town for a brief rest after the strenuous work of the close upon three years' struggle for postal reform, leaving strict orders at the South Australian Office that if any communication from the Government intended for him arrived there it should be forwarded without delay. The document did arrive, but was laid aside to await the wanderer's return because it bore in the left-hand corner what seemed to be the signature of a then well-known man connected with Australian affairs who, at the meetings of the Association, was much given to bestow on its members much unsought advice and worthless criticism; and was therefore, by unanimous consent, voted an insufferable bore. However, when a messenger came from the Treasury to ask why no notice had been taken of a letter from the Chancellor of the Exchequer, the alarmed clerk on duty hastened to send on the belated dispatch, wrapped up as a brown paper parcel, by railway, as being, to his mind, the most expeditious, apparently because most novel mode of conveyance. But parcels by rail made slower progress in those days than in these; and when at last this one reached its destination its date was hardly of the newest.

No. 1, ORME SQUARE.
The residence of Rowland Hill when Penny Postage was established.
The Tablet was put up by the L.C.C.
From a Photograph by Messrs. Whiteley & Co.

The first interview with the Chancellor of the Exchequer was scarcely satisfactory, but through no fault of Mr Baring, who was but the mouthpiece of the Cabinet. The Government, as we have seen, offered a temporary (two years') engagement to a man already provided with steady employment, and therefore in a fairly good financial position, as things were then accounted; required him to devote his whole time to the public service; and to this temporary engagement proposed to attach the salary of a head clerk. This, too, to a man who, with the help of thousands of supporters of every class, had just inaugurated an epoch-making reform destined to confer lasting benefit on his own country and on the entire civilised world; who was on the wrong side of forty; and who had a wife and young children to support. The offer—however intended—could only be described as shabby; and the fact that during the interview the amount of emolument was twice increased suggested a hard-bargain-driving transaction rather than a discussion between friendly negotiators. We have also seen that in 1837 Rowland Hill, through his friend Mr Villiers, offered to make a present to the Government of his plan—willing, because he was convinced of its soundness and workability, to let them have the full credit of its introduction, but stipulating that if the gift were refused he should refer his proposals to the Press, and to the country—a gift the Government had not the courage to accept. It is therefore clear that monetary greed found no place in my father's temperament, but only the dread which every prudent husband and father must feel when confronted with the prospect, in two years' time and at the age of forty-six, of recommencing the arduous battle of life.

He told Mr Baring that while he was willing to give his services gratuitously, or to postpone the question of remuneration till the new system should have had adequate trial, it would be impossible for him to enter on such an undertaking were he placed on a footing inferior to that of the Secretary to the Post Office—a necessary stipulation if the reformer was to have full power to carry his plan into operation. He was well aware that the post officials viewed it and him with unfriendly eyes; and his anxiety was not diminished by the knowledge that his reform would be developed under another roof than that of the Treasury, and by the very men who had pronounced the measure revolutionary, preposterous, wild, visionary, absurd, clumsy, and impracticable. His opponents had prophesied that the plan would fail; and as Matthew Davenport Hill, when writing of this subject, wittily and wisely said: "I hold in great awe prophets who may have the means of assisting in the fulfilment of their own predictions." It was therefore imperative that Rowland Hill's position should be a well-defined one, and he himself be placed on an equality with the principal executive officer among those with whose habits and prejudices he was bound to interfere. The labour would be heavy, and the conditions were unusual. He must try to turn enemies still smarting under the bitterness of defeat into allies willing as well as able to help on the reform they detested; and to persuade them not to place obstacles in its way. The innovations to be made would be numerous, because, while reduction of postage and modes of prepayment formed the principal features of the plan, they were far from being the only features. The projected increase of facilities for transmitting letters, etc., would cause an immense amount of extra work; and as in this matter he would have to contend with the Post Office almost single-handed, nothing would be easier than for its head officials to raise plausible objections by the score to every proposal made. Nor could the public, who had now secured cheap postage and an easier mode of paying for it—to superficial eyes the only part of the plan worth fighting for—be henceforth relied upon to give the reformer that support which was necessary to carry out other important details; the less so as the reformer would be debarred from appealing for outside help or sympathy, because, when once the official doorways are passed, a man's independence is lost, and his lips are perforce sealed.

The interview was brought to a close by Rowland Hill telling Mr Baring that before returning a definite answer he must consult his friends; and that as his eldest brother was away on circuit at Leicester, and he proposed to start at once for that town to seek fraternal advice, three days must elapse before the matter could be settled.

He found his brother lying on a couch in a state of exhaustion after a very hard day's work, and Rowland proposed to delay discussion of the question till the following day. But Matthew would not hear of this; and, getting more and more moved as the younger man proceeded with his tale, presently sprang upright, and, oblivious of fatigue, threw himself with ardour into the subject of the offered appointment. After a while, Matthew proposed to write a letter on his own account to Rowland, which the latter should hand to the Chancellor of the Exchequer. This was done the next day, the younger brother writing to the elder's dictation; and the letter is given at full length in my father's "Life" and in my brother's "The Post Office of Fifty Years Ago." In Matthew's own clear and eloquent language—for he was as admirable a writer as he was a speaker—are expressed the views enunciated above, which Rowland had already laid before Mr Baring at the interview just described.

Before the Chancellor of the Exchequer and my father met again the former wrote him a letter explanatory of the course of conduct to be adopted on his engagement at the Treasury, stating, among other things, that free access to the Post Office, and every facility of enquiry as to the arrangements made would be given, but that all "your communications will be to the Treasury, from which any directions to the Post Office will be issued; and you will not exercise any direct authority, or give any immediate orders to the officers of the Post Office." The explanation was said to be given "to prevent future misunderstanding"; and this was doubtless the euphonious mode of expressing apprehension of a state of things which, in view of the well-known hostility of St Martin's-le-Grand, the writer felt was likely to arise; and again mention was made of the condition that "the employment is considered as temporary, and not to give a *claim* to continued employment in office at the termination of those two years."[126]

The prospect was scarcely satisfactory; nevertheless, my father hoped that by the end of his term of engagement, and by unceasing effort on his part, he might find himself "in a recognised position, in direct communication with persons of high authority, and entrusted with powers which, however weak and limited in the outset, seemed, if discreetly used, not unlikely in due time to acquire strength and durability. I was far from supposing that the attainment of my post was the attainment of my object. The obstacles, numerous and formidable, which had been indicated in my brother's letter had all, I felt, a real existence; while others were sure to appear of which, as yet, I knew little or nothing. Still, I felt no way daunted, but, relying at once on the efficiency of my plan, I felt confident of succeeding in the end."[127]

The goal at which Rowland Hill aimed was, as he told Mr Baring at this second interview, the permanent headship—as distinguished from the political headship—of the Post Office, then filled by Colonel Maberly:[128] the only position in which the reformer could really acquire that authority which was essential to the development of his plan. But the Fates were stronger even than one strong-willed man; and Colonel Maberly held the post for fifteen years longer. Thus, when the helm came at last into Rowland Hill's hands, he was long past middle life; and his years of almost unrestricted influence were destined to be but few.

Further encouragement to accept the present position was given by Mr Baring's friendly, sympathetic attitude; and it should here be recorded that the longer Rowland Hill served under his chief the more cordial grew the relations between them. Ample proof of this confidence was seen in the Chancellor of the Exchequer's increased readiness to adopt suggestions from the new official, and to leave to him the decision on not a few questions of importance.

On the first day of my father's appointment he accompanied Mr Baring to the Post Office, that being the first time the reformer had set foot within its portals. He was much interested in the different processes at work, such as date-stamping, "taxing"—the latter destined soon, happily, to be abolished—sorting, etc. But the building, which had been erected at great expense only ten years previously, struck him as too small for the business carried on in it; badly planned, badly ventilated, and deficient in sanitary arrangements—a monument to the fatuity alike of architect and builder. This discovery led him to think of practicable alterations in the existing edifice and of devolution in the shape of erection of district offices; and by Mr Baring's wish he drew up a paper giving his views in detail, and including with his proposals that necessary accompaniment of amalgamation into one force of the two corps of letter-carriers, the general and the "twopenny post" men, which has already been alluded to. But this greatly needed measure was, perforce, deferred till after Colonel Maberly's retirement.

In order the better to get through as much of his projected work as he could accomplish in the twice twelvemonths before him, my father rose daily at six, and after an early breakfast set off for the Treasury, where at first his appearance at an hour when many officials were probably only beginning to rise caused considerable astonishment, and where he stayed as long as he could. If even under these circumstances the progress made seemed slow and unsatisfactory to the man longing to behold his scheme adopted in its entirety, how much worse would not the reform have fared had he kept strictly to the hours prescribed by official custom!

A few weeks after his acceptance of office, and at Mr Baring's suggestion, he visited Paris to inspect the postal system there. He found it in many respects well ahead of our own. In France the old system never weighed so heavily upon the people as did our own old system upon us. The charges were about two-thirds of our own for corresponding distances, but the number of a letter's enclosures was not taken into consideration, the postage varying according to weight. Though Paris was much smaller than London, its post offices were more numerous than ours, being 246 against our 237. There was a sort of book post, a parcel post for valuables of small dimensions at a commission paid of 5 per cent.—the Post Office, in case of loss, indemnifying the loser to the extent of the value of the article; and a money order system so far in advance of our own that the French people sent more than double as much money through the post as we did. The gross revenue was about two-thirds that of the British Post Office; the expenses 20 per cent. more; the nett revenue less than half.

Street letter-boxes were an old institution in France; our own, therefore, were but an adaptation. The larger towns of Germany possessed them, as did also the towns and villages of the Channel Isles. After his visit to France, Rowland Hill urged the Treasury to adopt street letter-boxes, and one was put up in Westminster Hall. But it was not till the early 'fifties that they were introduced to any great extent. Before the establishment of penny postage there were only some 4,500 post offices in the United Kingdom. In the year of my father's death (1879), the number had grown to over 13,000, in addition to nearly 12,000 pillar and wall boxes. And the advance since 1879 has, of course, been very great.[129] But it is not alone in number that the change is seen. In the case of post offices, a handsome edifice full of busy workers has, in many towns and districts, replaced an insignificant building managed by a few more or less leisurely officials, or by even one person.

AN OLD POST OFFICE.
A POST-OFFICE IN 1790.
By permission of the Proprietors of the *City Press*.

It was during this visit to Paris that my father became acquainted with M. Piron, *Sous Directeur des Postes aux Lettres*, a man whose memory should not be suffered to perish, since it was mainly through his exertions that the postal reform was adopted in France. For several years during the latter part of Louis Philippe's reign, M. Piron strove so persistently to promote the cause of cheap postage that he actually injured his prospects of rising in the Service, as the innovation was strenuously opposed both by the monarch and by the Postmaster-General, M. Dubost, the "French Maberly." Therefore, while the "citizen king" remained on the throne the Government gave little or no encouragement to the proposed reform. But M. Piron, too much in earnest to put personal advancement above his country's welfare, went on manfully fighting for cheap postage. He it was who made the accidental discovery among the archives of the French Post Office of documents which showed that a M. de Valayer had, nearly two hundred years before, established in Paris a private (penny?) post—of which further mention will be made in the next chapter. Neither Charles Knight, who first suggested the impressed stamp, nor Rowland Hill, who first suggested the adhesive stamp, had heard of M. de Valayer or of his private post; and even in France they had been forgotten, and might have remained so but for M. Piron's discovery. One is reminded of the re-invention of the mariner's compass and of many other new-old things.

Nine years after my father's official visit to Paris, that is, with the advent of the Revolution of 1848, the reforming spirit in France had stronger sway; and M. Piron's efforts were at last crowned with success. The uniform rate proposed by him (20 centimes) was adopted, and the stamp issued was the well-known black head of Liberty. In order to keep pace with the public demand, the first sheets were printed in such a hurry that some of the heads—the dies to produce which were then detached from one another—were turned upside down. M. Piron sent my father one of the earliest sheets with apologies for the reversals. These are now almost unobtainable, and are therefore much prized by philatelists.

During this visit to Paris, or at a later one, my father also made the acquaintance of M. Grasset, M. St Priest, and other leading post officials; and, among non-official and very interesting people, M. Horace Say, son to the famous Jean Baptiste Say, and father to the late M. Léon Say, three generations of illustrious Frenchmen.

Although travelling in France—or, indeed, in England or any other country—was in 1839 very different from what it has become in these luxurious days, for railways were established later in France than they were here, my mother had accompanied her husband. One day the pair set off in a *calèche* to visit some old friends who lived in a rather distant part of the country. Darkness came on, and ere long all trace of the road was lost. At last the wretched little vehicle broke down in a field; and the driver, detaching the horse, rode off to try to discover their whereabouts. The process was a slow one; and the travellers were left alone for what seemed to be many hours. Near the field was a wood in which wolves had been seen that day, and there was good reason to dread a visit from them. When at last the driver, having found the right road, reappeared, attached the horse to the *calèche*, and pushed on again, he drove his party by mistake to the back-door of their friends' house. It was now late at night, and the family, who had retired to rest, and were waked by the driver's loud knocking, mistook the belated travellers for robbers, and refused to unbar the door. It was only after a long parley that the wearied visitors were admitted, to receive, of course, the warmest welcome. The master of the house had been the hero of an unusually romantic story. As a young officer in the French army, he was captured at the time of the unfortunate Walcheren expedition, and carried to England, there to remain some years as a prisoner of war. While on *parole* he made many friends in this country, where he occupied part of his time by the study of English law, in which he became a proficient. During his novitiate he became acquainted with a young lady unto whom he was not long in losing his heart. As he came to know her and her widowed mother better, a suspicion crossed his mind that the daughter was being kept out of a handsome property, rightly hers, by a fraudulent relative. Examination of the case strengthened suspicion into conviction, and he undertook to champion her cause, his knowledge of English law coming in as a powerful weapon to his hand. On conclusion of the trial, he and some of those who had acted with him set off for the lady's home as fast as horses, post-boys, and money could take them. "They are scattering guineas!" exclaimed a bystander. "They have won the case!" It was so, and something more than the case, for the gallant young Frenchman was rewarded for his prowess by receiving in marriage the hand of the girl for whom he had accomplished so much. When the war was over, M. Chevalier returned to France together with his wife and her mother.

Heartily as Mr Baring approved of the new system, he still distrusted the principle of prepayment. In this opinion he was, as we have seen, not singular. By many people it was still pronounced "un-English" to prepay letters. But my father was so confident of the wisdom of the step that Mr Baring ultimately gave way, stipulating only that the responsibility should rest, not on the Chancellor of the Exchequer, but on the author of the reform. The condition was unhesitatingly accepted.

To ensure use of the stamps, Mr Baring, later, proposed that it should be made illegal to prepay postage other than by their means; but Rowland Hill, hating compulsion, and feeling confident of their ultimate acceptability, maintained that it would be better if at first the two modes of payment, money and stamps, contended for public favour on equal terms, and succeeded in convincing Mr Baring of the soundness of that view.

The question of the stamps was therefore one of the first to require my father's attention on his return from Paris; and he found much to occupy him in dealing with the many suggestions contained in the letters sent in by the public, and in the vast number of designs accompanying them. As the succeeding chapter will show, the subject, in one form or another, took up much of his time for a little over twelve months.

Early in December, at his suggestion, the tentative postal rate of 1d. for London, and 4d. for the rest of the kingdom was introduced, all tiresome extras such as the penny on each letter for using the Menai and Conway bridges, the halfpenny for crossing the Scottish border, etc., being abolished. This experiment was made to allow the postal staff to become familiarised with the new system, as a vast increase of letters, necessarily productive of some temporary confusion, was looked for on the advent of the uniform penny rate. Under the old system 4d. had been the lowest charge beyond the radius of the "twopenny post"; therefore, even the preliminary reduction was a relief. But although three years earlier a lowering of the existing rates to a minimum of 6d. or 8d. would have been eagerly welcomed, the public were now looking forward to yet lower charges; and the prospect of paying 4d. was viewed with great dissatisfaction. People began to suspect that the concession would go no further, that the Government intended to "cheat the public," and my father was accused of having "betrayed his own cause." Thus easily is a scare manufactured.

The result of the first day of this preliminary measure was awaited with some anxiety. The increase of the fourpenny letters was about 50, and of the penny letters nearly 150 *per cent.*, the unpaid letters being about as numerous as usual, prepayment being not yet made compulsory. This state of things my father considered "satisfactory"; Mr Baring "very much so." The next day the numbers fell off, and this gave the enemies of postal reform a delightful, and by no means neglected, opportunity of writing to its author letters of the "I told you so!" description.

The 10th of January 1840, when the uniform penny rate came into operation, was a busy day at the post offices of the country. Many people made a point of celebrating the occasion by writing to their friends, and not a few—some of the writers being entire strangers—addressed letters of thanks to the reformer.[130] One of these was from Miss Martineau, who had worked ably and well for the reform; and another from the veteran authoress, Miss Edgeworth, whom, some twenty years earlier, Rowland Hill had visited in her interesting ancestral home.[131]

At that time, and for many years after, there was at St Martin's-le-Grand a large centre hall open to the public, but, later, covered over and appropriated by the ever-growing Circulation Department. At one end of the hall was a window, which during part of the day always stood open to receive the different kinds of missives. These, as the hour for closing drew near, poured in with increasing volume, until at "six sharp," when the reception of matter for the chief outgoing mail of the day ended, the window shut suddenly, sometimes with a letter or newspaper only half-way through.[132] On the afternoon of the 10th, six windows instead of one were opened; and a few minutes before post time a seventh was thrown up, at which the chief of the Circulation Department himself stood to help in the receipt of letters. The crowd was good-tempered, and evidently enjoyed the crush, though towards the last letters and accompanying pennies were thrown in anyhow, sometimes separating beyond hope of reunion; and though many people were unable to reach the windows before six o'clock struck. When the last stroke of the hour had rung out, and the lower sash of every window had come down with a rush like the guillotine, a great cheer went up for "penny postage and Rowland Hill," and another for the Post Office staff who had worked so well.

So much enthusiasm was displayed by the public that the author of the new system fully expected to hear that 100,000 letters, or more than three times the number usually dispatched, had been posted. The actual total was about 112,000.

The reformer kept a constant watch on the returns of the number of inland letters passing through the post. The result was sometimes satisfactory, sometimes the reverse, especially when a return issued about two months after the establishment of the penny rate showed that the increase was rather less than two-and-three-quarters-fold. The average postage on the inland letters proved to be three halfpence; and the reformer calculated that at that rate a four-and-three-quarters-fold increase would be required to bring up the gross revenue to its former dimensions. Eleven years later his calculation was justified by the result; and in the thirteenth year of the reform the number of letters was exactly five times as many as during the last year of the old system.

Meanwhile, it was satisfactory to find that the reductions which had recently been made in the postage of foreign letters had led to a great increase of receipts, and that in no case had loss to the revenue followed.

One reason for the comparatively slow increase in the number of inland letters must be attributed to the persistent delay in carrying out my father's plan for extending rural distribution. In the minute he drew up, he says: "The amount of population thus seriously inconvenienced the Post Office has declared itself unable to estimate, but it is probable that in England and Wales alone it is not less than 4,000,000. The great extent of the deficiency [of postal facilities] is shown by the fact that, while these two divisions of the empire contain about 11,000 parishes, their total number of post offices of all descriptions is only about 2,000. In some places *quasi* post offices have been established by carriers and others, whose charges add to the cost of a letter, in some instances as much as sixpence. A penny for every mile from the post office is a customary demand."[133]

Of the beneficent effects of cheap postage, gratifying accounts were meanwhile being reported; some told in conversation, or in letters from friends or strangers, some in the Press or elsewhere.

One immediate effect was an impetus to education, especially among the less affluent classes. When one poor person could send another of like condition a letter for a penny instead of many times that amount, it was worth the while of both to learn to read and write. Many people even past middle age tried to master the twin arts; and at evening classes, some of which were improvised for the purpose, two generations of a family would, not infrequently, be seen at work seated side by side on the same school bench. Other poor people, with whom letter-writing, for lack of opportunity to practise it, had become a half-forgotten handicraft, made laborious efforts to recover it. And thus old ties were knit afresh, as severed relatives and friends came into touch again. Surely, to hinder such reunion by "blocking" rural distribution and other important improvements was little, if at all, short of a crime.

Mr Brookes, a Birmingham home missionary, reported that the correspondence of the poorer classes had probably increased a hundredfold; and that adults as well as young people took readily to prepayment, and enjoyed affixing the adhesive Queen's head outside their letters.

Professor Henslow, then rector of Hitcham, Suffolk, wrote of the importance of the new system to those who cultivated science and needed to exchange ideas and documents. He also stated that before penny postage came in he had often acted as amanuensis to his poorer parishioners, but that they now aspired to play the part of scribe themselves.

The servant class, hitherto generally illiterate, also began to indite letters home; and a young footman of Mr Baring's one day told my father that he was learning to write in order to send letters to his mother, who lived in a remote part of the country; and added that he had many friends who were also learning. Indeed, one poor man, settled in the metropolis, proudly boasted that he was now able to receive daily bulletins of the condition of a sick parent living many miles away.

Charles Knight found that the reduced rates of postage stimulated every branch of his trade—an opinion endorsed by other publishers and book-sellers; and the honorary secretary to the Parker Society, whose business was the reprinting of the early reformers' works, wrote, two years after the abolition of the old system, to tell the author of the new one that the very existence of the Society was due to the penny post.

"Dear Rowland," wrote Charles Knight, in a letter dated 10th May 1843, "The Poor Law 'Official Circular' to which par. No. 7 chiefly refers, is one of the most striking examples of the benefit of cheap postage. It could not have existed without cheap postage. The Commissioners could not have sent it under their frank without giving it away, which would have cost them £1,000 a year. It is sold at 4d., including the postage, which we prepay; and we send out 5,000 to various Boards of Guardians and others who are subscribers, and who pay, in many cases, by post office orders. The work affords a profit to the Government instead of costing a thousand a year."

After four years of the new system Messrs Pickford said that their letters had grown in number from 30,000 to 720,000 *per annum*. And testimony of similar character was given either in evidence before the Committee on Postage of 1843, or, from time to time, was independently volunteered.

The postal reform not only gave a vast impetus to trade and education, but even created new industries, among them the manufacture of letter-boxes and letter-weighing machines—which were turned out in immense quantities—to say nothing of the making of stamps and of stamped and other envelopes, etc.

In two years the number of chargeable letters passing through the post had increased from 72,000,000 *per annum* to 208,000,000. Illicit conveyance had all but ceased, and the gross revenue amounted to two-thirds of the largest sum ever recorded. The nett revenue showed an increase the second year of £100,000, and the inland letters were found to be the most profitable part of the Post Office business.[134] It is a marvel that the new system should have fared as well as it did, when we take into consideration the bitter hostility of the postal authorities, the frequent hindrances thrown in the path of reform, to say nothing of the terrible poverty then existing among many classes of our fellow country people under the blighting influence of Protection and of the still unrepealed Corn Laws; poverty which is revealed in the many official reports issued during that sad time, in "S.G.O.'s" once famous letters, and in other trustworthy documents of those days, whose hideous picture has, later, been revived for us in that stirring book, "The Hungry Forties."

The hindrances to recovery of the postal revenue were in great measure caused by the delay in carrying out the details of Rowland Hill's plan of reform. Especially was this the case in the postponement of the extension of rural distribution—to which allusion has already been made—one of the most essential features of the plan, one long and wrongfully kept back; and, when granted, gratefully appreciated. Issue of the stamps was also delayed, these not being obtainable for some months after the introduction of the new system; and there was a still longer delay in providing the public with an adequate supply.[135]

The increase of postal expenditure was another factor in the case. The total charge for carrying the inland mails in 1835—the year before "Post Office Reform" was written—was £225,920; and it remained approximately at that figure while the old system continued in force. Then it went up by leaps and bounds, till by the end of the first year of the new system (1840) it reached the sum of £333,418. It has gone on steadily growing, as was indeed inevitable, owing to the increase of postal business; but the growth of expenditure would seem to be out of all proportion to the service, great as that is, rendered. By 1868 the charge stood at £718,000,[136] and before the nineteenth century died out even this last sum had doubled.

The following instance is typical of the changes made in this respect. In 1844 the Post Office *received* from the coach contractors about £200 for the privilege of carrying the mail twice a day between Lancaster and Carlisle. Only ten years later, the same service performed by the railway cost the Post Office some £12,000 a year.[137]

Another form of monetary wastefulness through overcharge arose from misrepresentation as to the length of railway used by the Post Office on different lines, one Company receiving about £400 a year more than was its due—although, of course, the true distance was given in official notices and time-tables. Even when the error was pointed out, the postal authorities maintained that the charge was correct.

This lavish and needless increase of expenditure on the part of the Post Office made Mr Baring as uneasy as it did my father. Not infrequently when explanations were demanded as to the necessity for these enhanced payments, evasive or long-delayed replies were given. Thus Rowland Hill found himself "engaged in petty contests often unavailing and always invidious";[138] and in these petty contests and ceaseless strivings to push forward some item or other of his plan, much of his time, from first to last, was wasted. Thus, at the beginning of 1841, when he had been at the Treasury a year and quarter, it became evident that, unless some improvement took place, two years or even a longer period would not suffice to carry out the whole of his plan.

Before 1841 came to an end he was destined to find the opposing powers stronger than ever. In the summer of that year the Melbourne Ministry fell—to the harassed postal reformer a heavy blow. For, if during the past two years he had not succeeded in accomplishing nearly all he had hoped to do, still the record of work was far from meagre. But if, with Mr Baring as an ally, and under a Government among whose members, so far as he knew, he counted but a single enemy, progress was slow, he had everything to dread from a Ministry bound to be unfriendly.

With their advent, conviction was speedily forced upon him that the end was not far off. The amount and scope of his work was gradually lessened; minutes on postal matters were settled without his even seeing them; and minutes he had himself drawn up, with the seeming approbation of his official chiefs, were quietly laid aside to be forgotten. On the plea of insufficiency of employment—insufficiency which was the natural consequence of the taking of work out of his hands—the number of his clerks was cut down to one; and all sorts of minor annoyances were put in his way. Meanwhile, the demands from the Post Office for increased salaries, advances, allowances, etc., which during the past two years had been frequently sent up to the Treasury, became more persistent and incessant than ever.

Rural distribution was still delayed, or was only partially and unsatisfactorily carried out. Some places of 200 or 300 inhabitants were allowed a post office, while other centres peopled by 2,000 or 3,000 went without that boon. This plan of rural distribution, whose object was to provide post offices in 400 registrars' districts which were without anything of the sort, was, after long waiting, conceded by the Treasury before the break-up of the Melbourne Ministry; and my father, unused till latterly to strenuous modes of official evasion, believed the measure safe. He forgot to take into account the Post Office's power of passive resistance; and several months were yet to elapse ere he discovered that Mr Baring's successor had suspended his predecessor's minute; nor was its real author ever able to obtain further information concerning it.

Nor was this all. Letters written by Rowland Hill to the new Chancellor of the Exchequer on the subject of registration and other reforms remained unnoticed, as did also a request to be allowed to proceed with one or two more out of a list of measures which stood in need of adoption. Later, my father wrote urging that other parts of his reform should be undertaken, drawing attention to the work which had already been successfully achieved; and so forth. A brief acknowledgment giving no answer to anything mentioned in his letter was the only outcome. At intervals of two months between the sending of each letter, he twice wrote again, but of neither missive was any notice taken.

Among other projects it had been decided that Rowland Hill should go to Newcastle-on-Tyne to arrange about a day mail to that town; and the necessary leave of absence was duly granted. He was also desirous of visiting some of the country post offices; but, being anxious to avoid possible breach of rule, he wrote to Colonel Maberly on the subject. The letter was referred to the Postmaster -General, and, after him, to the Chancellor of the Exchequer: the result being that the sanction to any portion of the journey was withdrawn.

One of the worst instances of the official "veiled hostility" to reform and reformer appeared in a document which my father—who might easily have given it a harsher name—always called the "fallacious return," published in 1843. In this the Post Office accounts were so manipulated as to make it seem that the Department was being worked at an annual loss of £12,000 or more. The unfriendly powers had all along prophesied that the reform could not pay; and now, indeed, they had a fine opportunity of "assisting in the fulfilment of their own predictions."

Till the new postal system was established, the "packet service" for foreign and colonial mails had, "with little exception," been charged to the Admiralty. In the "fallacious return" the entire amount (£612,850) was charged against the Post Office. Now, in comparing the fiscal results of the old and new systems, it was obviously unfair to include the cost of the packet service in the one and exclude it from the other. Despite all statements made to the contrary—and a great deal of fiction relating to postal arithmetic has long been allowed to pass current, and will probably continue so to do all down the "ringing grooves of time"—the nett revenue of the Department amounted to £600,000 *per annum*.[139]

Another "mistake" lay in under-stating the gross revenue by some £100,000. On this being pointed out by my father to the Accountant-General, he at once admitted the error, but said that a corrective entry made by him had been "removed by order."[140] And not only was correction in this case refused, but other "blunders" in the Post Office accounts on the wrong side of the ledger continued to be made, pointed out, and suffered to remain.

In one account furnished by the Department it was found, says my father, "that the balance carried forward at the close of a quarter changed its amount in the transit; and when I pointed out this fact as conclusive against the correctness of the account, it was urged that without such modification the next quarter's account could not be made to balance."[141] Not a very bright example of the application of culinary operations to official book-keeping because of the ease with which it could be detected. What wonder that to any one whose eyes are opened to such ways, faith in official and other statistics should be rudely shaken!

The effect of these high-handed proceedings was naturally to foster mistaken ideas as to postal revenues.

In 1842 Lord Fitzgerald, during a debate on the income-tax, said that the Post Office revenue had perished. The statement was speedily disposed of by Lord Monteagle, who, after pointing out the falseness of the allegation, declared that the expense of the packet service had no more to do with penny postage than with the expense of the war in Afghanistan or China, or the expense of the Army and Navy.[142]

In the House of Commons, Peel, of course only quoting memoranda which had been provided for his use, repeated these misleading statistics; and, later, they have found further repetition even in some of the Postmaster-General's Annual Reports.

These frequently recurring instances of thwarting, hindering, and misrepresentation showed plainly that the working of the postal reform should not have been entrusted to men whose official reputation was pledged not to its success but to its failure; and that the "shunting" of its author on to a Department other than that in which if endowed with due authority he might have exercised some control, was, to put the case mildly, a great mistake.

One ray of comfort came to him in the midst of his troubles. In the hard times which prevailed in the early 'forties diminution of revenue was far from being peculiar to the Post Office. The country was undergoing one of the heaviest of those periodically recurrent waves of depression which lessen the product of all taxes (or the ability to pay them) when, in April 1843, my father was able to write in his diary that the Post Office "revenue accounts show an increase of £90,000 on the year.... The Post Office is the only Department which does not show a deficiency on the quarter."[143]

In July 1842, the Chancellor of the Exchequer wrote to Rowland Hill to remind him that his three years' engagement at the Treasury would terminate in the ensuing September, and adding that he did not consider it advisable to make any further extension of the period of engagement beyond the date assigned to it.

Dreading lest, when the official doors should close behind him, his cherished reform should be wrecked outright, its author offered to work for a time without salary. The offer was refused, and the intended dismissal was announced in Parliament. The news was received with surprise and indignation there and elsewhere.

The Liberal Press was unanimous in condemnation of the Government's conduct, and some of the papers on their own side, though naturally cautious of tone, were of opinion that Rowland Hill had been harshly used. The Ministers themselves were probably of divided mind; and my father, when commenting upon a letter which the Prime Minister about this time addressed to him, says: "I cannot but think that, as he wrote, he must have felt some little of that painful feeling which unquestionably pressed hard upon him in more than one important passage of his political career."[144]

At the last interview the postal reformer had with the Chancellor of the Exchequer, Mr Goulburn's courteous manner also went "far to confirm the impression that he feels he is acting unjustly and under compulsion."[145]

One of the most indignant and outspoken of the many letters which Rowland Hill received was from his former chief, Mr Baring, who stigmatised the conduct of the Government as "very shabby," more than hinted that jealousy was the cause of dismissal, and added that had the Postmaster-General's plan of letter-registration been carried into effect, it "would have created an uproar throughout the country." It was well known that the head of the Post Office did not feel too kindly towards the reform, and was bent on charging a shilling on every registered letter, while Rowland Hill stoutly maintained that sixpence would be sufficient.[146] Hence the allusion. The Postmaster-General is said to have demanded his opponent's dismissal, and as he was credited with being in command of several votes in the Lower House, his wishes naturally carried weight.

Cobden gave vent to his disgust in a characteristic letter in which he suggested that the programme of the Anti-Corn-Law League should be followed:—a national subscription raised, a demonstration made, and a seat in Parliament secured. But the programme was not followed.

Among other letters of sympathy came one from the poet who, as his epitaph at Kensal Green reminds us, "sang the *Song of the Shirt.*" Said Hood: "I have seen so many instances of folly and ingratitude similar to those you have met with that it would never surprise me to hear of the railway people, some day, finding their trains running on so well, proposing to discharge the engines."[147]

The public, used to nearly four years of the new system, took alarm lest it should be jeopardised; and the Mercantile Committee, well entitled as, after its arduous labours, it was to repose, roused itself to renewed action, and petitioned the Government to carry out the postal reform in its entirety.

But the ruling powers were deaf to all protests; and thus to the list of dismissed postal reformers was added yet one more. First, Witherings; then, Dockwra; next, Palmer; and now, Hill.

While giving due prominence to the more salient features of the intrigue against the postal reform and reformer, the painful narrative has been as far as possible curtailed. It is, however, well worth telling if only to serve as warning to any would-be reformer—perhaps in any field: in the Post Office certainly—of the difficulties that lie in the path he yearns to tread. Should the reader be inclined to fancy the picture overdrawn, reference to the "Life of Sir Rowland Hill," edited by Dr G. B. Hill, will show that in those pages the story is told with far more fulness of detail and bluntness of truth-speaking.

More than thirty years after Peel had "given Rowland Hill the sack," as at the time *Punch*, in a humorous cartoon, expressed it, the real story of the dismissal was revealed to its victim by one who was very likely to be well-informed on the subject. It is an ugly story; and for a long time my brother and I agreed that it should be told in these pages. Later, seeing that all whom it concerned are dead, and that it is well, however difficult at times, to follow the good old rule of *de mortuis nil nisi bonum*, it has seemed wiser to draw across that relic of the long-ago past a veil of oblivion.

But here a digression may be made into a several years' later history, because, however chronologically out of place, it fits in at this juncture with entire appropriateness.

It is obvious that no person could succeed in cleansing so Augean a stable as was the Post Office of long ago without making enemies of those whose incompetency had to be demonstrated, or whose profitable sinecures had to be suppressed. Thus even when Rowland Hill's position had become too secure in public estimation for open attack to be of much avail, he was still exposed to that powerful "back-stairs" influence which, by hindering the progress of his reform, had done both the public service and himself individually much harm.

Of the reality of this secret hostility, ample proof was from time to time afforded, none, perhaps, being more striking than the following. When Lord Canning had been political head of the Post Office for some months, he one day said to my father: "Mr Hill, I think it right to let you know that you have enemies in high places who run you down behind your back. When I became Postmaster-General, every endeavour was made to prejudice me against you. I determined, however, to judge for myself. I have hitherto kept my eyes open, saying nothing. But I am bound to tell you now that I find every charge made against you to be absolutely untrue. I think it well, however, that you should know the fact that such influences are being exerted against you."[148]

When, at the age of forty-seven, Rowland Hill had to begin the world afresh, one dread weighed heavily upon his mind. It was that Peel's Government might advance the postal charges to, as was rumoured, a figure twice, thrice, or even four times those established by the reformed system. It was a dread shared by Messrs Baring, Wallace, Moffatt, and very many more. Great, therefore, was the relief when the last-named friend reported that the new Postmaster-General had assured him that there was no danger of the postage rates being raised.[149]

After the dismissal by Peel, a long and anxious time set in for the little household in the then semi-rural precinct of Orme Square, Bayswater; and again my mother's sterling qualities were revealed. Reared as she had been in a circle where money was plentiful and hospitality unbounded, she wasted no time in useless lamentations, but at once curtailed domestic expenses—those most ruthlessly cut down being, as, later, our father failed not to tell us, her own. In his parents' home he had lived in far plainer style than that maintained in the house of which, for many years, owing to her mother's early death, she had been mistress. Yet in all that ministered to her husband's comfort she allowed scarcely any change to be made. At the same time, there was no running into debt, because she had a hearty contempt for the practice she was wont to describe as "living on the forbearance of one's tradespeople."

But at last anxiety was changed to relief. One morning a letter arrived inviting her husband to join the London and Brighton Railway Board of Directors. Owing to gross mismanagement, the line had long been going from bad to worse in every way; and an entirely new directorate was now chosen. The invitation was especially gratifying because it came from personal strangers.

My father's connection with the railway forms an interesting chapter of his life which has been told elsewhere. In a work dealing only with the postal reform, repetition of the story in detail would be out of place. One brief paragraph, therefore, shall suffice to recall what was a pleasant episode in his career.

The "new brooms" went to work with a will, and the railway soon began to prosper. The price of shares—notwithstanding the announcement that for the ensuing half-year no payment of dividends could be looked for—rose rapidly; ordinary trains were increased in speed and number, expresses started, and Sunday excursion trains, by which the jaded dwellers "in populous city pent" were enabled once a week to breathe health-giving sea-breezes, were instituted; the rolling stock was improved, and, by the building of branch lines, the Company was ere long enabled to add to its title "and South Coast." The invitation to my father to join the Board met, at the sitting which discussed the proposal, with but one dissentient voice, that of Mr John Meesom Parsons of the Stock Exchange. "We want no Rowland Hills here," he said, "to interfere in everything; and even, perhaps, to introduce penny fares in all directions"—a rate undreamed of in those distant days. He therefore resolved to oppose the unwelcome intruder on every favourable occasion. The day the two men first met at the Board, the magnetic attraction, instinct, whatever be its rightful name, which almost at once and simultaneously draws together kindred souls, affected both; and forthwith commenced a friendship which in heartiness resembled that of David and Jonathan, and lasted throughout life. Mr Parsons, as gleefully as any school-boy, told us the story against himself on one out of many visits which he paid us; and with equal gleefulness told it, on other occasions and in our presence, to other people.[150]

An incident which occurred four years after the termination of Rowland Hill's engagement at the Treasury seemed to indicate a wish on Peel's part to show that he felt not unkindly towards the reformer, however much he disliked the reform. In the seventh year of penny postage, and while its author was still excluded from office, the nation showed its appreciation of Rowland Hill's work by presenting him with a monetary testimonial. Sir

Robert Peel was among the earliest contributors, his cheque being for the maximum amount fixed by the promoters of the tribute. Again Mr "Punch" displayed his customary genius for clothing a truism in a felicitous phrase by comparing Peel's action with that of an assassin who deals a stab at a man with one hand, and with the other applies sticking-plaster to the wound.

FOOTNOTES:

[126] Letter to Rowland Hill from Mr Baring, dated "Downing Street, 14th September 1839."

[127] "Life," i. 371.

[128] An amusing character-sketch of Colonel Maberly is to be found in the pages of Edmund Yates's "Recollections and Experiences."

[129] In connection with the putting up of one receptacle in London not many years ago, a gruesome discovery was made. The ground near St Bartholomew's Hospital had been opened previous to the erection of a pillar letter-box, when a quantity of ashes, wood and human, came to light. "Bart's" looks upon Smithfield, scene of the burning of some of the martyrs for conscience' sake. No need, then, to ponder the meaning of these sad relics. They clearly pointed to sixteenth-century man's inhumanity to man.

[130] The first person to post a letter under the new system is said to have been Mr Samuel Lines of Birmingham, Rowland Hill's former drawing-master, whose portrait hangs in the Art Gallery of that city. He was warmly attached to his ex-pupil, who, in turn, held the old man in high esteem, and maintained an occasional correspondence with him till the artist's death. Determined that in Birmingham no one should get the start of him, Mr Lines wrote to my father a letter of congratulation, and waited outside the Post Office till at midnight of the 9th a clock rang out the last stroke of twelve. Then, knocking up the astonished clerk on duty, he handed in the letter and the copper fee, and laconically remarked: "A penny, I believe."

[131] Another well-known literary woman, the poetess, Elizabeth Barrett Browning, according to her "Letters" recently published, wrote to an American friend earnestly recommending adoption of "our penny postage, as the most successful revolution since 'the glorious three days' of Paris"— meaning, of course, the three days of July 1830 (i. 135).

[132] This window and the amusing scramble outside it are immortalised in Dickens's pleasant article on the Post Office in the opening number of *Household Words*, first edition, 30th March 1850. (Our friend, Mr Henry Wills, already mentioned in the Introductory Chapter, was Dickens's partner in *Household Words*, and brought the famous novelist to our house at

Hampstead to be dined and "crammed" before writing the article. It was a memorable evening. No doubt the cramming was duly administered, but recollection furnishes no incident of this operation, and only brings back to mind a vivid picture of Dickens talking humorously, charmingly, incessantly, during the too brief visit, and of his doing so by tacit and unanimous consent, for no one had the slightest wish to interrupt the monologue's delightful flow. His countenance was agreeable and animated; the impression made upon us was of a man, who, as the Americans aptly put it, is "all there." We often saw him both within doors and without, for one of his favourite walks, while living in Tavistock Square, was up to Hampstead, across the Heath—with an occasional peep in at "Jack Straw's Castle," where friends made a rendezvous to see him—and back again to town through Highgate. Every one knew him by sight. The word would fly from mouth to mouth, "Here comes Dickens!" and the lithe figure, solitary as a rule, with its steady, swinging pace, and the keen eyes looking straight ahead at nothing in particular, yet taking in all that was worth noting, would appear, pass, and be lost again, the while nearly every head was turned to look after him.) Whenever visitors were shown over the Post Office, they were advised so to time their arrival that the tour should end a little before 6 P.M., with a visit to a certain balcony whence a good view could be obtained of the scene. One day my father escorted the Duchess of Cambridge and her younger daughter—better known since as Duchess of Teck—over the Post Office. He was delighted with their society, being greatly struck with the elder lady's sensible, well-informed talk, and the lively, sociable manner of the younger one. Both were much amused by the balcony scene, and Princess Mary entered keenly into the fun of the thing. She grew quite excited as the thickening crowd pressed forward faster, laughed, clapped her hands, and audibly besought the stragglers, especially one very leisurely old dame, to make haste, or their letters would not be posted in time.

[133] "Life," i. 451. In 1841 the census gave the population of England and Wales as a little under 16,000,000. The delay above mentioned therefore affected at least a fourth of the number.

[134] "Report of the Committee on Postage" (1843), p. 29.

[135] See also chap. vi.

[136] "Life," i. 412.

[137] "First Annual Report of the Postmaster-General, 1854."

[138] "Life," i. 414.

[139] "Life," ii. 4, 5.

[140] "Life," ii. 87.

[141] *Ibid*, i. 448.

[142] "Hansard," lxiv. 321.

[143] "Life," i. 460.

[144] "Life," i. 471.

[145] *Ibid.*, i. 468.

[146] The registration fee is one of the postal charges which have become smaller since that time, to the great benefit of the public. It is pleasant to know that the threatened plan of highly-feed compulsory registration was never carried into effect.

[147] "Gentle Tom Hood," as the wittiest of modern poets has been called, was a friend of old standing. Though little read to-day, some of his more serious poems are of rare beauty, and his *Haunted House* is a marvel of what Ruskin used to call "word-painting." His letters to children were as delightful as those of the better-known "Lewis Carroll." Hood was very deaf, and this infirmity inclined him, when among strangers or in uncongenial society, to taciturnity. Guests who had never met him, and who came expecting to hear a jovial fellow set the table in a roar, were surprised to see a quiet-mannered man in evidently poor health, striving, by help of an ear-trumpet, to catch other people's conversation. But, at any rate, it was *not* in our house that the hostess, piqued at the chilly silence pervading that end of her table which should have been most mirthful, sent her little daughter down the whole length of it to beg the bored wit to "wake up and be funny!" Hood had many cares and sorrows, including the constant struggle with small means and ill-health; and it is pleasant to remember that when the final breakdown came, Sir Robert Peel— concealing under a cloak of kindly tactfulness, so kindly that the over-sensitive beneficiary could not feel hurt—bestowed on the dying man some sorely-needed monetary assistance.

[148] This and the previous paragraph are contributed by Mr Pearson Hill, who was always, and deservedly, entirely in our father's confidence.

[149] "Life," i. 436. The only time, later, when there seemed a chance of such increase was during the Crimean War, "when," said my father in his diary, "being called upon to make a confidential report, I showed that, though some immediate increase of revenue might be expected from raising the rate to twopence, the benefit would be more than counterbalanced by the check to correspondence; and upon this the project was abandoned."

[150] It was during Rowland Hill's connection with the Railway Company that a riddle appeared in a certain newspaper which was copied into other papers, and was therefore not slow in reaching our family circle. It was worded much as follows: "When is Mr Rowland Hill like the rising sun?— When he tips the little Hills with gold." We never knew who originated this delightful *jeu d'esprit*, but our father was much amused with it, and we children had the best possible reason for being grateful to its author. The riddle cropped up afresh in Lord Fitzmaurice's "Life of Lord Granville" (i. 174); but the Duke of Argyll, then Postmaster-General, is therein made the generous donor.

CHAPTER VI

THE STAMPS

BETWEEN the date of Rowland Hill's leaving the Treasury, and that of his appointment to the Post Office to take up afresh the work to which, more than aught else, he was devoted, an interval of about four years elapsed, during a great part of which, as has just been mentioned, he found congenial employment on the directorate of the London and Brighton railway; a little later becoming also a member of the Board of Directors of two minor lines of railway. But as this episode is outside the scope of the present work, the four-years-long gap may be conveniently bridged over by the writing of a chapter on postage stamps.

Since their collection became a fashion—or, as it is sometimes unkindly called, a craze—much has been written concerning them, of which a great part is interesting, and, as a rule, veracious; while the rest, even when interesting, has not infrequently been decidedly the reverse of true. This latter fact is especially regrettable when the untruths occur in works of reference, a class of books professedly compiled with every care to guard against intrusion of error. Neglect of this precaution, whether the result of carelessness or ignorance, or from quite dissimilar reasons, is to be deplored. No hungry person cares to be offered a stone when he has asked for bread; nor is it gratifying to the student, who turns with a heart full of faith to a should-be infallible guide into the ways of truth, to find that he has strayed into the realm of fiction.

The present chapter on stamps merely touches the fringe of the subject, in no wise resembles a philatelist catalogue, and may therefore be found to lack interest. But at least every endeavour shall be made to avoid excursion into fableland.

Since the story of the postal labels should be told from the beginning, it will be well to comment here on some of the more glaring of the misstatements regarding that beginning contained in the notice on postage stamps which forms part of the carelessly-written article on the Post Office which appeared in the ninth edition of the "Encyclopædia Britannica," vol. xix. p. 585.

(1) "A postpaid envelope," the writer declares, "was in common use in Paris in the year 1653."

So far from being "in common use," the envelope or cover was the outcome of an aristocratic monopoly granted, as we have seen in a previous chapter, to M. de Valayer, who, "under royal approbation" set up "'a private' [penny?][151] post, placing boxes at the corners of the streets for the reception of letters wrapped up in envelopes which were to be bought at offices established for that purpose."[1] To M. de Valayer, therefore, would seem to belong priority of invention of the street letter-box, and perhaps of the impressed stamp and envelope; although evidence to prove that the boon was intended for public use seems to be wanting. In the days of Louis XIV. how many of the "common"alty were able to make use of the post? M. de Valayer also devised printed forms of "billets," prepaid, and a facsimile of one is given in the *Quarterly Review's* article.[152] Like our own present-day postcards, one side of the billet was to be used for the address, the other for correspondence; but the billet was a sheet of paper longer than our postcard, and no doubt it was folded up—the address, of course, showing—before being posted. There is no trace on the facsimile of an adhesive stamp. Neither is mention made of any invention or use of such stamp in France or elsewhere in the year 1670, although some seeker after philatelist mare's-nests a while since read into the article aforesaid fiction of that sort.

(2) "Stamped postal letter paper (*carta postale bollata*) was issued to the public by the Government of the Sardinian States in November 1818; and stamped postal envelopes were issued by the same Government from 1820 till 1836."

There was no such issue "to the public." For the purpose of collecting postal duties, "stamped paper or covers of several values, both with embossed and with impressed stamps, appear to have been used in the kingdom of Sardinia about the year 1819." [153] The use of these stamped covers, etc., was almost entirely limited to one small class of the community, namely the Ministers of State, and was in force from about 1819 to 1821 only. "In March 1836, a formal decree was passed suppressing their further use, the decree being required simply to demonetise a large stock found unused in the Stamp Office at Turin."[1] The Sardinian experiment, like the earlier one of M. de Valayer in Paris, had but a brief existence, the cause of failure in both cases being apparently attributable to the absence of uniformity of rate.

(3) "Stamped wrappers for newspapers were made experimentally in London by Mr Charles Whiting, under the name of 'go-frees,' in 1830."

In this country Charles Knight—in as complete ignorance as was my father of M. de Valayer's experiment in the mid-seventeenth century—has always been considered the first to propose the use of stamped covers or wrappers for newspapers; and this he did in 1834, his covers being intended to take the place, as payers of postage, of the duty stamp, when that odious "tax on knowledge" should be abolished. Had it been possible under the old postal system to prepay letter-postage as well as newspaper-postage, what more likely than that a man so far-seeing as was Mr Knight would also have suggested the application of his stamp to all mail matter? *Letter* postage stamps and prepayment had, of necessity, to await the advent of 1840 and uniformity of rate.[154]

(4) "Finally, and in its results most important of all, the adhesive stamp was made experimentally by Mr James Chalmers in his printing office at Dundee, in 1834."

An untruth followed by other untruths equally astounding.

Mr Chalmers, when writing of his stamps, has   happily supplied refutation of the fraudulent claim set up for him since his own death and that of the postal reformer; and as Mr Chalmers is the person chiefly concerned in that claim, and was a man as honourable as he was public-spirited, his evidence must necessarily be more valuable than that of any other witness. He published his suggestions as to postal reform, etc., in full, with his name and address added, in the *Post Circular*[155] of 5th April 1838, his paper being dated 8th February of the same year. Specimens of his stamps accompanied his communication; and in a reprint of this paper made in 1839 he claimed November 1837 as the date of his *"first"* experiments in stamp-making—the italics being his own. In none of his writings is there mention of any earlier experiments; neither is allusion made to any such in the numerously-signed "certificate" addressed by his fellow-citizens of Dundee to the Treasury in September 1839. The certificate eulogises Mr Chalmers' valuable public services, speaks of his successful efforts in 1825 to establish a 48 hours' acceleration of the mail-coaches plying between Dundee and London, and recommends to "My Lords" the adoption of the accompanying "slips" proposed by him. But nowhere in the certificate is reference made to the mythical stamps declared, nearly half a century later, to have been made in 1834. Yet some of these over one hundred signatories must have been among the friends who, according to the fable, visited Mr Chalmers' printing office in that year to inspect those early stamps. An extraordinary instance of wholesale forgetfulness if the stamps had had actual existence.[156] The "slips" made *"first"* in November 1837 were narrow pieces of paper of which one end bore the printed stamp, while the other end was to be slipped under the envelope flap—a clumsy device, entailing probable divorce between envelope and "slip" during their passage through the post. The fatal objection to all his stamps was that they were type-set, thereby making forgery easy. In every case the stamps bear the face-value proposed by Rowland Hill in his plan of reform—a penny the half, and twopence the whole ounce. Not only did Mr Chalmers *not* invent the stamp, adhesive or otherwise, but of the former he disapproved on the ground of the then supposed difficulty of gumming large sheets of paper.[157]

It may be added that copies of the *Post Circular* figure in the "Cole Bequest" to the South Kensington Museum; and if a very necessary caution addressed to the custodians there while the Chalmers claim was being rather hotly urged has received due attention, those documents should still be in the Museum, unimpeachable witnesses to the truth.

This claim to priority of invention, or of *publication* of invention, of the stamps which, with culpable carelessness, obtained recognition in the pages of the "Encyclopædia Britannica" has no foundation in fact. The writer of the article on the Post Office in "Chambers's Encyclopædia," ix. 677 (edition 1901), is far better informed on the subject of which he treats, though even he says that "Both" [men] "seem to have hit on the plan independently; but," he adds, with true discernment of the weakest feature of the claim, "the use of adhesive postage stamps, without uniform rates, and at a time when the practice of sending letters unpaid was almost universal, would obviously have been impossible."

This impossibility has already been demonstrated in the present work in the chapter on "The Old System." The simple explanation of the cause which prompted Mr Chalmers, late in 1837, to make designs for the stamps is not far to seek. At some time during the intervening months he had read "Post Office Reform,"[158] opened up a correspondence with its author—till then an entire stranger—and joined the ranks of those who were helping on the reform. It is a pity that in the attempt to fix upon this public-spirited man credit for an invention which was not his, the good work he actually accomplished should be frequently lost sight of.

The "Dictionary of National Biography" also too readily gave countenance to the Chalmers fable, a decision perhaps explained by the priority of position accorded in the alphabet to C over H. An accident of this sort gives a misstatement that proverbial long start which is required for its establishment, and naturally handicaps truth in the race; the consequence being that rectification of error is not made, and the later article is altered to bring it into seeming agreement with the earlier.[159]

On the other hand, the conductors of "Chambers's Encyclopædia" evidently recognise that a work of reference should be a mine of reliable information, one of their most notable corrections in a later edition of a mistake made in one earlier being that attributing the suppression of garrotting to the infliction on the criminals of corporal punishment—an allegation which, however, often asserted by those outside the legal profession, has more than once been denied by some of the ablest men within it.

No notice would have been taken in these pages of this preposterous claim were it not that the two works of reference whose editors or conductors seem to have been only too easily imposed upon have a wide circulation, and that until retraction be made—an invitation to accord which, in at least one case, was refused for apparently a quite frivolous reason—the foolish myth will in all probability be kept alive. The fraud was so clumsily constructed that it was scarcely taken seriously by those who know anything of the real history of the stamps, impressed and adhesive; and surprise might be felt that sane persons should have put even a passing faith in it, but for recollection that—to say nothing of less notorious cases—the once famous Tichborne claimant never lacked believers in his equally egregious and clumsily constructed imposture.

How little the Chalmers claimant believed in his own story is shown by his repeated refusal to accept any of the invitations my brother gave him to carry the case into Court. Had the claim been genuine, its truth might then and there have been established beyond hope of refutation.

In all probability most of the claimants to invention of the postage stamp—they have, to our knowledge, numbered over a dozen, while the claimants to the entire plan of reform make up at least half that tale—came from the many competitors who, in response to the Treasury's invitation to the public to furnish designs, sent in drawings and written suggestions.[160] What more natural than that, as years went past and old age and weakened memory came on, these persons should gradually persuade themselves and others that not only had they invented the *designs* they sent up for competition, but also the very *idea* of employing stamps with which to pay postage? Even in such a strange world as this, it is not likely that *all* the claimants were wilful impostors.[161]

Rowland Hill's first proposal in regard to the postage stamps was that they and the envelopes should be of one piece, the stamps being printed on the envelopes. But some days later the convenience of making the stamp separate, and therefore adhesive, occurred to him; and he at once proposed its use, describing it, as we have seen, as "a bit of paper just large enough to bear the stamp, and covered at the back with glutinous wash," etc. As both stamps are recommended in "Post Office Reform" as well as in its author's examination before the Commissioners of Post Office Inquiry in February 1837, it is clear that priority of *suggestion* as well as of *publication* belong to Rowland Hill.[162]

By 1838 official opinion, though still adverse to the proposal to tax letters by weight, had come to view with favour the idea of prepayment by means of stamps. Still, one of the chief opponents enumerated as many as nine classes of letters to which he thought that stamps would be inapplicable. The task of replying to eight of these objections was easy enough; with the ninth Rowland Hill was fain to confess his inability to deal. Stamps, it was declared, would be unsuitable to "half-ounce letters weighing an ounce or more."[163]

That the stamps—whatever should be the design chosen—would run risk of forgery was a danger which caused no little apprehension; and the Chairman of the Board of Stamps and Taxes (Inland Revenue) proposed to minimise that risk by having them printed on paper especially prepared. In the case of the envelopes bearing the embossed head, the once famous "Dickinson" paper, which contained fine threads of silk stretched across the pulp while at its softest, was that chosen. It was believed to be proof against forgery, and was in vogue for several years, but has long fallen into disuse.

The Government, as we have seen, decided in July 1839 to adopt the plan of uniform penny postage, including the employment of "stamped covers, stamped paper, and stamps to be used separately,"[164] and invited the public to furnish designs for these novel objects. In answer to the appeal came in some 2,600 letters containing suggestions and many sets of drawings, of which forty-nine varieties alone were for the adhesive stamps. It was, if possible, an even less artistic age than the present—though, at least, it adorned the walls of its rooms with something better than tawdry bric-à-brac, unlovely Japanese fans, and the contents of the china-closet—and in most cases beauty of design was conspicuous by its absence, a fault which, coupled with others more serious, especially that of entire lack of security against forgery, fore-doomed the greater number of the essays to rejection.[165]

To become a financial success it was necessary that the stamps should be produced cheaply, yet of workmanship so excellent that imitation could be easily detected. Now there is one art which we unconsciously practise from infancy to old age—that of tracing differences in the human faces we meet with. It is this art or instinct which enables us to distinguish our friends from strangers; and it was, perhaps, recognition of this fact that long ago led to the placing on the coinage of the portrait of the reigning monarch because it was familiar to the public eye, and therefore less likely than any other face to be counterfeited. In an engraving of some well-known countenance, any thickening or misplacing of the facial lines makes so great an alteration in features and expression that forgery is far more easily detected than when the device is only a coat-of-arms or other fanciful ornament.[166] For this reason, therefore, it was decided in 1839 to reproduce on the postage stamp the youthful Queen's head in profile designed by Wyon for the money of the then new reign, daily use of which coinage was making her face familiar to all her people. The head is also identical with that on the medal—likewise by Wyon—which was struck to commemorate her first State visit to the city in November 1837.

The stamp then being difficult to counterfeit, and worth but little in itself, while the machinery employed to produce it was costly, the reason is obvious why, so far as is known, only two attempts, and those so clumsy that one wonders who could have wasted time in forging the things, were made to imitate the finely executed, earliest "Queen's head."[167]

The design was engraved by hand on a single steel matrix, the head, through the agency of this costly machinery, being encompassed by many fine, delicately-wrought lines. The matrix was then hardened, and used to produce impressions on a soft steel roller of sufficient circumference to receive twelve repetitions, the beautiful work of the original matrix being therefore repeated, line for line, in every stamp printed. The roller, being in turn hardened, reproduced, under very heavy pressure, its counterpart on a steel plate a score of times, thus making up the requisite 240 impressions which cause each sheet to be of the value of one sovereign.[168]

Absolute uniformity was thus secured at comparatively little cost. The ingenious process was invented by Mr Perkins,[169] of the firm of Perkins, Bacon & Co. of Fleet Street, who, during the first forty years of the reformed postal system, printed some 95/100ths of our postage stamps, and in that space of time issued nearly 21,000,000,000 of penny adhesives alone.[170] Later, the contract passed into the hands of Messrs De La Rue, who hitherto, but long after 1840, had merely printed stamps of a few higher values than the penny and twopenny issue. In at least one work of fiction, however, the impression is conveyed that the latter firm from the first enjoyed the monopoly of stamp production of all values.

About midway in the 'fifties a serious fire broke out on Messrs Perkins & Co.'s premises, and much valuable material was destroyed. Investigation of the salvage showed that barely two days' supply of stamps remained in stock; and some anxiety was felt lest these should become exhausted before fresh ones could be produced, as even a temporary return to prepayment by coin of the realm would by this time have been found irksome. But with characteristic zeal, the firm at once recommenced work, and only a few people were ever aware how perilously near to deadlock the modern postal machine had come. It was after this fire that the crimson hue of the penny adhesive was altered to a sort of brick-red. The change of colour—one of several such changes exhibited by the red stamp—is duly recorded in Messrs Stanley Gibbon & Co.'s catalogue, though the probably long-forgotten accident with which it would seem to be connected is not mentioned.

The reasons for the four months' long delay in the issue of the stamps were twofold. They were, first, the more or less open hostility of the Post officials to both reform and reformer, which, as has been stated, caused all sorts of hindrances to be strewn in the path of progress; and, secondly, the apprehension still felt by the Government that the public would not take kindly to prepayment. The stamps ought, of course, to have been issued in time to be used by the 10th January 1840, when the new system came into force. When they were at last forthcoming, none were forwarded to the receiving offices till complaint was made. The fault was then found to lie with the wording of the Treasury letter giving the requisite directions. Later, another difficulty arose. The Stamp Office persisted in issuing the stamped covers in entire sheets as they were printed, and the Post Office refused to supply them uncut to the receivers. Three days alone were wasted over this wrangle. A week later the Post Office, which had formally undertaken the distribution of the covers, discovered that such work was beyond its powers. For a month after the first issue of the stamps the receiving offices remained unsupplied.

While the Government and others still cherished the delusion that the recipient of a letter would feel insulted if denied the time-honoured privilege of paying for it, the delayed publication of the stamps was less to be regretted since it enabled the experiment to be first tried with money only.

The official forecast was at fault. From the very start, and with the best will in the world, the public, when posting letters, put down pennies and missives together, and when the stamps—called by would-be wits the "Government sticking-plasters"—at last appeared, the difficulty was not to persuade people to make use of them, but to get them supplied fast enough to meet the popular demand.

While the stamps were still new that large section of mankind which never reads public instructions was occasionally at a loss where to affix the adhesive. Any corner of the envelope but the right one would be chosen, or, not infrequently, the place at the back partly occupied by the old-fashioned seal or wafer. Even the most painstaking of people were sometimes puzzled, and a certain artist, accustomed, like all his brethren of the brush, to consider that portion of his canvas the right hand which faced his left, was so perplexed that he carried to the nearest post office his letter and stamp, knocked up the clerk, and when the latter's face appeared at the little unglazed window of the ugly wooden screen which is now superseded everywhere, perhaps save at railway booking offices, by the more civilised open network, asked politely, "Which do you call the right hand of a letter?" "We've no time here for stupid jokes," was the surly answer, and the window shut again directly.

A similar rebuff was administered to a man who, while travelling, called for letters at the post office of a provincial town. He was the unfortunate possessor of an "impossible" patronymic. "What name?" demanded the supercilious clerk. "Snooks," replied the applicant; and down went the window panel with a bang, accompanied by a forcibly expressed injunction not to bother a busy man with idiotic jests.

To the post office of, at that time, tiny Ambleside, came one day a well-to-do man to buy a stamp to put on the letter he was about to post. "Is this new reform going to last?" he asked the postmaster. "Certainly," was the reply; "it is quite established." "Oh, well, then," said the man, resolved to give the thing generous support, "give me *three* stamps!" Not much of a story to tell, perhaps, but significant of the small amount of letter-writing which in pre-penny postage days went on even among those well-to-do people who were not lucky enough to enjoy the franking privilege.

The postal employees also showed their strangeness to the new order of things by frequently forgetting to cancel the stamps when the letters bearing them passed through the post—thereby enabling dishonest people to defraud the Department by causing the unobliterated labels to perform another journey. Many correspondents, known and unknown, sent Rowland Hill, in proof of this carelessness, envelopes which bore such stamps. Once a packet bearing four uncancelled stamps reached him.

The Mulready envelope had met with the cordial approbation of the artist's fellow Royal Academicians when it was exhibited in Council previous to its official acceptance; though one defect, palpable to any one of fairly discerning ability, had apparently escaped the eighty possibly somnolent eyes belonging to "the Forty"—that among the four winged messengers whom Britannia is sending forth in different directions seven legs only are apportioned. The envelope failed to please the public; it was mercilessly satirised and caricatured, and ridicule eventually drove it out of use. So vast a number of "Mulreadies" remained in stock, however, that, on their withdrawal, a machine had to be constructed to destroy them. There were no philatelists then to come to their rescue.

THE MULREADY ENVELOPE.

Forgery of the stamps being out of the question, fraudulent people devoted their energies to getting rid of the red ink used to obliterate the black "pennies" in order to affix these afresh to letters as new stamps. The frauds began soon after the first issue of the adhesives, for by the 21st of May my father was already writing in his diary of the many ingenious tricks which were practised. Cheating the Post Office had so long been an established rule, that even when postage became cheap, and the public shared its benefits impartially—peer and Parliamentarian now being favoured no more highly than any other class—the evil habit did not at once die out.

In some cases the fraud was palpable and unabashed. For example, Lord John Russell one day received a sheet of paper, the label on which had been washed so mercilessly that the Queen's features were barely discernible. The difficulty of dealing with the trouble was, of course, intensified by the fact that whereas the stamps were impressed on the paper by powerful machinery, and had had time to dry, the obliterations were made by hand,[171] and were fresh—a circumstance which, in view of the tenacity of thoroughly dried ink, gave a great advantage to the dishonest.

At this juncture an ink invented by a Mr Parsons was favourably reported on as an obliterant, but it shortly yielded to the skill of Messrs Perkins & Co.; and the stamp-cleaning frauds continuing, several of our leading scientific men, including Faraday, were consulted. As a result, new obliterating inks, red and black, were successively produced, tested, and adopted, but only for a while. Some of the experiment-makers lived as far off as Dublin and Aberdeen; and Dr Clark, Professor of Chemistry at the University of the latter city, came forward on his own account, and showed his interest in the cause by making or suggesting a number of experiments. Many people, indeed, went to work voluntarily, for the interest taken in the matter was widespread, and letters offering suggestions poured in from many quarters. But apparently the chemically skilled among the rogues were abler than those employed by the officials, since the "infallible" recipes had an unlucky knack of turning out dismal failures. Therefore, after consultation with Faraday, it was resolved that, so soon as the stock of stamps on hand became exhausted, an aqueous ink should be used both for the stamps and for the obliteration, ordinary black printing ink being meanwhile employed for the latter process. Professor Phillips and Mr Bacon, of the firm of Perkins & Co., at the same time undertook to procure a destructive oleaginous ink to be used in the printing of the new stamp.

It was hoped that thoroughly good printer's ink would be found efficacious for obliterating purposes; but ere long a chemist named Watson completely removed the obliteration. He then proposed for use an obliterative ink of his own invention, which was tried, but proved to be inconveniently successful, since it both injured the paper and effaced the writing near the stamp. Its use had therefore to be abandoned.

The trouble did not slacken, for while Mr Watson was laboriously removing the black printing ink from the black pennies, and making progress so slowly that, at a like rate, the work could not have repaid any one, honest or the reverse, for the time spent upon it, Mr Ledingham, my father's clerk, who had throughout shown great enthusiasm in the cause, was cleaning stamps nine times as fast, or at the rate of one a minute—a process rapid enough to make the trick remunerative.

Ultimately, it occurred to Rowland Hill that "as the means which were successful in removing the printing ink obliterant were different from those which discharged Perkins' ink, a secure ink might perhaps be obtained by simply mixing the two."[172] The device succeeded, the ink thus formed proving indestructible; and all seemed likely to go well, when a fresh and very disagreeable difficulty made its unwelcome appearance. To enable this ink to dry with sufficient rapidity, a little volatile oil had been introduced, and its odour was speedily pronounced by the postal officials to be intolerable. Happily, means were found for removing the offence; and at length, a little before the close of the year, all requirements seemed to be met.[173]

It had been a time of almost incessant anxiety. For more than six months there had been the earlier trouble of securing a suitable design for the stamps, and then, when selected, the long delay in effecting their issue; and now, during another six months, this later trouble had perplexed the officials and their many sympathisers. In the end, the colour of the black penny was changed to red, the twopenny stamp remaining blue. Thenceforth, oleaginous inks were used both for printing and for obliterating; the ink for the latter purpose being made so much more tenacious than that used to print the stamp that any attempt to remove the one from the other, even if the destruction of both did not follow, must at least secure the disappearance of the Queers head. A simple enough remedy for the evil, and, like many another simple remedy, efficacious; yet some of the cleverest men in the United Kingdom took half a year to find it out.

Before trial it was impossible to tell which of the two kinds of stamps would be preferred: the one impressed upon the envelope and so forming a part of it, or the other, the handy little adhesive. Rowland Hill expected the former to be the favourite on account of its being already in place, and therefore less time-consuming. Moreover, as a man gifted with a delicate sense of touch, the tiny label which, when wet, is apt to adhere unpleasantly to the fingers, attracted him less than the cleanlier embossed stamp on the envelope; and perhaps he thought it not unlikely that other people would be of like mind. But from the first the public showed a preference for the adhesive; and to this day the more convenient cover with the embossed head has been far seldomer in demand. It is not impossible that if the present life of feverish hurry and high pressure continues, and even intensifies, the reformer's expectations as regards the choice of stamps may yet be realised. It may have been the expression of this merely "pious opinion" on his part which gave rise to some absurd fables—as, for instance, that he recommended the adhesive stamp "very hesitatingly," and only at the eleventh hour; that he sought to restrict the public to the use of the impressed stamp because he preferred it himself; and rubbish of like sort.

From the time that Rowland Hill first planned his reform till the day when his connection with the Post Office terminated, his aim ever was to make of that great Department a useful servant to the public; and all who knew what was his career there were well aware that when at length he had beaten down opposition, that object was attained. He was the last man likely to allow personal predilections or selfish or unworthy considerations of any kind to stand before the welfare of the service and of his country.

SIR ROWLAND HILL.
From a Photograph by Maull and Polyblank.

FOOTNOTES:

[151] "Life," i. 377. It is curious that neither in the article on the French Post Office in the "Encyclopædia Brittanica" nor in that in Larousse's "*Dictionnaire du XIXe Siècle*" is mention made of M. de Valayer or M. Piron. Whether the real worthies are excluded from the articles in order to make room for the fustian bound to creep in, it would be difficult to say. But, while perusing these writings, a saying of my brother's often returns to mind. "I have never," he declared, "read any article upon the postal reform, friendly or the reverse, which was free from misstatements."

[152] No. 128, p. 555.

[153] "The Origin of Postage Stamps," p. 7. By Pearson Hill. Here is a story of a "find" that is more interesting than that at Turin or that of M. Piron already alluded to, because it comes nearer home to us. About the middle of the nineteenth century, and during the demolition in London of some old houses which had long been appropriated to governmental use, and were now abandoned, the discovery was made of a large number of the paper-duty stamps, issued by George III.'s Ministry in order to tax the "American Colonies." When the obnoxious impost was cancelled, and the many years long revolt had become a successful revolution, the ex-colonies thenceforth assuming the title of "The United States," the stamps became waste material, and were thrown into a cupboard, and forgotten. At the time of their reappearance, the then Chairman of the Board of Stamps and Taxes (Inland Revenue Office), Mr John Wood, gave half a dozen of them to Rowland Hill, as curiosities; and one is still in my possession. Another was given by my father to the American philanthropist, Mr Peabody, then visiting this country, who was greatly interested in the discovery. Now it

would be just as correct to say that the tax had been imposed on the American Colonies—of course it never *was* imposed, since, as we know, payment was from the first refused—till the middle of the nineteenth century, simply because the stamps were only found some eighty years after their supersession, as it is to say that the Sardinian "stamped postal letter paper" and "stamped postal envelopes" were employed till 1836, in which year, after long disuse, they were formally abolished. But the manner and matter of the "Encyclopædia Britannica's" article on the Post Office and the stamps are not what they should be, and much of them would reflect discredit on the average school-boy.

[154] Prepayment, as has been stated, was not actually unknown, but was so rare as to be practically non-existent.

[155] The *Post Circular* was a paper set up temporarily by the "Mercantile Committee" to advocate the reform. It was ably edited by Mr Cole, and had a wide circulation.

[156] The stamps were probably exhibited at the Dundee printing office, any time between November 1837 and September 1839—at which later date they were sent to London.

[157] Published in February of that year.

[158] Published in February of that year.

[159] Dr Birkbeck Hill, on one occasion, told me that in the article on my father which he was asked to write for the D.N.B. he said of the adhesive stamp that its invention had been "wrongfully attributed to Mr James Chalmers"—words which nowhere appear in the article as it now stands. "The proprietors of the 'Encyclopædia Britannica,'" wrote my brother in "The Origin of Postage Stamps," pp. 14, 15 (note), "did not avail themselves of the offer I had made to place them in communication with those from whom official information could be best obtained—indeed, they appear to have made no application to the Post Office for information of any kind.... Meanwhile, as it afterwards turned out, they were abundantly supplied with Mr P. Chalmers' *ex parte*, and, to say the least, singularly inaccurate statements. With the editor of the 'Dictionary of National Biography' I had no communication whatever." Is it after this careless fashion that much of our "island story" is compiled? If so, what wonder that long before the present day wise men should have declared that all history needed to be rewritten?

[160] One of these claimants was a man connected with a well-known national museum; and his pretensions were to us a never-failing source of amusement. He was distinguished for two peculiarities: one being a passion for slaughtering the reputations of his friends; the other, the

misappropriation to his own credit of all originality in any reforms or inventions projected by them. So far as I am aware, only one claimant was of my own sex; and she, at least, had the courage of her opinions, for, instead of biding her time till the postal reformer was no more, the poor insane creature wrote direct to him, saying she was the originator of the entire plan, and begging him to use his influence with the Government to obtain for her an adequate pension. The stories connected with some of the other claims are quite as curious as the foregoing.

[161] Inaccuracy of memory applies to other things than invention of postage stamps. Here is a curious instance. "Sir John Kaye, in writing his history of the Sepoy War, said he was often obliged to reject as convincing proof even the overwhelming assertion, 'But I was there.' 'It is hard,' he continues, 'to disbelieve a man of honour when he tells you what he himself did; but every writer long engaged in historical enquiry has had before him instances in which men, even after a brief lapse of time, have confounded in their minds the thought of doing, or the intent to do, a certain thing with the fact of actually having done it. Indeed, in the commonest affairs of daily life we often find the intent mistaken for the act, in retrospect.' Kaye was writing at a period of not more than ten to twelve years after the events which he was narrating. When you extend ten years to twenty or twenty-four, memories grow still more impaired, and the difficulty of ensuring accuracy becomes increasingly greater." (Thus "The Reformer," A. and H. B. Bonner, vii. 36, 37.) Most of the claims to invention of the postage stamp seem to have been made considerably more than ten, twelve, twenty, or twenty-four years after its introduction—some of them curiously, or, at any rate, opportunely enough, forty years or so after; that is about the time of Rowland Hill's death, or but little later.

[162] For the adhesive stamp, see "Post Office Reform," p. 45, and "Ninth Report of the Commissioners of Post Office Inquiry," p. 38. The impressed stamp is mentioned in "Post Office Reform" at p. 42, and also in that "Ninth Report." The writer of the "Encyclopædia Britannica's" article (xix. 585), while quoting Rowland Hill's description of the adhesive stamp, adds: "It is quite a fair inference that this alternative had been suggested from without," but gives no reason for hazarding so entirely baseless an assertion. The article, indeed, bears not a few traces of what looks like personal malice; and it is a pity that the editorial revising pen, whether from indolence or from misunderstanding of the subject on its wielder's part, was suffered to lie idle.

[163] These are the actual words made use of. See "Second Report of the Commissioners of Post Office Inquiry," Question 11,111.

[164] Thus the Treasury Minute.

[165] "In the end there were selected from the whole number of competitors four whose suggestions appeared to evince most ingenuity," wrote my father. "The reward that had been offered was divided amongst them in equal shares, each receiving £100" ("Life," i. 388). Sir Henry Cole gives their names as follows:—"Mr Cheverton, Mr C. Whiting, myself, and, I believe, Messrs Perkins, Bacon & Co. After the labour," he adds, "of reading the two thousand five" (?six) "hundred proposals sent to the Treasury, 'My Lords' obtained from them no other modes of applying the postage stamp than those suggested by Mr Hill himself—stamped covers or half sheets of paper, stamped envelopes, labels or adhesive stamps, and stamps struck on letter-paper itself."—("Fifty Years of Public Life," i. 62, 65, 66.)

[166] So profoundly did Rowland Hill feel the importance of this fact that he invariably scouted a suggestion occasionally made in the early days of the postal reform that his own head should appear on at least one of the stamps. The some-time postmaster of New Brunswick, who caused his portrait to adorn a colonial stamp now much sought after by philatelists on account, perhaps, of its rarity, for it was speedily abolished, seems to have been of quite a different frame of mind.

[167] This earliest stamp was a far finer and more artistic piece of workmanship than any of its successors; and has only to be compared with the later specimens—say, for example, with King Edward's head on the halfpenny postcards and newspaper bands—to see how sadly we have fallen behind some other nations and our own older methods, at any rate in the art of engraving, or, at least, of engraving as applied to the postage stamp.

[168] In the paper drawn up by Rowland Hill, "On the Collection of Postage by Means of Stamps," and issued by the Mercantile Committee in June 1839, he had recommended that, for convenience' sake, the stamp should be printed on sheets each containing 240, arranged in twenty rows of twelve apiece; and they are so printed to this day. It has been asserted that at first the sheets were printed in strips of twelve stamps each; but there is no truth in the statement. Archer's perforation patent, which makes separation of the adhesives easy, and is therefore a boon to the many of us who are often in a hurry, was not adopted before the mid-'fifties.

[169] His father, an American, was the inventor of the once famous air-gun.

[170] Fifteen years after the issue of the first stamps, during which time more than 3,000,000,000 had been printed, it was deemed advisable to make a second matrix by transfer from the first. It had become necessary to deepen the graven lines by hand, but the work was so carefully done that the deviation in portraiture was very slight.

[171] And a hasty hand, too, for in those days of manual labour there was a keen race among the stampers as to who, in a given time, should make the greatest number of obliterations. The man whose record stood habitually highest was usually called on to exhibit his prowess to visitors who were being escorted over the Department.

[172] Rowland Hill's Journal, 9th November 1840.

[173] "Life," i. 399-407.

CHAPTER VII

AT THE POST OFFICE

AS the evident weakening of Peel's Government became more marked, the thoughts of the man who had been sacrificed to official intrigues, and unto whom it was, as he pathetically writes, "grief and bitterness to be so long kept aloof from my true work," turned longingly towards the Post Office and to his insecurely established and only partially developed plan. With a change of Ministry, better things must surely come.

His hopes were realised. In 1846 the Peel Administration fell, and Lord John (afterwards Earl) Russell became Prime Minister. The public voice, clearly echoed in the Press, demanded Rowland Hill's recall to office, there to complete his reform.[1174]

One of the first intimations he received of his probable restoration was a letter from Mr Warburton advising him to be "within call if wanted." A discussion had risen overnight in Parliament. Mr Duncombe had complained of the management of the Post Office, and so had Mr Parker, the Secretary to the Treasury. The new Postmaster-General, Lord Clanricarde, it was reported, had found "the whole establishment in a most unsatisfactory condition"; and the new Prime Minister himself was "by no means satisfied with the state of the Post Office," and did not "think the plans of reform instituted by Mr Hill had been sufficiently carried out." Messrs Hume and Warburton urged Mr Hill's recall.[1175]

Several of the good friends who had worked so well for the reform both within and without Parliament also approached the new Government, which, indeed, was not slow to act; and my father entered, not, as before, the Treasury, but his fitter field of work—the Post Office. The whirligig of time was indeed bringing in his revenges. An entire decade had elapsed since the reformer, then hopeful and enthusiastic, inwardly digested the cabful of volumes sent him by Mr Wallace, and dictated to Mrs Hill the pages of "Post Office Reform." He had at the time been denied admission to the Post Office when seeking for information as to the working of the old system he was destined to destroy. He now found himself installed within the official precincts, and in something resembling authority there.

Thus before the passing of the year 1846 he was able to comment yet further in his diary on the curious parallel between his own treatment and that of Dockwra and Palmer. "Both these remarkable men," he wrote, "saw their plans adopted, were themselves engaged to work them out, and subsequently, on the complaint of the Post Office, were turned adrift by the

Treasury." We "were all alike in the fact of dismissal.... I alone was so far favoured as to be recalled to aid in the completion of my plan."[176]

At the time when Dockwra, the most hardly used of all, was driven from office a ruined man, and with the further aggravation of responsibility for the costs of a trial which had been decided unjustly against him, the "merry monarch's" numerous progeny were being lavishly provided for out of the national purse. The contrast between their treatment and that of the man who had been one of the greatest benefactors to his country renders his case doubly hard.

In an interview which Mr Warburton had with the Postmaster-General preparatory to Rowland Hill's appointment, the Member for Bridport pointed to the fact that his friend was now fifty-one years of age, and that it would be most unfair to call on him to throw up his present assured position only to run risk of being presently "shelved"; and further urged the desirability of creating for him the post of Adviser to the Post Office, in order that his time should not be wasted in mere routine duty. At the same time, Mr Warburton stipulated that Rowland Hill should not be made subordinate to the inimical permanent head of the Office. Had Mr Warburton's advice been followed, it would have been well for the incompleted plan, the reformer, and the public service. Rowland Hill himself suggested, by way of official designation, the revival of Palmer's old title of Surveyor-General to the Post Office; but the proposal was not received with favour. Ultimately he was given the post of Secretary to the Postmaster-General, a title especially created for him, which lapsed altogether when at last he succeeded to Colonel Maberly's vacated chair. The new office was of inferior rank and of smaller salary than his rival's; and, as a natural consequence, the old hindrances and thwartings were revived, and minor reforms were frequently set aside or made to wait for several years longer. Happily, it was now too late for the penny post itself to be swept away; the country would not have allowed it; and in this, the seventh year of its establishment, its author was glad to record that the number of letters delivered within 12 miles of St Martin's-le-Grand was already equal to that delivered under the old system throughout the whole United Kingdom.

By 1846 Rowland Hill was occupying a better pecuniary position than when in 1839 he went to the Treasury. He had made his mark in the railway world; and just when rumours of his retirement therefrom were gaining ground, the South Western Railway Board of Directors offered him the managership of that line. The salary proposed was unusually high, and the invitation was transparently veiled under a Desdemona-like request that he would recommend to the Board some one with qualifications "as much like your own as possible." But he declined this and other flattering offers, resigned his three directorships, and thus relinquished a far larger income than that which the Government asked him to accept. The monetary sacrifice, however, counted for little when weighed in the balance against the prospect of working out his plan.

His first interview with Lord Clanricarde was a very pleasant one; and he left his new chief's presence much impressed with his straightforward, business-like manner.

On this first day at St Martin's-le-Grand's Colonel Maberly and Rowland Hill met, and went through the ceremony of shaking hands. But the old animosity still possessed considerable vitality. The hatchet was but partially interred.

With Lord Clanricarde my father worked harmoniously; the diarist after one especially satisfactory interview writing that he "never met with a public man who is less afraid of a novel and decided course of action."

Early in his postal career, my father, by Lord Clanricarde's wish, went to Bristol to reorganise the Post Office there, the first of several similar missions to other towns. In nearly every case he found one condition of things prevailing: an office small, badly lighted, badly ventilated, and with defective sanitary arrangements; the delivery of letters irregular and unnecessarily late; the mail trains leaving the provincial towns at inconvenient hours; and other vexatious regulations, or lack of regulations. He found that by an annual expenditure of £125 Bristol's chief delivery of the day could be completed by nine in the morning instead of by noon. Although unable to carry out all the improvements needed, he effected a good deal, and on the termination of his visit received the thanks of the clerks and letter-carriers.[177]

In 1847 a thorough revision of the money order system was entrusted to him; and, thenceforth, that office came entirely under his control. Seventeen years later, Lord Clanricarde, in the Upper House, paid his former lieutenant, then about to retire, a handsome tribute of praise, saying, among other things, that, but for Mr Hill, the business of that office could hardly have been much longer carried on. No balance had been struck, and no one knew what assets were in hand. On passing under Mr Hill's management, the system was altered: four or five entries for each order were made instead of eleven; and official defalcation or fraud, once common, was now no more heard of.[178]

Lord Clanricarde placed the management of that office under my father's command in order that the latter should have a free hand; and it was settled that all returns to Parliament should be submitted to Rowland Hill before being sent to the Treasury, with leave to attack any that seemed unfair to penny postage. Previous to this act of friendliness and justice on the Postmaster-General's part, papers had generally been submitted to the permanent head of the office and even to officers of lower rank, but had been withheld from the reformer's observation.[179]

"Eternal vigilance" is said to be the necessary price to pay for the preservation of our liberties; and, half a century ago, a like vigilance had to be exercised whenever and wherever the interests of the postal reform were concerned.

The arrears in the Money Order Departments of the London and provincial offices were so serious that to clear them off would, it was declared, fully employ thirty-five men for four years. The Post Office had always maintained that the Money Order Department yielded a large profit; but a return sent to Parliament in 1848 showed that the expenditure of the year before the change of management exceeded the receipts by more than £10,000. In 1849 my father expressed "a confident expectation" that in the course of the year the Money Order Office would become self-supporting. By 1850 that hope was realised. By 1852 the office showed a profit of £11,664, thereby, in six years, converting the previous loss into a gain of more than £22,000;[180] and during the last year of Rowland Hill's life (1878-79) the profits were £39,000.

A reduction of size in the money order forms and letters of advice, and the abolition of duplicate advices effected a considerable saving in stationery alone; while the reduction of fees and the greater facilities for the transmission of money given by cheap postage raised the amount sent, in ten years only, twenty-fold. In 1839 about £313,000 passed through the post; and in 1864, the year of my father's resignation, £16,494,000. By 1879 the sum had risen to £27,000,000; and it has gone on steadily increasing.

Perhaps the following extract from Rowland Hill's journal is satisfactory, as showing improvement in account-keeping, etc. "July 8th, 1853.—A recent return to Parliament of the number and cost of prosecutions [for Post Office offences] from 1848 to 1852 inclusive, shows an enormous decrease—nearly, I think, in the ratio of three to one. This very satisfactory result is, I believe, mainly owing to the improved arrangements in the Money Order Office."[181]

The new postal system, indeed, caused almost a revolution in official account-keeping. Under the old system the accounts of the provincial postmasters were usually from three to six months in arrear, and no vouchers were demanded for the proper disbursement of the money with which the postmasters were credited. In consequence of this dilatoriness, the officials themselves were often ignorant of the actual state of affairs, or were sometimes tempted to divert the public funds to their own pockets, while the revenue was further injured by the delay in remitting balances. Under the new system each postmaster rendered his account weekly, showing proper vouchers for receipts and payments and the money left in hand, to the smallest possible sum. This improvement was accompanied by lighter work to a smaller number of men, and a fair allowance of holiday to each of them.

When, in 1851, my father's attention was turned to the question of facilitating life insurance for the benefit of the staff, and especially of its humbler members, it was arranged with Sir George Cornwall Lewis,[182] at that time Chancellor of the Exchequer, that, to aid in making up the requisite funds, the proceeds of unclaimed money orders, then averaging £1,100 a year, and all such money found in "dead" letters as could not be returned to their writers, should be used. Accumulations brought the fund up to about £12,000. In this manner "The Post Office Widows' and Orphans' Fund Society" was placed on a firm footing. A portion of the void order fund was also employed in rescuing from difficulties another society in the London office called "The Letter-Carriers' Burial Fund."[183]

Although in 1857 my father, with the approval of Lord Colchester, the then Postmaster-General, had proposed the extension of the money order system to the Colonies, it was not till the Canadian Government took the initiative in 1859 that the Treasury consented to try the experiment. It proved so successful that the measure was gradually extended to all the other colonies, and even to some foreign countries.

Like Palmer, Rowland Hill was a born organiser, and work such as that effected in the Money Order Office was so thoroughly congenial that it could scarcely fail to be successful. The race of born organisers can hardly be extinct. Is it vain to hope that one may yet arise to set in order the said-to-be-unprofitable Post Office Savings Bank, whose abolition is sometimes threatened? As a teacher of thrift to one of the least thrifty of nations, it is an institution that should be mended rather than ended. Mending must surely be possible when, for example, each transaction of that Bank costs 7.55d. exclusive of postage—or so we are told—while other savings banks can do their work at a far lower price.[184]

The following story is illustrative of the strange want of common-sense which distinguishes the race, especially when posting missives. "Mr Ramsey, (missing-letter clerk)," writes Rowland Hill in his diary of 27th May 1847, "has brought me a packet containing whole banknotes to the amount of £1,500 so carelessly made up that they had all slipped out, and the packet was addressed to some country house in Hereford, no post-town being named. It had found its way, after much delay, into the post office at Ross, and had been sent to London by the postmistress."

It is not often that the head of so dignified and peaceful an institution as the Post Office is seen in a maimed condition, and that condition the result of fierce combat. Nevertheless, in that stirring time known as "the year of revolutions" (1848), a newly-appointed chief of the French Post Office, in the pleasant person of M. Thayer, arrived in this country on official business. He came supported on crutches, having been badly wounded in the foot during the June insurrection in Paris. He told us that his family came originally from London, and that one of our streets was named after them. If, as was surmised, he made a pilgrimage to Marylebone to discover it, it must have looked to one fresh from Paris a rather dismal thoroughfare.

About 1849 Rowland Hill instituted periodical meetings of the Post Office Surveyors to discuss questions which had hitherto been settled by the slower method of writing minutes. These postal parliaments were so satisfactory that henceforth they were often held. They proved "both profitable and pleasant, increased the interest of the surveyors in the work of improvement, and by the collision of many opinions, broke down prejudices, and overthrew obstacles."

One of the greatest boons which, under my father's lead, was secured to the letter-carriers, sorters, postmasters, and others, all over the kingdom, was the all but total abolition of Post Office Sunday labour. In a single day 450 offices in England and Wales were relieved of a material portion of their Sunday duties. Three months later the measure was extended to Ireland and Scotland, 234 additional offices being similarly relieved. While these arrangements were in process of settlement, Rowland Hill, in the autumn of 1849, resolved to still further curtail Sunday labour. Hitherto the relief had been carried out in the Money Order Department only, but it was now decided to close the offices entirely between the hours of ten and five. To make this easier, it became necessary to provide for the transmission of a certain class of letters through London on the Sunday, and to ask a few men to lend their services on this account. Compulsion there was none: every man was a volunteer; and for this absence of force my father, from beginning to end of the movement, resolutely bargained. Previous to the enactment of this measure of relief, 27 men had been regularly employed every Sunday at the General Post Office. Their number was temporarily increased to 52 in order that some 5,829 men—all of whom were compulsory workers—should elsewhere be relieved, each of some five-and-three-quarters hours of labour every "day of rest." In a few months, all the arrangements being complete, and the plan got into working order, the London staff was reduced to little more than half the number employed before the change was made. Ultimately, the services even of this tiny contingent were reduced, four men sufficing; and Sunday labour at the Post Office was cut down to its minimum amount—a state of things which remained undisturbed during my father's connection with that great public Department.

The actual bearing of this beneficent reform was, strange to say, very generally misunderstood, and perhaps more especially by "The Lord's Day Society." Thus for some months Rowland Hill was publicly denounced as a "Sabbath-breaker" and a friend and accomplice of His Satanic Majesty. The misunderstanding was not altogether discouraged by some of the old Post Office irreconcilables; but it is only fair to the memory of the chief opponent to record the fact that when the ill-feeling was at its height Colonel Maberly called his clerks together, told them that, owing to unjust attacks, the Department was in danger, and exhorted them to stand forth in its defence.[185]

When the turmoil began the Postmaster-General was inclined to side with some of the leading officials who advocated compulsion should the number volunteering for the London work be insufficient. Happily, the supply was more than ample. But when the trouble subsided Lord Clanricarde generously admitted that he had been wrong and my father right.

Some of the provincial postmasters and other officials, misunderstanding the case, joined in the clamour, and went far on the way to defeat a measure planned for their relief. Others were more discerning, and the postmaster of Plymouth wrote to say that at his office alone thirty men would be relieved by an enactment which was "one of the most important in the annals of the Post Office."

The agitation showed how prone is the public to fly to wrong conclusions. Here was Rowland Hill striving to diminish Sunday work, and being denounced as if he was seeking to increase it! It goes without saying that, during the agitation, numerous letters, generally anonymous, and sometimes violently abusive, deluged the Department, and especially the author of the relief; and that not even Rowland Hill's family were spared the pain of receiving from candid and, of course, entirely unknown friends letters of the most detestable description. Truly, the ways of the unco gude are past finding out.

While the conflict raged, many of the clergy proved no wiser than the generality of their flocks, and were quite as vituperative. Others, to their honour be it recorded, tried hard to stem the tide of ignorance and bigotry. Among these enlightened men were the Hon. and Rev. Grantham Yorke, rector of St Philip's, Birmingham; the Professor Henslow already mentioned; and Dr Vaughan, then head-master of Harrow and, later, Dean of Llandaff. All three, although at the time personal strangers, wrote letters which did their authors infinite credit, and which the recipient valued highly. The veteran free-trader, General Peronnet Thompson, also contributed a series of able articles on the subject to the then existing *Sun*.

Some of the newspapers at first misunderstood the question quite as thoroughly as did the public; but, so far as we ever knew, only the *Leeds Mercury*—unto whose editor, in common with other editors, had been sent a copy of the published report on the reduction of Sunday labour—had the frankness to express regret for having misrepresented the situation.[186] Other newspapers were throughout more discriminating; and the *Times*, in its issue of 25th April 1850, contained an admirable and lengthy exposition of the case stated with very great clearness and ability.[187]

"Carrying out a plan of relief which I had suggested as a more general measure when at the Treasury," says Rowland Hill in his diary, " I proposed to substitute a late Saturday night delivery in the nearer suburbs for that on Sunday morning. By this plan more than a hundred men would be forthwith released from Sunday duty in the metropolitan district alone."[188] He further comments, perhaps a little slyly, on the "notable fact that while so much has been said by the London merchants and bankers against a delivery where their places of business are, of course, closed, not a word has been said against a delivery in the suburbs where they live."[189]

To give further relief to Sunday labour, Rowland Hill proposed "so to arrange the work as to have the greatest practicable amount of sorting done in the travelling offices on the railways; the earlier portion ending by five on Sunday morning, and the later not beginning till nine on Sunday evening. The pursuit of this object led to a singular device."[190] He was puzzling over the problem how to deal with letters belonging to good-sized towns too near to London to allow of sorting on the way. The railway in case was the London and North-Western; the towns St Albans and Watford. The thought suddenly flashed upon him that the easiest way out of the difficulty would be to let the *down* night mail train to Liverpool receive the St Albans and Watford *up* mails to London; and that on arrival at some more remote town on the road to Liverpool they should be transferred, sorted, to an *up* train to be carried to London. No time would be really lost to the public, because, while the letters were performing the double journey their destined recipients would be in bed; nor would any additional expense or trouble be incurred. The plan was a success, was extended to other railways, and the apparently eccentric proceeding long since became a matter of everyday occurrence.

In 1851 prepayment in money of postage on inland letters was abolished at all those provincial offices where it had thus far been allowed. Early in the following year the abolition was extended to Dublin, next to Edinburgh, and, last of all, to London—thus completing, throughout the United

Kingdom, the establishment of prepayment by stamps alone, and thereby greatly simplifying the proceedings at all offices. To save trouble to the senders of many circulars, the chief office, St Martin's-le-Grand, continued to receive prepayment in money from 10 A.M. to 5 P.M., in sums of not less than £2 at a time: an arrangement, later, extended to other offices.

An extract from Rowland Hill's diary, under date 29th October 1851, says: "A clerkship at Hong-Kong having become vacant by death, the Postmaster-General has, on my recommendation, determined not to fill it, and to employ part of the saving thus effected in giving to the postmaster and each of the remaining clerks in turn leave of absence for a year and a half,[191] with full salary, and an allowance of £100 towards the expense of the voyage. By these means, while ample force will still be left, the poor fellows will have the opportunity of recruiting their health."

Early in 1852 Rowland Hill also writes in his diary that "The Postmaster-General has sanctioned a measure of mine which, I expect, will have the effect of converting the railway stations in all the larger towns into gratuitous receiving offices." The plan, convenient as it has proved, was, however, long in being carried out.

The agitation to extend penny postage beyond the limits of the British Isles is much older than many people suppose. Far back in the 'forties Elihu Burritt[192] strove long and manfully in the cause of "*ocean* penny postage"; and in my father's diary, under date 5th March 1853, it is recorded that the Postmaster-General received a deputation "which came to urge the extension of penny postage to the Colonies."[193] It was a reform long delayed; and as usual the Post Office was reproached for not moving with the times, etc. That a large portion of the blame lay rather with the great steamship companies, which have never failed to charge heavily for conveyance of the mails, is far too little considered.

But the great steamship companies are not alone in causing the Post Office to be made a scapegoat for their own sins in the way of exacting heavy payments. In 1853 Rowland Hill gave evidence before a Parliamentary committee to consider railway and canal charges; and showed that, owing to the strained relations between the Post Office and the railway companies, the use of trains for mail conveyance was so restricted as to injure the public and even the companies themselves; also that, while the cost of carrying passengers and goods had been greatly reduced on the railways, the charge for carrying the mails had grown by nearly 300 per cent., although their weight had increased by only 140 per cent. He also laid before the Committee a Bill—approved by two successive Postmasters-General—framed to prescribe reasonable rates, and laying down a better principle of arbitration in respect of trains run at hours fixed by the Postmaster-General. The Committee, as shown by their Report, mainly adopted Rowland Hill's views, which were indeed perfectly just, and, if adopted, would, in his estimation, have reduced the annual expenditure in railway conveyance—then about £360,000—by at least £100,000. The proposals were made to secure fair rates of charge in all new railway bills, but it was intended to extend the arrangement eventually to already existing railways. But the railway influence in Parliament was too strong to allow adoption of these improvements; and attempts subsequently made were unavailing to alter the injurious law enacted early in the railway era, and intended to last only till experience of the working of the lines should have afforded the requisite data for laying down a scale of charges.[194] Being of opinion that, in order to serve the public more effectually, far greater use should be made of the railways, the reformer tried to procure for the Post Office the unrestricted use of all trains for a moderate fixed charge. Owing, however, to the existing law, the uncertainty of rates of payment, the excessive awards frequently made, and other causes, this useful measure was not adopted, with the result that the subsidies to the companies went on increasing in magnitude.

In the same year the Great Northern Railway had spontaneously begun to run a train at night, at such speed as to outstrip the night mail on the London and North-Western line. Believing that the object was to tempt the public into agitating for the use of the rival train and line, my father applied to the North-Western Railway company for such acceleration as would obviate the possibility of such a demand being made. He also suggested the introduction of what are now called limited mails; but this idea was not adopted for some years.[195] Till the acceleration was accomplished the answer to a letter leaving London by the night mail for Edinburgh or Glasgow could not be received till the afternoon of the next day but one.

Increased speed, however, was found to produce unpunctuality, misunderstandings, and other evils; and the public grew dissatisfied. Of course the railway companies blamed the Post Office, and, equally, of course, though with better reason, the Post Office blamed the railway companies. My father proposed that each side should be subjected to fines whenever irregularity occurred, and that punctuality should receive reward. But the proposal was not accepted. In 1855, however, the attempt was again made to induce the railway companies to agree to the payment of mutual penalties in case of unpunctuality, coupled with reward to the companies, but not to the Office, for punctual performance. Only one company—the North British—accepted the proposal, the result being that the instances of irregularity were in half a year brought down from 112 to 9, the company at the same time receiving a reward of £400.

Later, the railway companies agreed to accelerate their night mails between London and Edinburgh and Glasgow. An *additional* payment of some £15,000 a year had to be made, but the benefit to the two countries was so great that the outlay was not grudged. The effort to extend a like boon to Ireland was not so successful. The companies which had begun with moderate demands, suddenly asked for lessened acceleration and increased remuneration; and the Government adopted their views in preference to those of the Postmaster-General and the postal reformer. As a natural consequence, an annual subsidy of over £100,000 had to be paid in addition to the necessary cost of provision for letter-sorting in the trains and steamships. Punctuality also was often disregarded, and penalties were suspended on the score of insufficient pier accommodation at Holyhead.

Some of the companies were short-sighted enough to refuse what would have been remunerative work offered by the Post Office. On one short line of 23 miles, £3,000 per annum was demanded for the carriage of a night mail; and, although the Office offered to furnish a train of its own, as by law any one was entitled to do, and to pay the appointed tolls, though legally exempt from so doing—such payment to be settled by arbitration—the proposal was rejected. Ultimately, a more circuitous route was adopted at a third of the cost first demanded.

There was great need of reorganisation and common-sense rearrangement in these matters. Why, for instance, when carrying a letter between Land's End and John O'Groat's should twenty-one separate contracts, irrespective of engagements with rural messengers and of plans for the conveyance of mail-bags to and from railway stations and post offices, have been required?

With a view to the reduction of these extravagant subsidies, Rowland Hill proposed that "Government should, on ample security, and to a limited extent, advance loans on the terms on which it could itself borrow to such companies as were willing to adopt a reasonable tariff of charge for postal services." He hoped by these means to reduce the annual payments to the companies by about £250,000. The Duke of Argyll, then Postmaster-General, and Mr Hutchinson, Chairman of the Stock Exchange, highly approved of the plan; but, though it evoked much interest, and came up again as a public question more than once in later years, no progress was made. Were State purchase of the railways to become the law of the land, solution of the difficulty might yet be discovered.

One of the measures Rowland Hill hoped to see accomplished was the conveyance of mails on one of the principal lines by special trains absolutely limited to Post Office service. The cost would be moderate if the companies could be induced to join in an arrangement under which, the bare additional expense in each instance being ascertained by a neutral authority, a certain fixed multiple of that amount should be paid. Captain (afterwards Sir Douglas) Galton, of the Board of Trade, and Sir William Cubitt heartily approved of the plan, the latter estimating the cost in question at 1s. to 1s. 3d. a mile, and advising that two and a half times that amount should be offered. Under this rule the Post Office would pay less for the whole train than it already paid for a small part of one. The plan of charge by fixed scale found little favour with the companies; but the proposed special mail service was ultimately adopted.

The Postmaster-General (Lord Canning's) Commission in 1853 on the Packet Service—which included among its members Lord Canning himself and the then Sir Stafford Northcote—did much useful work, and published an able Report giving a brief history of "contract mail-packets"; explaining why, under older conditions, heavy subsidies were necessary, and expressing their opinion that, as now the steamers so employed carry passengers and freight, these large subsidies could no longer be required. When a new route has been opened for the extension of commerce, further continuance of the Service, unless desirable on account of important political reasons, should depend on its tendency to become self-supporting. Among other recommendations made were the omission in future contracts of many conditions whose effect is increase of cost; a reduction of the contract to an undertaking (subject to penalties for failure) to convey the mails at fixed periods and with a certain degree of speed, and an agreement that, except in the case of a new route, contracts should not be allowed to exist for a long period.

When at last the management of the Packet Service was transferred from the Admiralty to the Post Office, a useful—indeed necessary—reform was accomplished. While in the hands of the former Department, the Service had become a source of very heavy expense, owing, in great part, to its extension for political reasons very far beyond postal requirements.

Great inconvenience had resulted also from the slight control possessed by the Post Office over the Service. In 1857, for example, the contract with the West Indian Packet Company was renewed without the knowledge of either the Postmaster-General or of Rowland Hill. The absence in the contracts of stipulations as to punctuality likewise had ill effects. The most punctual service at this time was that between Devonport and the Cape of Good Hope, as the Union Steamship Company, into whose contract such stipulations had been introduced in strong form, made during 1859 every one of its voyages within the appointed time.

Investigation of the Packet Service accounts showed how abundant was the room for diminution of cost. The annual charge to the Home Government for conveying the mails to and from Honduras was, as a consequence, readily cut down from £8,000 to £2,000, and eventually to £1,500. There had always been a heavy loss on the foreign and colonial service. That to the Cape of Good Hope and Natal was reduced in six years from £28,000 to £5,400 per annum. Much of the merit of this diminution of cost, as regards the Packet Service, was always attributed by my father to his youngest brother Frederic; and while that department remained under the latter's control the large annual loss was reduced by more than £200,000—one-half the sum—by the cutting down of expenditure, the other half by increased yield from the correspondence. The cost to the British taxpayer was further lightened by calling upon the colonists, who had hitherto been exempt from all such charges, henceforth to bear their fair share of the expense. Thus both punctuality and economy were insisted upon.

About 1857 a persistent demand arose for a mail service to Australia by the Panama route, the Press vigorously taking up the agitation, and the Government being accused of "red tapeism" because they did not move in the matter, or not until the outcry grew so loud that it was deemed expedient to apply to the shipping agencies for tenders. Being one day at the Athenæum Club, Rowland Hill met a friend, a man of superior education and varied knowledge, who had long held an important post in the Far East, almost on the shores of the Pacific. "Why," asked this friend, "do you not establish an Australian mail by the Panama route?" "Why should we?" was the counter-question. "Because it is the shortest," replied the friend. At once Rowland Hill proposed an adjournment to the drawing-room, where stood a large globe; the test of measurement was applied, and thereupon was demonstrated the fallacy of a widespread popular belief, founded on ignorance of the enormous width of the Pacific Ocean—a belief, as this anecdote shows, shared even by some of those who have dwelt within reach of its waters.[196]

But convincing friends was of far less moment than convincing the public; and Rowland Hill drew up a Report on the subject which, backed by the Postmaster-General, Lord Colchester, had the desired effect of preventing, for the time being, what would have been a heavy and useless expenditure of public money.[197]

It is found that great public ceremonies affect the weekly returns of the number of letters passing through the post. Sometimes the result is a perceptible increase; at other times a decrease. The funeral of the great

Duke of Wellington was held on the 18th November 1852, and "all London" was in the streets to look at it. The weekly return, published on the 22nd, showed that the number of letters dispatched by the evening mail from the metropolis on that memorable 18th fell off by about 100,000. The next day's letters were probably increased by an extra 10,000. The revolutionary year, 1848, also had a deteriorating influence on correspondence, the return published in 1849 for the previous twelvemonths showing a smaller increase than, under ordinary circumstances, might have been expected.

In 1853 Docker's ingenious apparatus for the exchange of mail-bags at those railway stations through which trains pass without stopping was introduced. The process is described by the postal reformer as follows:— "The bags to be forwarded, being suspended from a projecting arm at the station, are so knocked off by a projection from the train as to fall into a net which is attached to the mail carriage, and is for the moment stretched out to receive them; while, at the same time, the bags to be left behind, being hung out from the mail carriage, are in like manner so struck off as to be caught in a net fixed at the station; the whole of this complex movement being so instantaneous that the uninformed eye cannot follow it." It was this inability to understand the movement which led to a ridiculous error. On the first day of the experiment people assembled in crowds to witness it. At Northallerton "half Yorkshire" gathered—according to the mail inspector—and many were under the impression that the outgoing set of bags they saw hanging to the projecting arm in readiness for absorption by the passing train, and the incoming set hanging out from the mail carriage, ready to be caught in the net fixed at the station, were one and the same thing. Though what useful purpose could be served by the mere "giving a lift" of a hundred yards or so to one solitary set of bags is rather hard to perceive.

AN EARLY TRAVELLING POST OFFICE WITH MAIL BAGS EXCHANGE APPARATUS.
By permission of the Proprietors of the *"City Press."*

The invention was not altogether a success, very heavy bags—especially when the trains were running at great speed—being sometimes held responsible for the occurrence of rather serious accidents. It even became necessary to cease using the apparatus till the defect, whatever it might be, could be put right. Several remedies were suggested, but none proved effectual till my brother, then only twenty-one years of age, hit upon a simple contrivance which removed all difficulties, and thenceforth the exchange-bag apparatus worked well. Sir William Cubitt, who had unsuccessfully striven to rectify matters, generously eulogised his youthful rival's work.

The stamp-obliterating machines which superseded the old practice of obliteration by hand were also my brother's invention. In former days the man who could stamp the greatest number of letters in a given time was usually invited to exhibit his prowess when visitors were shown over the office. The old process had never turned out impressions conspicuous for legibility, and means of improvement had been for some time under consideration. But it was a trial presided over by Lord Campbell in 1856 which precipitated matters. An important question turned upon the exact date at which a letter had been posted, but the obliterating stamp on the envelope was too indistinct to furnish the necessary evidence. Lord Campbell sharply animadverted upon the failure, and his strictures caused the Duke of Argyll—then Postmaster-General—to write to Rowland Hill upon the subject. The use of inferior ink was supposed to be responsible for the trouble, and various experiments were tried, without effecting any marked beneficial result. Objection was made to abolition of the human hand as stamper on the ground that thus far it had proved to be the fastest worker. Then my brother's mechanical skill came to the rescue, and complaints as to clearness and legibility soon became rare.[198] By the machines the obliterations were made faster than by the best hand-work, the increase of speed being at least 50 per cent. About the year 1903 my brother's machines began, I am told, to be superseded by others which are said to do the work faster even than his. Judging by some of the obliterations lately made, presumably by these later machines, it is evident that, so far as clearness and legibility are concerned, the newer process is not superior to the older.

My brother was a born mechanician, and, like our uncle Edwin Hill, could, out of an active brain, evolve almost any machine for which, in some emergency, there seemed to be need. To give free scope to Pearson's obvious bent, our father had, in his son's early youth, caused a large four-stalled stable adjoining our house at Hampstead to be altered into a well-equipped workshop; and in this many a long evening was spent, the window being often lighted up some hours after the rest of the family had retired to bed, and my brother being occasionally obliged to sing out, through the one open pane, a cheery "good-night" to the passing policeman, who paused to see if a burglarious conspiracy was being devised during the nocturnal small hours, from the convenient vantage-ground of the outhouse.

The dream of my brother's life was to become a civil engineer, for which profession, indeed, few young men could have been better fitted; and the dream seemed to approach accomplishment when, during a visit to our father, Sir William (afterwards first Lord) Armstrong spoke most highly of Pearson's achievements—he had just put into completed form two long-projected small inventions—and offered to take the youth into his own works at Newcastle-on-Tyne. But the dream was never destined to find realisation. Sir William's visit and proposal made a fitting opportunity for the putting to my brother of a serious question which had been in our father's head for some time. In his son's integrity, ability, and affection, Rowland Hill had absolute trust. Were the younger man but working with him at the Post Office, the elder knew he could rely on unswerving support, on unwavering fidelity. The choice of callings was laid before my brother: life as a civil engineer—a profession in which his abilities could not fail to command success—or the less ambitious career of a clerk at St Martin's-le-Grand. Our father would not dwell upon his own strong leaning towards the latter course, but with the ever-present mental image of harassing official intrigues against himself and his hard-won reform, it is not difficult to picture with what conflicting emotions he must have waited his son's decision. This was left entirely in the young man's hands; and he chose the part which he knew would best serve his father. The cherished dream was allowed to melt into nothingness, and my brother began his postal career not as a favoured, but as an ordinary clerk, though one always near at hand, and always in the complete confidence of his immediate chief. Whatever regrets for the more congenial life Pearson may have harboured, he never, to my knowledge, gave them audible expression, nor could any father have had a more loyal son. When, many years later, it seemed desirable that some official should be appointed to report on the value of the mechanical inventions periodically offered to the Post Office, and to supervise those already in operation, it seemed when my brother was selected for that post as if he had only received his due, and that merely in part.

He had also administrative ability of no mean order; and when only twenty-eight years of age was selected by the Postmaster-General to go to Mauritius to reorganise the post office there, which through mismanagement had gradually drifted into a state of confusion, apparently beyond rectification by the island authorities. He speedily brought the office into good working order; but perhaps his Mauritian labours will be best remembered by his substitution of certain civilised stamps—like those then used in some of the West Indian isles—in place of the trumpery red and blue, penny and twopenny, productions which were the handiwork of some local artist, and which are now so rare that they command amazingly large sums of money in the philatelist world.

PEARSON HILL.
By permission of the Proprietor of Flett's Studios, late London School of Photography.

FOOTNOTES:

[174] The people of to-day who have never known the old postal system can have no idea of the unanimity and strength of that voice. Memory of the former state of things was still fresh in men's minds; and, with perhaps one exception, no person wished for its return. "Hill, you are the most popular man in the kingdom," one day exclaimed an old friend. The exception—there might have been more than one, but if so, we were none the wiser—was one of the Bentincks who, so late as the year 1857, suggested in the House of Commons a return to franking on the score that penny postage was one of the greatest jobs and greatest financial mistakes ever perpetrated. Sir Francis Baring advised Mr Bentinck to try to bring back the old postal rates, when he would see what the country thought of the proposal.—("Hansard," cxlvi. 188, 189.)

[175] By this time Mr Wallace had retired from public life, and only a short while later became involved in pecuniary difficulties. By the exertions of his friends and admirers, an annuity was secured to him—a provision which, though small in comparison with his former prosperity, placed the venerable ex-Parliamentarian well above want. He died in 1855, aged eighty-two.

[176] "Life," ii. 9, 10.

[177] "Life," ii. 58.

[178] The *Times* (Parliamentary Debates), 15th June 1864. The Money Order Office dates from 1792. It was first known as "Stow & Co.," being started as a private undertaking by three Post Office clerks; and its mission

was to enable small sums of money to be safely transmitted to our sailors and soldiers. Later, all classes of the community were included in the benefit, the remittances to be forwarded being still restricted to small sums. Each of the three partners advanced £1,000 to float the enterprise, and division of the profits gave to each about £200 a year. The commission charged was 8d. in the pound, of which 3d. each went to the two postmasters who received and paid the orders, and 2d. to the partners. The Postmaster-General sanctioned the measure, which clearly supplied a felt want, but refrained from interference with its management. In 1838 "Stow & Co." ceased to exist, becoming thenceforth an official department, and the then partners receiving compensation for the surrender of their monopoly. The fees were thereupon fixed at 6d. for sums not exceeding £2, and 1s. 6d. for sums of £2 to £5, the rates being still further reduced in 1840.

[179] "Life," ii. 59, 60.

[180] "Life," ii. 257.

[181] "Life" ii. 260.

[182] Reputed author of the well-known saying that "Life would be endurable were it not for its pleasures."

[183] "Life," ii. 304-307. In 1871 the amount of unclaimed money orders was £3,390. In that year the Lords of the Treasury put an end to this disposal of unclaimed money except in regard to the then existing recipients of the aid; and the accumulated capital, together with the interest thereon, about £20,707, was paid into the Exchequer.—(Editor, G.B.H.'s, note at p. 306.)

[184] "Life," ii. 365. (Note by its Editor.)

[185] "Life," ii. 122. On the famous 10th of April 1848 (Chartist day) Colonel Maberly likewise showed his martial spirit and strong sense of the virtue of discipline when he requested Rowland Hill to place his own clerks and those of the Money Order Office—in all about 250—under his, the Colonel's, command, thus making up a corps of special constables some 1,300 strong. All over London, on and before that day, there was great excitement; a large supply of arms was laid in, defences were erected at Governmental and other public buildings, very little regular work was done, and there was any amount of unnecessary scare, chiefly through the alarmist disposition of the Duke of Wellington—seldom, rumour said, averse from placing a town in a more or less state of siege, and ever ready to urge upon successive Governments the desirability of spending huge sums on fortifications whose destiny ere long was to become obsolete— though partly also because there were many people still living who could

remember the Gordon riots immortalised in "Barnaby Rudge," and who feared a repetition of their excesses. But the Chartists were a different set of men from Gordon's "tag, rag, and bobtail" followers. On the morning of the 10th, my father, driving to the Post Office, came up in Holborn with the long procession marching in the direction of Kennington Common (now a park), preparatory to presenting themselves with their petition at the Houses of Parliament. Calling on the cabman to drive slowly, my father watched the processionists with keen interest, and was much struck with their steady bearing, evident earnestness, and the bright, intelligent countenances of many of them. On close inspection, not a few terrible revolutionists are found to look surprisingly like other people, though the comparison does not invariably tell in favour of those other people.

[186] The *Mercury's* article (25th April 1850) was so good that it seems worth while to quote some of it. "Macaulay informs us that the post, when first established, was the object of violent invective as a manifest contrivance of the Pope to enslave the souls of Englishmen; and most books of history or anecdote will supply stories equally notable. But we really very much doubt whether any tale of ancient times can match the exhibition of credulity which occurred in our own country, and under our own eyes, within these last twelve months.... Nearly 6,000 people have been relieved from nearly six hours' work every Sunday by the operation of a scheme which was denounced as a deliberate encouragement to Sabbath-breaking and profanity."

[187] *À propos* of never answering attacks in the Press and elsewhere, my father was not a little given to quote the opinion of one of the Post officials who "goes so far as to declare that if he found himself charged in a newspaper with parricide, he would hold his tongue lest the accusation should be repeated next day with the aggravation of matricide."—"Life," ii. 235.

[188] This relief, proposed in November 1849, became an accomplished fact a few days before the year died out.

[189] "Life," ii. 138.

[190] *Ibid.* ii. 137.

[191] In those slower-going days a large part of the holiday would be taken up by the journey home and back.

[192] A frequent and always welcome visitor at my father's house was this son of America—"the learned blacksmith," as he was habitually called. He was one of the most interesting as well as most refreshingly unconventional of men, but was never offensively unconventional because he was one of "Nature's noblemen." Sweet-tempered, gentle-mannered, and pure-minded,

he won our regard—affection even—from the first. He could never have been guilty of uttering an unkind word to any one, not even to those who were lukewarm on the slavery question, who did not feel inspired to join the Peace Society, or who were languid in the cause of "ocean penny postage." On the last-named subject he had, as an entire stranger, written to my father a long letter detailing his scheme, and urging the desirability of its adoption; and it was this letter which led to our making Elihu Burritt's acquaintance. He became a great friend of my elder sister, and maintained with her a many years' long correspondence. Once only do I remember seeing him angry, and then it was the righteous indignation which an honest man displays when confronted with a lie. It was when unto him had been attributed the authorship of my father's plan. He would have nothing to do with a fraudulent claim to which sundry other men have assented kindly enough, or have even, with unblushing effrontery, appropriated of their own accord. Elihu Burritt and Cardinal Mezzofanti were said to be the two greatest linguists of the mid-nineteenth century; and I know not how many languages and dialects each had mastered—the one great scholar a distinguished prince of the Roman Catholic Church, the other an American of obscure birth and an ex-blacksmith. Another trans-atlantic postal reformer, though one interested in the reform as regarded his own country rather than ours, was Mr Pliny Miles, who in outward appearance more closely resembled the typical American of Dickens's days than that of the present time. In his own land Mr Miles travelled far and wide, wrote much, spoke frequently, and crossed the Atlantic more than once to study the postal question here. He was an able man, and a good talker. I well remember his confident prophecy, some few years before the event, of a fratricidal war between the Northern and Southern States; how bitterly he deplored the coming strife; and how deeply impressed were all his hearers both with the matter and manner of his discourse. I believe he had "crossed the bar" before hostilities broke out.

[193] "Life," ii. 241.

[194] "Life," ii. 227-230.

[195] "My notion is," wrote the diarist, "to run a train with only one or two carriages in addition to those required for the mail, and to stop only once in about 40 miles." A long distance run in those days. The speed was fixed at 40 miles an hour, stoppages included. This was considered very quick travelling in the 'fifties.

[196] "It is curious," says my father, "how inveterate is the mistake in question. Columbus expected to reach Cathay more quickly by sailing westward, but was stopped by the American continent. The projectors of the 'Darian Scheme' hoped to enrich themselves by making their settlement

a great *entrepot* between Europe and the East Indies; and Macaulay, in his interesting narrative of the enterprise ('History of England,' vol. v. p. 200), considers their mistake to consist mainly in the assumption that Spain would permit a settlement on its territory; but it seems not to have occurred to him that, in any event, the scheme was intrinsically hopeless, seeing that the old route by the Cape of Good Hope, besides avoiding the cost and delay of transhipment, surpasses the Darian route even in shortness" ("Life," ii. 292). It is also well known that the discoverer of certain rapids on the great river St Lawrence believed himself to be nearing the country of Confucius when he called them "La Chine."

[197] Thus the agitation for an "all red route" is a mere revival.

[198] Sixth Annual Report of the Postmaster-General.

CHAPTER VIII

AT THE POST OFFICE—*Continued*

THE important Commission appointed in 1853 to revise the scale of salaries of the Post Office employees held many sittings and did valuable work.[199] Its report was published in the following year. Rowland Hill's examination alone occupied eight days; and he had the satisfaction of finding the Commissioners' views in accordance with his own on the subject of patronage, promotion, and classification.

On the score that the business of the Post Office is of a kind which peculiarly requires centralisation, the Commission condemned the principle of the double Secretariate, and recommended that the whole should be placed under the direction of a single secretary; that in order to enable "every deserving person" to have within his reach attainment to "the highest prizes," the ranks of the Secretary's Office should be opened to all members of the establishment; and that throughout the Department individual salaries should advance by annual increments instead of by larger ones at long intervals: all advancements to be contingent on good conduct. It was also advised that, to attract suitable men, prospects of advancement should be held out; that improvement in provincial offices—then much needed—should be secured by allowing respective postmasters, under approval and in accordance with prescribed rules, to appoint their own clerks; and that promotion should be strictly regulated according to qualification and merit—a rule which in time must raise any department to the highest state of efficiency. The abolition of a crying evil was also advised. At the time in question all appointments to the office rested not with the Postmaster-General but with the Treasury, the nomination being in effect left to the Member of Parliament for the district where a vacancy occurred, provided he were a general supporter of the Government. It was a system which opened the way to many abuses, and was apt to flood the service with "undesirables." The Commissioners advised the removal of the anomaly both for obvious reasons and "because the power which the Postmaster-General would possess of rewarding meritorious officers in his own department by promoting them to the charge of the important provincial offices would materially conduce to the general efficiency of the whole body." The relinquishment of patronage—a privilege always held dear by politicians—was conceded so far as to allow to the Postmaster-General the appointing of all postmasterships where the salary exceeded £175 a year, thus avoiding the application in all cases where the Post Office is held in conjunction with a private business or profession. A subsequent concession reduced the minimum to £120. The relinquishment of so much patronage reflected great credit on the Administration then in power.[200]

It is pleasant to remember that when, in after years, the postal reform, by its complete success, had proved the soundness of its author's reasoning, the Conservatives and "Peelites," who of old had opposed the Penny Postage Bill, seemed sometimes to go out of their way to show him friendliness. One of the kindest of his old opponents was Disraeli—not yet Earl of Beaconsfield—who, as Chancellor of the Exchequer, invited the reformer to share his hospitality, and especially singled out the new guest for attention. The first Postmaster-General to invite Rowland Hill to his house was his second chief, the Tory Lord Hardwicke, who had also asked Colonel Maberly, but was careful to put the two men one at each end of the very long table.

When, therefore, at last (in 1854) my father was given the post Colonel Maberly had so long filled, and became thenceforth known to the world as Secretary to the Post Office, it was with deep gratification that he recorded the fact in his diary that "all those to whom I had on this occasion to return official thanks had been members of the Government by which, twelve years before, I had been dismissed from office.[201] I could not but think that the kind and earnest manner in which these gentlemen now acted proceeded in some measure from a desire to compensate me for the injustice of their former leader; and this view made me even more grateful for their consideration."[202]

The old hostility between Colonel Maberly and Rowland Hill was scarcely likely to decrease while they remained, to use the sailor Postmaster-General's favourite expression, "two kings of Brentford." Colonel Maberly had never been sparing of his blows during the long agitation over the postal reform previous to its establishment; and a dual authority is hardly calculated to transform opponents into allies. It was therefore fortunate that the peculiar arrangement, after enduring, with considerable discomfort, for seven and a half years, was brought to a close.

We all have our strong points; and one of Colonel Maberly's was a happy knack of selecting heads of departments, the chief Secretary's immediate subordinates. They were an able staff of officers, unto whom my father always considered that the good reputation the Post Office enjoyed while he was its permanent head was largely due. With their aid the reformer devised and matured measures of improvement more rapidly than before— more rapidly because there was now far less likelihood, when once authorisation had been obtained for carrying them out, of seeing his proposals subjected to tiresome modifications or indefinite delays, too often leading to entire abandonment. Thus he was enabled to give most of his time to the work of organisation, to him always, as he has said, "of all occupations the least difficult and the most pleasant." He encouraged his newly-acquired staff "to make what proved to be a valuable change in their mode of proceeding; for whereas the practice had been for these officers simply to select the cases requiring the judgment of the Secretary, and to await his instructions before writing their minutes thereon, I gradually induced them to come prepared with an opinion of their own which might serve in a measure for my guidance." This placing of confidence in able and experienced men had, as was but natural, excellent results.

The arrangement of secretarial and other duties being now settled, reforms proceeded satisfactorily; new and greatly improved post offices were erected, and older ones were cleared of accumulated rubbish, and made more habitable in many ways. It was found that at the General Post Office itself no sort of provision against the risk of fire existed—an extraordinary state of things in a building through which many documents, often of great value and importance, were continually passing. Little time was lost in devising measures to remedy this and other defects.

But, strange to say, in 1858 the construction and alteration of post office buildings was transferred by the Treasury to the Board of Works. Knowing that the change would lead to extravagance, Rowland Hill essayed, but quite unsuccessfully, to effect a reversal of this measure; and in support of his views instanced a striking contrast. A new post office had been erected at Brighton, the cost, exclusive of a moderate sum expended to fit it up as a residence, being about £1,600. A similar building had now to be put up at Dundee, whose correspondence was half that of Brighton. The Board of Works' estimate came to four or five times that amount, and all that Rowland Hill could accomplish was to bring the cost down to £5,700.

The first of the long series of "Annual Reports of the Postmaster-General" was published in 1854. It was prefaced with an interesting historical sketch of the Post Office from its origin, written by Matthew Davenport Hill's eldest son Alfred, unto whom my father was further beholden for valuable assistance as arbitrator in the already mentioned disputes between the Post Office and the railway companies. The modern weakness of apathy—most contagious of maladies—seemed after a while to settle even on the Post Office, for, late in the 'nineties, the issue was for a time discontinued.

One passage alone in the First Report shows how satisfactory was the progress made. "On the first day of each month a report is laid before the Postmaster-General showing the principal improvements in hand, and the stage at which each has arrived. The latest of these reports (which is of the usual length) records 183 measures, in various stages of progress or completed during the month of December 1854. Minor improvements, such as extension of rural posts, etc., are not noticed in these reports."[203]

Another small periodical publication first appeared in 1856, which, revised and issued quarterly, is now a well-known, useful little manual. This was the *British Postal Guide*. Its acceptability was made evident by its ready sale, amounting, not long after its issue, to 20,000 or 30,000 copies. Two years later an old publication known as the *Daily Packet List* was rearranged, enlarged, and turned into a weekly edition, which, as the *Postal Circular*, accomplished much useful service. Had the Treasury allowed the extension of the sphere of this little work, as recommended by the Postmaster-General and Rowland Hill, it could have been so extended as to become a postal monitor, correcting any possible misconceptions, and keeping the public constantly informed as to the real proceedings of the Post Office.

By November 1854 the diarist was able to write that his "plan has been adopted, more or less completely, in the following States: Austria, Baden, Bavaria, Belgium, Brazil, Bremen, Brunswick, Chile, Denmark, France, Frankfort, Hamburg, Hanover, Lubeck, Naples, New Grenada, Netherlands, Oldenburg, Peru, Portugal, Prussia, Russia, Sardinia, Saxony, Spain, Switzerland, Tuscany, United States, and Wurtemberg." It seems worth while to repeat the long list just as my father gave it, if only to show how much, since that time, the political geography of our own continent has altered, most of the tiny countries and all the "free cities" of mid-nineteenth-century Europe having since that date become absorbed by larger or stronger powers. It will be noticed that Norway and Sweden had not yet followed the example of the other western European countries. But the then "dual kingdom" did not long remain an exception.

Among the first European powers to adopt the postal reform were, strange to say, Spain and Russia, neither of which was then accounted a progressive country. In September 1843 the Spanish ambassador wrote to Rowland Hill asking for information about postal matters, as his Government contemplated introducing the postage stamp, and, presumably, a certain amount of uniformity and low rates. Not long after, news came that Russia had adopted stamps. The chief motive in each case was, however, understood to be the desire to prevent fraud among the postmasters.

Although Spain moved early in the matter of postal reform, Portugal sadly lagged behind, no new convention having been effected with that country, and, consequently, no postal improvements, save in marine transit, made for fifty years. In 1858, however, mainly through the good offices of the British Ministers at Madrid and Lisbon, and of Mr Edward Rea, who was sent out from London by the Postmaster-General for the purpose, better postal treaties were made, both with Spain and Portugal. Even with such countries as Belgium, Germany (the German Postal Union), and the United States, progress in the way of treaties was very slow.

The postal revenues of all these European countries were smaller than our own, Portugal's being less than that of the city of Edinburgh. Small indeed is the connection between the amount of a country's correspondence and the number of its population. According to an official return published in the *Journal de St Petersburg* in 1855, the letters posted during the year throughout the huge empire of Russia were only 16,400,000, or almost the same number as those posted during the same year in Manchester and its suburbs.

By 1853 a low uniform rate of postage was established over the length and breadth of our even then vast Indian Empire; a few outlying portions alone excepted. For many years after the introduction of the new system, involving, as it did, complete adoption of Rowland Hill's plan, the Indian Post Office did not pay expenses; but by 1870 it became self-supporting.[204]

It has sometimes been asserted that, in his eagerness to make his reform a financial success, Rowland Hill cut down the wages of the lower strata of employees. Nothing could be more untrue. Economy, he believed, was to be obtained by simpler methods and better organisation, not by underpaying the workers. While at the Post Office he did much to improve the lot of these classes of men. Their wages were increased, they had greater opportunity of rising in the service, a pension for old age combined with assistance in effecting life assurance, gratuitous medical advice and medicines,[205] and an annual holiday without loss of pay. The number of working hours was limited to a daily average of eight, and a regulation was made that any letter-carrier who, taking one day with another, found his work exceed that limit, should be entitled to call attention to the fact and obtain assistance. An exhaustive enquiry was made as to the scale of wages paid, the hours of work required, etc.; and the report, when published, told the world that the men of similar rank in other callings, such as policemen, railway porters, and several more, were not so well treated as their brethren in the postal service. So clearly, indeed, was this proved that public endorsement of the fact was at once evidenced by a marked increase of applications for situations as sorters, letter-carriers, etc.

A striking proof of this recognition of a truth came at first hand to Rowland Hill's knowledge. He was consulting an old medical friend, and in the course of conversation the latter said that his footman wished to obtain an appointment as letter-carrier. Whereupon my father pointed out that the man was better off as footman, because, in addition to receiving good wages, he had board, lodging, and many other advantages. This, answered the doctor, had already been represented to the man; but his reply was that in the Post Office there was the certainty of continuity of employment and the pension for old age. The fact that the employees in a public department are not, like many other workers, liable at any moment to be sent adrift by the death or impoverishment of their employers, constitutes one of the strongest attractions to the service. Has this circumstance any connection with the growing disinclination of the poorer classes to enter domestic service?

In 1854 rural distribution was greatly extended, 500 new offices being opened. This extension, it may be remembered, was one of several measures which were persistently opposed by the enemies of the postal reform. How much the measure was needed, and, when granted, how beneficial were its results, is shown by the fact that it was followed by the largest increase of letters which had taken place in any year since 1840, or a gain on 1853 of 32,500,000.

The measure affected several hundreds of different places and a very large percentage of the entire correspondence of the United Kingdom. Formerly there were to every office limits, sometimes narrow, sometimes wide, beyond which there was either no delivery, or one made only at additional charge, generally of a penny a letter: an arrangement which, in spite of my father's repeated efforts to amend it, outlived the introduction of the new postal system for more than fourteen years, and in the districts thus affected partially nullified its benefits. Not until this and other survivals of the older state of things were swept away could his plan be rightly said to be established.

London—whose then population formed one-tenth and its correspondence one-fourth of the United Kingdom—was also not neglected. It was divided into ten postal districts,[206] each of which was treated as a separate town with a local chief office in addition to its many minor offices. The two corps of letter-carriers—the general postmen and those who belonged to the old "twopenny post"—which till this time existed as distinct bodies of employees, were at last amalgamated; their "walks" were rearranged, and a new plan of sorting at the chief office was instituted, while the letters and other missives intended for the different districts, being sorted before they reached London, were no longer, as of old, sent to St Martin's-le-Grand, but were at once dispatched for distribution to the local chief office whose initials corresponded with those upon the covers. Door letter-boxes increased in number in the houses of the poorer as well as of the richer classes; and the use, in addition to the address, on the printed heading of a letter of the initials denoting the postal district from which it emanated, and on the envelope of that where it should be delivered—a use to which the public generally accustomed itself kindly—greatly facilitated and expedited communication within the 12 miles circuit, so that thenceforth it became possible to post a letter and receive its reply within the space of a few hours—a heartily appreciated boon in the days when the telephone was not. As a natural consequence, the number of district letters grew apace, and the congestion at St Martin's-le-Grand was perceptibly lessened. At the same time, the Board of Works to some extent amended the nomenclature of the streets and the numbering of houses. The most important delivery of the day, the first, was accelerated by two hours; in some of the suburbs by two and a half hours. That is, the morning's letters were distributed at nine o'clock instead of at half-past eleven. Since that time, and for many years now, the delivery has been made at or before eight o'clock. Nothing facilitated these earlier deliveries more than the sorting of letters *en route*; and the practice also enabled more frequent deliveries to be made. Improved communication with the colonies and foreign countries, through better treaties, was likewise effected; and each improvement was rendered easier by the rapid growth everywhere of railways and shipping companies, and the increased speed of trains and steamships.

In 1855 "the system of promotion by merit," recommended by my father and endorsed with approval by the Civil Service Commissioners "was brought into full operation. In the three metropolitan offices, when a vacancy occurred application for appointment was open to all; the respective claims were carefully compared, and, without the admission of any other consideration whatever, the claim which was adjudged to be best carried the day. To keep our course free from disturbing influences, it was laid down that any intercession from without in favour of individual officers should act, if not injuriously, at least not beneficially, on the advancement of those concerned." ... "By the transfer to the Post Office of appointment to all the higher postmasterships, opportunity for promotion was greatly enlarged, and posts formally bestowed for political services now became the rewards of approved merit. This change obviously involved great improvement in the quality of the persons thus entrusted with powers and duties of no small importance to the public. In the provincial offices a corresponding improvement was, in great measure, secured by delegating the power of appointing their subordinates, under certain restrictions, to the respective postmasters, who, being themselves responsible for the good working of their offices, were naturally led to such selection as would best conduce to that end. This delegation, so far as related to clerks, was made on the recommendation of the Civil Service Commissioners; and the trust being satisfactorily exercised, was subsequently extended to the appointment of letter-carriers also." The measure worked well. "From the different departments of the metropolitan offices, and from the provincial surveyors the reports of its operation were almost uniformly satisfactory.

Officers were found to take more personal interest in their duties, to do more work without augmentation of force, to make up in some degree by additional zeal for the increased yearly holiday that was granted them, and to discharge their duties with more cheerfulness and spirit, knowing that good service would bring eventual reward."[207]

The new system of promotion by merit worked far better than that of the Commissioners' examinations for admission to the Civil Service. As regards the letter-carriers, it has always been found that the men best fitted for this duty were those whose previous life had inured them to bodily labour and endurance of all kinds of weather. The new educational requirements in many instances excluded these people, while giving easy admission to shopmen, clerks, servants, and others accustomed to indoor and even sedentary life, who were little fitted to perform a postman's rounds. The Duke of Argyll, then Postmaster-General, requested the Commissioners to adopt a somewhat lower standard of acquirement. At the same time he authorised the subjection of candidates for the office of letter-carriers to a stricter test as regards bodily strength, with the result that about one man in every four was rejected. By these means, and the greater attention paid to the laws of sanitation in offices and private dwellings, the health of the department gradually reached a high standard.

That the plan of confining admission to the service to candidates who have passed the Civil Service examinations is not without its drawbacks, is seen by the following extract from a Report by Mr Abbott, Secretary to the Post Office in Scotland. "Considering," he says, "the different duties of the account, the secretary's and the sorting branches, I am inclined to believe that the examination should have more special reference to the vacancy the candidate is to fill than to his general knowledge on certain subjects proposed for all in the same class, more especially as regards persons nominated to the sorting office, where manual dexterity, quick sight, and physical activity are more valuable than mere educational requirements."[208]

As may be surmised by the foregoing, Rowland Hill was one of the many clear-sighted men who declined to yield unquestioning approbation to the system of competitive examinations introduced by the Civil Service Commissioners; nor did longer acquaintance with it tend to modify his opinion on the subject. The scheme, he thought, "worked unsatisfactorily, the criteria not being the best, and the responsibility being so divided that no one is in effect answerable for an appointment made under it. The consequence of its adoption has been, in many instances, the rejection of men who gave promise of great usefulness, and the admission of others whose usefulness has proved very small.[209] If no way had been open to the public service but through competitive examination as now conducted, I cannot say what might have been my own chance of admission, since on the plan adopted, no amount of knowledge or power in other departments is regarded as making up for deficiency in certain prescribed subjects. Under such a system neither George Stephenson nor Brindley would have passed examination as an engineer, nor perhaps would Napoleon or Wellington have been admitted to any military command. The principle, if sound, must be equally applicable to manufacturing and commercial establishments, but I have heard of none that have adopted it. Indeed, a wealthy merchant lately declared (and I believe most of his brethren would agree with him) that if he had no clerks but such as were chosen for him by others, his name would soon be in the *Gazette*. I have always been of opinion that the more the appointments to the Post Office, and indeed to other departments, are regulated on the principles ordinarily ruling in establishments conducted by private individuals, the better it will be for the public service. The question to be decided between candidates should be, I think, simply which is best fitted for the duties to be performed; and the decision should be left to the person immediately answerable for the right performance of the duty."[210]

While tranquillity reigned at St Martin's-le-Grand from, and long after, 1854, not only among the heads of departments, but generally throughout the office, and while reports from all quarters, metropolitan and provincial, bore testimony to efficient work accomplished and good conduct maintained, it was inevitable that in a body so numerous as was that of the lower grade employees some amount of discontent should arise. Promotion by merit, in whatever class, has few charms in the eyes of those who are deficient in the very quality which insures promotion, and who, perhaps for many years, have drawn steady payment for ordinary duty so performed as to become scarcely more than nominal. In every large community there are certain to be some "bad bargains" who, though practically useless as workers, have often abundant capacity for giving trouble, especially, maybe, in the way of fomenting a spirit of mutiny.[211]

At the Post Office this spirit manifested itself even while every care was being taken to ameliorate the condition of this multitudinous class of employees, and to rectify individual cases of hardship, and while, even during the time of insubordination, many respectable men outside the postal walls were showing their appreciation of the advantage of a letter-carrier's position over that of men of like class in other callings, by applying for appointment to that corps. Misrepresentation is a principal factor in stimulating disaffection, and, for reasons other than sympathy with the alleged victims of supposed tyrannical employers, is sometimes, though, happily, rarely, employed by those who, as non-officials, are sheltered by anonymity as well as by extraneity from participation in such punishment as may befall the better-known disaffected.

From an early period of Rowland Hill's career at the Post Office he was subjected to almost constant personal attacks on the part of a certain weekly newspaper. Many were written with considerable plausibility, but all were void of substantial truth, while others were entire fabrications. All too were of the sort which no self-respecting man condescends to answer, yet which, perhaps all the more on account of that contemptuous silence, do infinite harm, and by an unthinking public are readily believed. Many of these attacks were traced to men who had left the postal service—to the no small advantage of that service—and whose dismissal was supposed to be the work of the permanent postal head; and one such man at least, a scribe with a ready pen, and ink in which the ingredient gall was over-liberally mingled, vented his spleen during a long succession of years with a perseverance worthy a better cause. As the newspaper in question had rather a wide circulation—since when did harmful literature fail to meet ready sale?—and the postal employees were, in many cases, no wiser than their fellow-readers, it was perhaps not unnatural that the attacks, which were directed more frequently and angrily against the postal reformer than against his colleagues, should meet with credence. "It certainly was rather ill-timed," says Rowland Hill, on hearing[212] of a particularly vicious libel, "for in the previous month (November 1858) I had induced the Treasury to abandon its intention of issuing an order forbidding the receipt of Christmas boxes, and also had obtained some improvement in their scale of wages, the Treasury granting even more than was applied for."[213]

It was not long before the agitation assumed a still more serious form, no fewer than three anonymous letters threatening assassination being received at short intervals by the harassed reformer. The heads of the different postal departments, becoming alarmed for the safety of the permanent chief's life, advised his temporary absence from the Office; and Mr Peacock, its solicitor, who knew that an expert had satisfied himself and others that the handwriting of the first of these letters could be traced to a certain postman who had been giving much trouble of late, proposed immediate arrest and prosecution. But, on comparing the suspected man's actual handwriting with that, disguised though it was, of the anonymous letter, Rowland Hill disagreed with the expert's view, and refused assent to so drastic a proceeding; happily so, for later circumstances seemed to point to justification of the adverse opinion. My father also declined to absent himself from the Office, and even when a fourth letter appeared, in which were mentioned the place, day, and hour when the fatal blow would be struck, he still, as was his custom, walked the last half mile of his way to work, armed only with his umbrella, and on the fateful occasion passed the indicated spot without encountering harm of any kind. Later than this, somehow, word of the anonymous letters reached my mother's ears, though not, of course, through her husband; and thenceforth she made it her daily practice to drive down to the Post Office, and accompany him home.

This episode would hardly be worth the telling did it not serve to show how little need there generally is to pay attention to letters, however threatening, when written by persons who dare not reveal their identity. On occasions of this sort memory brings back to mind the story of the brave Frenchman who at the time of the Franco-German war wrote to the then newly-proclaimed German Emperor, William I., at Versailles, to remind him of sundry ugly passages in his life, and to threaten him with condign punishment—the writer being a near neighbour, and appending to his letter his actual name and address. This man at least had the courage of his opinions. The anonymous scribbler is seldom so valorous.

In 1858 "The Post Office Library and Literary Association" was established, the institution being aided by the delivery of lectures, an enterprise in which several of the leading officials participated. Mr West gave a fascinating discourse on etymology; and Rowland Hill took his turn by lecturing on the annular eclipse of the sun ("visible at Greenwich") which happened in that year.[214] In 1859 similar institutions were started at most of the London district offices, and in some provincial towns.

When the volunteer movement was in the heyday of its youth, the Post Office was one of the earliest of the great public departments to establish a corps of its own, whose exploits were humorously related by "Ensign" Edmund Yates, under the heading "The Grimgribber Rifle Volunteers," in several numbers of *All the Year Round* of the period. The corps became amalgamated with the "Civil Service" volunteer force, of which fine body it was perhaps the pioneer company.

"I wrote," says Rowland Hill, "to the Postmaster-General, Lord Colchester, on the subject (of raising a volunteer corps), and obtained his ready sanction. Upon my communicating with the heads of departments, I was told that there would be readiness enough to volunteer if only the expenses could be provided for, or reduced to a low rate; that the men would willingly give their time, but thought it somewhat unreasonable that there should be a demand for their money also. The difficulty was overcome by the same means, and I suppose to about the same extent, as in other corps; but from that day to this I have been unable to understand the policy or propriety of making men pay for liberty to serve their country, a practice which must, in the nature of things, debar large numbers from enrolment. The movement was not limited to the chief office, and was especially satisfactory at Edinburgh."[215]

In July 1859 Sir Edward Baines, proprietor of the *Leeds Mercury*, wrote to introduce to Rowland Hill the inventor of the Post Office Savings[216] Bank scheme, Mr (afterwards Sir) Charles Sikes, a banker of Huddersfield—a scheme which has been a great convenience to people of limited means. Depositors and deposits have increased, till the modest venture launched in 1860, under the auspices of the Chancellor of the Exchequer, Mr Gladstone, has grown into a colossal undertaking. Sir Charles, with characteristic lack of self-advertisement, never sought reward of any kind for the good work he had initiated. He was satisfied with the knowledge that it had proved of immense benefit to his fellow-men. He long survived the carrying into practical shape of his scheme; and now that he is dead, his invention has, of course, been claimed by or for others.

The postal reform is one which, save as regards its most salient features, has been established somewhat on the "gradual instalment system," each instalment, as a rule, coming into operation after a hard struggle on the part of its promoter, and several years later than when first proposed. Prepayment of postage, for example, one of the most essential parts of my father's plan, was long allowed to remain optional, although he had "counted upon universal prepayment as an important means towards simplifying the accounts, with consequent economy of time and expense, the expedient of double postage on post-payment being regarded as a temporary mode of avoiding the difficulties naturally attending a transition state; and though hitherto deferring the measure to more pressing matters, I had always looked forward to a time suitable for taking the step necessary to the completion of my plan. The almost universal resort to prepayment had rendered accounts of postage very short and easy, but obviously universal practice alone could render them altogether unnecessary."[217]

The attempt to make prepayment compulsory was renewed in 1859, the proportion of unpaid letters having by that date become very small. But the public generally were insensible to the advantage to the service which economy of time and labour must secure, while the few active malcontents who thought themselves qualified to be a law unto themselves, if not to others, raised so much clamour that it was considered advisable to postpone issue of the edict. An error of judgment, perhaps, since the public soon becomes accustomed to any rule that is at once just and easy to follow; as indeed had already been shown by the readiness—entirely contrary to official prediction—with which prepayment had, from the first, been accepted. After all, submission to compulsory prepayment of our postage is not one whit more slavish than submission to compulsory prepayment of our railway and other vehicular fares, a gentle form of coercion to which even those of us who are the most revolutionary of mind assent with exemplary meekness.

So far back as 1842[218] Rowland Hill had recommended the establishment of a parcel post, but, although renewing his efforts both in

1858 and 1863, he was forced to leave accomplishment of this boon to later reformers. In the last-named year, however, the pattern post came into operation.

In 1862 he was able to make important alterations in the registration of letters. Allusion has already been made to the ancient quarrel between a former Postmaster-General and my father over the amount of fee, the political head of the office wishing to keep it at 1s., Rowland Hill to reduce it to 6d., a reduction easily obtained when in 1846 the latter entered the Post Office. A largely increased number of registered letters had been the result. The fee was now still further reduced, the reduction being followed by an even larger increase of registered letters; while the registration of coin-bearing letters was at last made compulsory. Before 1862 coins had often been enclosed in unregistered letters, at times so carelessly that their presence was evident, and abstraction easy. As a natural consequence, misappropriation was not infrequent. After the passing of this necessary enactment the losses diminished rapidly; the number of letters containing money posted in the second half of that year increased to about 900,000, and the number of those which failed to reach their destination was only twelve.

While it is undeniable that occasionally a letter-carrier or sorter has been responsible for the disappearance of some articles—at times of great value—entrusted to the care of the department, the public itself is frequently very far from blameless. As has already been shown, carelessness that can only be called culpable sometimes throws temptation in the men's way. In the course of a single twelvemonths, nearly 31,000 letters entirely unaddressed were posted, many of which contained money whose sum total amounted to several thousands of pounds.

The number of things lost in the post through negligence to enclose them in properly secured covers, or through placing them in covers which are imperfectly addressed or not addressed at all, so that sometimes neither sender nor intended recipient can be traced, is very great. In one twelvemonths alone the accumulations at the Dead Letter Office sold at auction by order of the Postmaster-General comprised almost every description of wearing apparel from socks up to sealskin jackets and suits of clothing, Afghan, Egyptian, and South African war medals, a Khedive's Star, a pearl necklace, some boxes of chocolate, a curious Transvaal coin, and several thousands of postage stamps. Did none of the losers dream of applying for repossession of their property ere it passed under the auctioneer's hammer; or did they resign themselves to the less troublesome assumption that the things had been stolen?

Simply to avoid payment of the registration fee—whose present amount can hardly be found burdensome—people will hide money or other valuables in some covering material that is inexpensive, or that may be useful to the recipient, such as butter, puddings, etc., which are sent off by the yet cheaper parcel post. One of the most flagrant cases of deception was that of a lady living in Siam, who dispatched to the old country several packages said to contain stationery and walking-sticks, and valued at £7, 10s. 0d. Suspicion was aroused—perhaps by the odd combination of treasures—and the parcels were opened, when the "stationery and walking-sticks" of modest value resolved themselves into a superb collection of diamonds and other jewels worth about £25,000.

The Post Office is often reproached for slowness or unwillingness to adopt new ways; and, as a rule, the accusations are accompanied by brilliant and highly original witticisms, in which figure the contemptuous words "red tape." For the apparent lack of official zeal, the reproaching public itself is often to blame. Its passion—dating from long past times, yet far from moribund—for defrauding the department which, on the whole, serves it so well, yet with so few thanks and so many scoldings, is one chief bar to possible reforms. When, for example, the book-post was established in 1846,[219] all sorts of things which had no right to be where they were found used to be hidden between the pages. In one instance, a watch was concealed in an old volume, within whose middle leaves a deep hole had been excavated which was artfully covered over by the outside binding and by several pages at the beginning and end of the book. To the casual observer it therefore presented an innocent appearance, but fell victim to post-official, lynx-eyed investigation.

"With every desire to give the public all possible facilities," wrote my father in his diary, "we were often debarred from so doing by the tricks and evasions which too frequently followed any relaxation of our rules."

Even the great Macaulay transgressed strict postal regulations, being in the habit, as his nephew tells us in one of the most delightful biographies ever written, of sending him, when a school-boy, letters fastened with sealing-wax, the seal hiding the welcome golden "tip." As the use of seals has almost entirely died out, and sealed missives, even in Macaulay's time, were coming to be looked at with suspicion—as probably containing something worth investigation—by those through whose hands they pass, the boy was fortunate in that his uncle's letters reached him safely.

Very unreasonable, and sometimes downright absurd, are many complaints made by the public. A lady once wrote to the authorities saying that whereas at one time she always received her letters in the morning, they now only reached her in the evening. The fact was that, through the making of better arrangements, the letters which used to come in with the matutinal tea and toast were now delivered over-night.

The following is a rather curious story of theft. The cook in a gentleman's family residing at Harrow one day received an unregistered letter from Hagley, near Birmingham, which, when posted, contained a watch. On reaching its destination the cover was found to enclose a couple of pebbles only. She at once went to her master for advice. An eminent geologist was dining at the house. When he saw the enclosures, he said: "These are Harrow pebbles; no such stones could be found at Hagley." This showed that the letter must have been tampered with at the Harrow end of the journey. The postal authorities were communicated with, and an official detective was sent to Harrow to make enquiries. Something about the letter had, it seems, attracted notice at the local post office—perhaps the watch had ticked—which proved that the packet was intact when handed to the letter-carrier for delivery. He had not, however, given the letter to the cook, but to the butler, who passed it on to the cook. The delinquent, then, must be either the letter-carrier or the butler. The letter-carrier had been long in the postal service, and bore an excellent character. Suspicion therefore pointed to the butler. He was called into the dining-room, and interrogated. He denied all knowledge of the watch, and declared he had given the packet to the cook exactly as he had received it. But while the interrogation was proceeding, his boxes were being examined; and, although no watch was found in any, the searchers came upon some things belonging to his master. Taxed with their theft, the man pleaded guilty, but once more disclaimed all knowledge of the watch. On some pretext he was allowed to leave the room, when he retired to the pantry, and there committed suicide.

As time wore on, during the ten years which followed 1854 and my father's appointment as Secretary to the Post Office, he sometimes found that his earlier estimate of former opponents was a mistake. When on the eve of entering the Post Office in 1846, he was, for instance, especially advised to get rid of Mr Bokenham, the head of the Circulation Department.[220] The new-comer, however, soon learned to appreciate at their just value Mr Bokenham's sterling qualities both in official and private life. So far from "inviting him to resign," my father, unasked, moved for and obtained that improvement in position and salary which his ex-adversary so thoroughly well deserved, and which any less disinterested man would probably have secured for himself long before. Nor was Mr Bokenham's the only instance of genuine worth rewarded by well-merited promotion in position or salary, or both.

Another former strong opponent had been Mr William Page, unto whose efforts the successful conclusion of that treaty, known as "The

Postal Union," which enables us to correspond with foreign nations for 2-½d. the half-ounce, was largely due. At the present day 2-½d. seems scarcely to deserve the term "cheap" postage, but in the middle of the nineteenth century it was a reduction to rejoice over. No visitor was more welcome to our house than Mr Page, who was one of the most genial and least self-seeking of men. He was a staunch "Maberlyite," and, even when most friendly with us, never concealed his attachment to the man to whom he owed much kindness, as well as his own well-deserved advancement, and the appointment to the postal service of his two younger brothers. This unswerving loyalty to a former chief naturally made us hold Mr Page in still warmer esteem, since the worship of the risen sun is much more common and much less heroic than is that of the luminary which has definitely set. When my father died, Mr Page, at once and uninvited, cut short an interesting and much-needed holiday in Normandy because he knew we should all wish him to be present at the funeral.

But although the situation at the Post Office greatly improved after the chief opponent's translation to another sphere of usefulness, the old hostility to the reform and reformer did not die out, being in some directions scotched merely, and not killed.

One of the most prominent among the irreconcilables was the novelist, Anthony Trollope. But as he was a surveyor, which means a postal bird of passage or official comet of moderate orbit regularly moving on its prescribed course, with only periodic appearances at St Martin's-le-Grand, he did not frequently come into contact with the heads there. He was an indefatigable worker; and many of his novels were partly written in railway carriages while he was journeying from one post town to another, on official inspection bent. On one occasion he was brought to our house, and a most entertaining and lively talker we found him to be. But somehow our rooms seemed too small for his large, vigorous frame, and big, almost stentorian voice. Indeed, he reminded us of Dickens's Mr Boythorn, minus the canary, and gave us the impression that the one slightly-built chair on which he rashly seated himself during a great part of the interview, must infallibly end in collapse, and sooner rather than later. After about a couple of hours of our society, he apparently found us uncongenial company; and perhaps we did not take over kindly to him, however keen our enjoyment, then and afterwards, of his novels and his talk. He has left a record in print of the fact that he heartily detested the Hills, who have consoled themselves by remembering that when a man has spent many years in writing romance, the trying of his hand, late in life, at history, is an exceedingly hazardous undertaking. In fact, Trollope's old associates at the Post Office were in the habit of declaring that his "Autobiography" was one of the greatest, and certainly not the least amusing, of his many works of fiction.

But Anthony Trollope had quite another side to his character beside that of novelist and Hill-hater, a side which should not be lost sight of. In 1859 he was sent out to the West Indies on official business; and, although a landsman, he was able to propose a scheme of steamer routes more convenient and more economical than those in existence, "and, in the opinion of the hydrographer to the Admiralty, superior to them even in a nautical point of view."[221] Nevertheless, the scheme had to wait long for adoption. Indeed, what scheme for betterment has *not* to wait long?

Whenever my father met with any foreign visitors of distinction, he was bound, sooner or later, to ask them about postal matters in their own country. The examined were of all ranks, from the King of the Belgians to Garibaldi, the Italian patriot, whom he met at a public banquet, and presently questioned as to the prospects of penny postage in Italy. Garibaldi's interest in the subject was but languid; the sword with him was evidently a more congenial weapon than the pen—or postage stamp. When, later, Rowland Hill told his eldest brother of the unsatisfactory interview, the latter was greatly amused, and said: "When you go to Heaven I foresee that you will stop at the gate to enquire of St Peter how many deliveries they have a day, and how the expense of postal communication between Heaven and the other place is defrayed."

To the year 1862 belongs a veracious anecdote, which, although it has no relation to postal history, is worth preserving from oblivion because its heroine is a lady of exalted rank, who is held in universal respect. In connection with the Great Exhibition of that year, whose transplanted building has since been known as the Alexandra Palace of North London, my father came to know the Danish Professor Forchammer; and, when bound for the Post Office, often took his way through the Exhibition, then in Hyde Park, and the Danish Section in particular. One morning he found the Professor very busy superintending a rearrangement of the pictures there. A portrait had just been taken from the line in order that another, representing a very attractive-looking young lady, which had previously been "skied," might be put into the more important place. The young lady's father had not yet become a king, and the family was by no means wealthy, which combination of circumstances perhaps accounted for the portrait's former inconspicuous position. On my father's asking the reason for the change, Professor Forchammer replied that a great number of people was expected to visit that Section to-day to look at the portrait, and it was imperative that it should be given the best place there, in consequence of the announcement just made public that the original was "engaged to marry your Prince of Wales."

My father parted with great regret from Lord Clanricarde when the Russell Administration went out of office. His kindness and courtesy, his aptitude for work, his good sense and evident sincerity, had caused the "Secretary to the Postmaster-General," after a service of nearly six years, to form a very high opinion of his chief.[222]

Lord Clanricarde's successor, Lord Hardwicke, belonged to the rough diamond species; yet he tried his hardest to fulfil intelligently and conscientiously the duties of his novel and far from congenial office. He had a cordial dislike to jobbery of any kind, though once at least he came near to acquiescing in a Parliamentary candidate's artfully-laid plot suggesting the perpetration of a piece of lavish and unnecessary expenditure in a certain town, the outlay to synchronise with the candidate's election, and the merit to be claimed by him. Happily, Lord Hardwicke's habitual lack of reticence gave wiser heads the weapon with which to prevent so flagrant a job from getting beyond the stage of mere suggestion. It was the man's kind heart and dislike to give offence which doubtless led him into indiscretions of the sort; but amiable as he was, he had at times a knack of making people feel extremely uncomfortable, as when, in conformity with his own ideas on the subject, he sought to regulate the mutual relations of the two chief Secretaries, when he called in all latchkeys—his own, however, included—and when, during his first inspection of his new kingdom, he audibly asked, on entering a large room full of employees, if he had "the power to dismiss all these men." The old sailor aimed at ruling the Post Office as he had doubtless ruled his man-of-war, wasted time and elaborate minutes on trivial matters—such as a return of the number of housemaids employed—when important reforms needed attention, and had none of the ability or breadth of view of his predecessor.

Lord Canning was my father's next chief, and soon showed himself to be an earnest friend to postal reform. It was while he was Postmaster-General, and mainly owing to his exertions, that in 1854 fulfilment was at last made of the promise given by Lord John Russell's Government, to place the author of Penny Postage at the head of the great department which controlled the country's correspondence—a promise in consideration of which Rowland Hill, in 1846, had willingly sacrificed so much. When Lord Canning left the Post Office to become Governor-General of India, my father felt as if he had lost a lifelong friend; and he followed with deep interest his former chiefs career in the Far East. During the anxious time of struggle with the Mutiny, nothing pained my father more than the virulent abuse which was often levelled at the far-seeing statesman whose wise and temperate rule contributed so largely to preserve to his country possession of that "brightest jewel of the crown" at a season when most people in Britain lost their senses in a wild outburst of fury. Lord Canning's management of India won, from the first, his ex-lieutenant's warmest admiration. The judgment of posterity—often more discerning, because less heated, than contemporaneous opinion—has long since decided that "Clemency Canning" did rightly. The nickname was used as a reproach at the time, but the later title of "The Lord Durham of India" is meant as a genuine compliment, or, better still, appreciation.[223]

The Duke of Argyll—he of the "silvern tongue"—succeeded Lord Canning, and showed the same aptitude for hard work which had distinguished his predecessors. His quickness of apprehension, promptitude in generalisation, and that facility in composition which made of his minutes models of literary style, were unusually great. When he left the Post Office he addressed to its Secretary a letter of regret at parting—an act of courtesy said to be rare. The letter was couched in the friendliest terms, and the regret was by no means one-sided.

Lord Colchester, the Postmaster-General in Lord Derby's short-lived second Administration, was another excellent chief, painstaking, hard-working, high-minded, remarkably winning in manner, cherishing a positive detestation of every kind of job, and never hesitating to resist pressure on that score from whatever quarter it might come. His early death was a distinct loss to the party to which he belonged.

For Lord Elgin, who, like Lord Canning, left the Post Office to become Governor-General of India, my father entertained the highest opinion alike as regarded his administrative powers, his calm and dispassionate judgment, and his transparent straightforwardness of character. "He is another Lord Canning," the postal reformer used to say; and that was paying his new chief the greatest compliment possible.

So far, then, as my father's experience entitled him to judge, there are few beliefs more erroneous than that which pictures these political, and therefore temporary masters of the Post Office—or, indeed, of other Governmental departments—as mere "ornamental figure-heads," drawing a handsome salary, and doing very little to earn it. The same remark applies to my father's last chief, who was certainly no drone, and who was ever bold in adopting any improvement which seemed to him likely to benefit the service and the public.

Hitherto the reformer had been fortunate in the Postmasters-General he had served under; and by this time—the beginning of the 'sixties—everything was working harmoniously, so that Mr (afterwards Sir John) Tilly, the then Senior Assistant Secretary, when contrasting the present with the past, was justified when he remarked that, "Now every one seems to do his duty as a matter of course."

But with the advent to power in 1860 of the seventh chief under whom my father, while at the Post Office, served, there came a change; and the era of peace was at an end. The new head may, like Lord Canning, have had knowledge of that hostility to which the earlier Postmaster-General, in conversation with Rowland Hill, alluded. But if so, the effect on the later chief was very different from that upon Lord Canning. At this long interval of time, there can be no necessity to disinter the forgotten details of a quarrel that lasted for four years, but which will soon be half a century old. Perhaps the situation may be best expressed in the brief, and very far from vindictive reference to it in my father's diary. "I had not," he wrote, "the good fortune to obtain from him that confidence and support which I had enjoyed with his predecessors." Too old, too utterly wearied out with long years of almost incessant toil and frequently recurring obstruction, too hopelessly out of health[224] to cope with the new difficulties, the harassed postal reformer struggled on awhile, and in 1864 resigned.

He was sixty-eight years of age, and from early youth upward, had worked far harder than do most people. "He had," said an old friend, "packed into one man's life the life's work of two men."[225]

FOOTNOTES:

[199] The Commissioners were Lord Elcho, Sir Stafford Northcote, Sir Charles Trevelyan, and Mr Hoffay.

[200] "Life," ii. 245-249.

[201] These were, of course, the "Peelites"—the members who, together with their leader, had seceded from the Tory party on the Free Trade question.

[202] "Life," ii. 225, 226.

[203] "Life," ii. 267.

[204] "Life," ii. 317.

[205] A medical man had now been added to the staff, the first so appointed being Dr Gavin, a much-esteemed official, who perished untimely, if I remember rightly, at Newcastle-on-Tyne, during the awful visitation there of the cholera epidemic of 1853.

[206] Afterwards diminished to eight.

[207] "Life," ii. 298-301.

[208] "Life," ii. 300. At this time the Post Office staff numbered over 24,000, of whom more than 3,000 served in the London district.

[209] A thirty or more years old example of this rejection returns to memory. A young man—a born soldier, and son to a distinguished officer in the Engineers—failed to pass the inevitable Army examination. The

subject over which he broke down was some poem of Chaucer's, I think the immortal Prologue to *The Canterbury Tales*—that wonderful collection of masterly-drawn portraits of men and women who must have been living people over five hundred years ago. Even an ardent lover of him "whose sweet breath preluded those melodious bursts that fill the spacious times of great Elizabeth with sounds that echo still," has never yet been able to perceive what connection the strains of "Dan Chaucer, the first warbler," can have with the science of modern warfare. The born soldier, it was said, was fain to turn ranchman in the American Far West.

[210] As regards this oft-discussed matter, it seems that Herbert Spencer was of like mind with my father. Speaking in his "Autobiography of Edison," the great philosopher says that "that remarkable, self-educated man" was of opinion that "college-bred men were of no use to him. It is astonishing," continues Herbert Spencer, "how general, among distinguished engineers, has been the absence of education, or of high education. James Brindley and George Stephenson were without any early instruction at all: the one taught himself writing when an apprentice, and the other put himself to school when a grown man. Telford too, a shepherd boy, had no culture beyond that which a parish school afforded. Though Smeaton and Rennie and Watt had the discipline of grammar schools, and two of them that of High Schools, yet in no case did they pass through a *curriculum* appropriate to the profession they followed. Another piece of evidence, no less remarkable, is furnished by the case of Sir Benjamin Baker, who designed and executed the Forth Bridge—the greatest and most remarkable bridge in the world, I believe. He received no regular engineering instruction. Such men who, more than nearly all other men, exercise constructive imagination, and rise to distinction only when they are largely endowed with this faculty, seem thus to show by implication the repressive influence of an educational system which imposes ideas from without instead of evolving them from within." ("Autobiography," i. 337, 338.) The remarks are the outcome of Herbert Spencer's perusal of a biographical sketch of the celebrated engineer, John Ericsson. In this occurred a significant passage: "When a friend spoke to him with regret of his not having been graduated from some technical institute, he answered that the fact, on the other hand, was very fortunate. If he had taken a course at such an institution, he would have acquired such a belief in authority that he would never have been able to develop originality and make his own way in physics and mechanics."

[211] In writing of the discontents which occasionally troubled the postal peace during the mid-nineteenth century, it must be clearly understood that no allusion is intended to those of later times. In this story of an old reform the latest year at the Post Office is 1864; therefore, since this is a chronicle

- 175 -

of "ancient history" only, comments on the troubles of modern days, which the chronicler does not profess to understand, shall be scrupulously avoided.

[212] He never wasted his time in reading the attacks, even when some good-natured friend occasionally asked: "Have you seen what Blank has just written about you?"

[213] "Life," ii. 328.

[214] Some of us enjoyed a capital view of the eclipse at Swindon in fine weather and pleasant company. Our friend, Mr W. H. Wills, who was also present, wrote an amusing account of the eclipse—appending to it, however, a pretty story which never happened—in *Household Words*. The eclipse was soon over, but the great astronomical treat of the year was, of course, Donati's unforgettable comet, "a thing of beauty," though unfortunately not "a joy for ever," which blazed magnificently in the northern hemisphere for some few weeks.

[215] "Life," ii. 334.

[216] Here was another reformer from outside the Post Office. Yet one more was Sir Douglas Galton, who first proposed that the Post Office should take over the telegraphic system. His father-in-law, Mr Nicholson of Waverley Abbey, sent the then Captain Galton's paper on the subject to Rowland Hill in 1852. The communication being private, my father replied also privately, giving the project encouragement, and leaving Captain Galton to take the next step. He submitted his plan to the Board of Trade, whence it was referred to the Post Office. The Postmaster-General, Lord Hardwicke, did not view the scheme with favour, and it was dropped, to be resumed later within the Office itself. Had Captain Galton's proposals been resolutely taken up in 1852, the British taxpayers might have been spared the heavy burden laid upon them when, nearly twenty years later, the State purchase of the Telegraphs was effected "at a cost at once so superfluous and so enormous." ("Life," ii. 251, 252.)

[217] "Life," ii. 335.

[218] "Report of the Select Committee on Postage (1843)," p. 41. Also "Life," ii. 336.

[219] Professor de Morgan was one of the many literary and scientific men who took an interest in the book-post when first proposed. At the outset it was intended that no writing of any sort, not even the name of owner or donor, should be inscribed in a volume so sent, but the Professor descanted so ably and wittily on the hardship of thus ruling out of transit an innocent book, merely because, a century or more ago, some hand had written on its

fly-leaf, "Anne Pryse, her boke; God give her grace therein to loke," that not even the hardest-hearted official, and certainly not my father, could have said him nay; and by this time any writing, short of a letter, is allowed. The Professor had a wonderfully-shaped head, his forehead towards the top being abnormally prominent. He was devoted to mathematics, and gave much time to their study; thus it used to be said by those who could not otherwise account for his strange appearance, that the harder he worked at his favourite study the keener grew the contest between the restraining frontal bones and protruding brain, the latter perceptibly winning the day. A delightful talker was this great mathematician, also a pugilistic person, and on occasion not above using his fists with effect. One day he was summoned for an assault, and duly appeared in the police court. "I was walking quietly along the street," began the victim, "when Professor de Morgan came straight up to me——" "That's a lie!" exclaimed the disgusted mathematician. "I came up to you at an angle of forty-five degrees." This anecdote has been given to several eminent men, but Professor de Morgan was its real hero.

[220] By shear ability, industry, and steadiness, Mr Bokenham had worked himself up from a humble position to high rank in the Post Office. One day a rough but pleasant-looking man of the lower agricultural class came to London from his and Mr Bokenham's native East Anglia, and called at St Martin's-le-Grand. "What! Bill Bokenham live in a house of this size!" he exclaimed. He had taken the imposing, but far from beautiful edifice built in 1829 for his cousin's private residence.

[221] "Life," ii. 288.

[222] In Edmund Yates's "Recollections" many pleasant stories are told of Lord Clanricarde, to whose kindness indeed the author owed his appointment to the Post Office.

[223] "The close of his career as Postmaster-General," wrote my father many years later, "was highly characteristic. For some reason it was convenient to the Government that he should retain his office until the very day of his departure for the East. Doubtless it was expected that this retention would be little more than nominal, or that, at most, he would attend to none but the most pressing business, leaving to his successor all such affairs as admitted of delay. When I found that he continued to transact business just as usual, while I knew that he must be encumbered with every kind of preparation, official, personal, and domestic, I earnestly pressed that course upon him, but in vain; he would leave no arrears, and every question, great or small, which he had been accustomed to decide was submitted to him as usual to the last hour of his remaining in the country. Nor was decision even then made heedlessly or hurriedly, but, as before,

after full understanding. ... In common with the whole world, I regarded his premature death as a severe national calamity. He was earnest and energetic in the moral reform of the Post Office, and had his life been longer spared, might perhaps have been the moral reformer of India.... That such a man, after acquiring a thorough knowledge of myself, should have selected me for the difficult and responsible post of Secretary to the Post Office, and have continued throughout my attached friend, is to me a source of the highest gratification." ("Life," ii. 353-355.)

[224] He had been still further crippled in 1860 by a paralytic seizure which necessitated entire abstention from work for many months, and from which he rallied, but with impaired health, although he lived some nineteen years longer.

[225] "Life," ii. 353-363. Yates, in his "Recollections," gives a vivid character sketch of this political head of the office. The portrait is not flattering. But then Yates, who, like other subordinates at St Martin's-le-Grand, had grievances of his own against the man who was probably the most unpopular Postmaster-General of his century, does not mince his words.

CHAPTER IX

THE SUNSET OF LIFE

IN February 1864, Rowland Hill sent in his resignation to the Lords of the Treasury. Thenceforward, he retired from public life, though he continued to take a keen interest in all political and social questions, and especially in all that concerned the Post Office.[226] In drawing his pen-portrait, it is better that the judgment of a few of those who knew him well should be quoted, rather than that of one so nearly related to him as his present biographer.

SIR ROWLAND HILL.
From a Portrait in "THE GRAPHIC."

In the concluding part to the "Life of Sir Rowland Hill and History of Penny Postage," partly edited, partly written by Dr G. Birkbeck Hill, the latter, while reviewing the situation, justly holds that "In the Post Office certainly" his uncle "should have had no master over him at any time." ... "Under the able chiefs whom he served from 1854 to 1860, he worked with full contentment." When "this happy period came to an end, with the appointment of" the Postmaster-General under whom he found it impossible to work, "his force was once more, and for the last time, squandered. How strangely and how sadly was this man thwarted in the high aim of his life! He longed for power; but it was for the power to carry through his great scheme. 'My plan' was often on his lips, and ever in his thoughts. His strong mind was made up that it should succeed."... "There was in him a rare combination of enthusiasm and practical power. He clearly saw every difficulty that lay in his path, and yet he went on with unshaken firmness. In everything but in work he was the most temperate of men. His health was greatly shattered by his excessive toils and his long struggles. For the last few years of his life he never left his house, and never even left the floor on which his sleeping room was. But in the midst of this confinement, in all the weakness of old age and sickness, he wrote: 'I accept the evil with the good, and frankly regard the latter as by far the weightier of the two. Could I repeat my course, I should sacrifice as much as before, and regard myself as richly repaid by the result.' With these high qualities was united perfect integrity. He was the most upright and the most truthful of men. He was often careless of any gain to himself, but the good of the State never for one moment did he disregard. His rule was stern, yet never without consideration for the feelings of others. No one who was under him ever felt his self-respect wounded by his chief.[227] He left behind him in all ranks of the service a strong sense of public duty which outlived even the evil days which came after him. One of the men who long served under him bore this high testimony to the character of his old chief: 'Sir Rowland Hill was very generous with his own money, and very close with public money. He would have been more popular had he been generous with the public money and close with his own.'"[228]

When Mr Gladstone was Chancellor of the Exchequer, my father often worked with him, their relations being most harmonious. Shortly before the postal reformer's resignation, the great statesman wrote that "he stands pre-eminent and alone among all the members of the Civil Service as a benefactor to the nation." At another time Mr Gladstone assured his friend that "the support you have had from me has been the very best that I could give, but had it been much better and more effective, it would not have been equal to your deserts and claims." And at a later season, when Rowland Hill was suffering from an especially virulent outbreak of the misrepresentation and petty insults which fall to the lot of all fearlessly honest, job-detesting men, the sympathising Chancellor wrote: "If you are at present under odium for the gallant stand you make on behalf of the public interests, at a period, too, when chivalry of that sort by no means 'pays,' I believe that I have, and I hope still to have, the honour of sharing it with you."[229] Writing soon after my father's death, the then leader of the Opposition used words which Rowland Hill's descendants have always prized. "In some respects his lot was one peculiarly happy even as among public benefactors, for his great plan ran like wildfire through the civilised world; and never, perhaps, was a local invention (for such it was) and improvement applied in the lifetime of its author to the advantage of such vast multitudes of his fellow-creatures." Ten years later, the same kindly critic, in the course of a speech delivered at Saltney in October 1889, said: "In the days of my youth a labouring man, the father of a family, was practically prohibited from corresponding with the members of his household who might be away. By the skill and courage and genius of Sir Rowland Hill, correspondence is now within reach of all, and the circulation of intelligence is greatly facilitated."[230]

A very busy man himself, my father was naturally full of admiration for Gladstone's marvellous capacity for work and for attending to a number of different things at once. One day, when the Secretary to the Post Office went to Downing Street to transact some departmental business with the Chancellor of the Exchequer, he found the latter engaged with his private secretaries, every one of whom was hard at work, a sculptor being meanwhile employed upon a bust for which the great man was too much occupied to give regular sittings. Every now and then during my father's interview, Mrs Gladstone, almost, if not quite, as hard-working as her husband, came in and out, each time on some errand of importance, and all the while letters and messengers and other people were arriving or departing. Yet the Chancellor of the Exchequer seemed able to keep that wonderful brain of his as clear as if his attention had been wholly concentrated on the business about which his postal visitor had come, and this was soon discussed and settled in Gladstone's own clear and concise manner, notwithstanding the should-have-been-bewildering surroundings, which would have driven my father all but distracted. A characteristic, everyday scene of that strenuous life.

On Rowland Hill's retirement, he received many letters of sympathy and of grateful recognition of his services from old friends and former colleagues, most of them being men of distinguished career. They form a valuable collection of autographs, which would have been far larger had not many of his early acquaintances, those especially who worked heartily and well during the late 'thirties to help forward the reform, passed over already to the majority. One letter was from Lord Monteagle, who, as Mr Spring Rice, Chancellor of the Exchequer in the Melbourne Administration, had proposed Penny Postage in the Budget of 1839.

Prolonged rest gave back to Rowland Hill some of his old strength, and allowed him to serve on the Royal Commission on Railways, and to show while so employed that his mind had lost none of its clearness. He was also able on several occasions to attend the meetings of the Political Economy Club and other congenial functions, and he followed with keen interest the doings of the Royal Astronomical Society, to which he had belonged for more than half a century.[231] He also spent much time in preparing the lengthy autobiography on whose pages I have largely drawn in writing this story of his reform. He survived his retirement from the Post Office fifteen years; and time, with its happy tendency to obliterate memory of wrongs, enabled him to look back on the old days of storm and stress with chastened feelings. Over several of his old opponents the grave had closed, and for the rest, many years had passed since they and he had played at move and counter-move. Thus, when the only son of one of his bitterest adversaries died under especially sad circumstances, the news called forth the aged recluse's ever ready sympathy, and prompted him to send the bereaved parent a genuinely heartfelt message of condolence. Increasing age and infirmities did not induce melancholy or pessimistic leanings, and although he never ceased to feel regret that his plan had not been carried out in its entirety—a regret with which every reformer, successful or otherwise, is likely to sympathise—he was able in one of the concluding passages of his Autobiography to write thus cheerfully of his own position and that of his forerunners in the same field: "When I compare my experience with that of other reformers or inventors, I ought to regard myself as supremely fortunate. Amongst those who have laboured to effect great improvements, how many have felt their success limited to the fact that by their efforts seed was sown which in another age would germinate and bear fruit! How many have by their innovations exposed themselves to obliquy, ridicule, perhaps even to the scorn and abhorrence of at least their own generation; and, alas, how few have lived to see their predictions more than verified, their success amply acknowledged, and their deeds formally and gracefully rewarded!"[232]

Owing to the still quieter life which, during his very latest years, he was obliged to lead through broken health, advancing age, and the partial loneliness caused by the passing hence of his two eldest brothers, one of his children, and nearly all his most intimate friends, he was nearly forgotten by the public, or at any rate by that vastly preponderating younger portion of it, which rarely studies "the history of our own times," or is only dimly aware that Rowland Hill had "done something to the Post Office." Many people believed him to be dead, others that he was living in a retirement not altogether voluntary. Thus one day he was greatly amused while reading his morning paper, to learn that at a spiritualist meeting his wraith had been summoned from the vasty deep, and asked to give its opinion on the then management of the Post Office. The helm at that time was in the hands of one of the bitterest of his old opponents, and sundry things had lately taken place—notably, if memory serves me aright, in the way of extravagant telegraphs purchase—of which he strongly disapproved. But that fact by no means prevented the spirit from expressing entire satisfaction with everything and everybody at St Martin's-le-Grand, or from singling out for particular commendation the then novel invention of halfpenny postcards. These the living man cordially detested as being, to his thinking, a mischievous departure from his principle of uniformity of rate.[233] Later, he so far conformed to the growing partiality for postcards as to keep a packet or two on hand, but they diminished in number very slowly, and he was ever wont to find fault with the unfastidious taste of that large portion of mankind which writes descriptions of its maladies, details of its private affairs, and moral reflections on the foibles of its family or friends, so that all who run, or, at any rate, sort and deliver, may read.

During the quarter-century which elapsed between Rowland Hill's appointment to the Treasury and his resignation of the chief secretaryship to the Post Office, many generous tributes were paid him by the public in acknowledgment of the good accomplished by the postal reform.

The year after the establishment of penny postage, Wolverhampton, Liverpool, and Glasgow, each sent him a handsome piece of plate, the Liverpool gift, a silver salver, being accompanied by a letter from Mr Egerton Smith, the editor of the local *Mercury*. Mr Smith told my father that the salver had been purchased with the pence contributed by several thousands of his fellow-townsmen, and that Mr Mayer, in whose works it had been made, and by whom it was delivered into the postal reformer's hands, had waived all considerations of profit, and worked out of pure gratitude. The other pieces of plate were also accompanied by addresses couched in the kindliest of terms.

From Cupar Fife came a beautiful edition of the complete works of Sir Walter Scott—ninety-eight volumes in all. In each is a fly-leaf stating for whom and for what services this unique edition was prepared, the inscription being as complimentary as were the inscriptions accompanying the other testimonials. My father was a lifelong admirer of Scott; and when the Cupar Fife Testimonial Committee wrote to ask what form their tribute should take, he was unfeignedly glad to please his Scots admirers by choosing the works of their most honoured author, and, at the same time, by possessing them, to realise a very many years long dream of his own. As young men, he and his brothers had always welcomed each successive work as it fell from pen and press, duly receiving their copy direct from the publishers, and straightway devouring it. Younger generations have decided that Scott is "dry." Had they lived in those dark, early decades of the nineteenth century, when literature was perhaps at its poorest level, they also might have greeted with enthusiasm the creations of "the Great Unknown," and wondered who could be their author.[234] My father set so high a value on these beautiful presentation volumes that, from the first, he laid down a stringent rule that not one of them should leave the house, no matter who might wish to borrow it.

The National Testimonial—to which allusion has already been made—was raised about three years after Rowland Hill's dismissal from the Treasury, and before his restoration to office by Lord John Russell's Administration, by which time the country had given the new postal system a trial, and found out its merits. In 1845 Sir George Larpent, in the name of the Mercantile Committee, sent my father a copy of its Resolutions, together with a cheque for £10,000, the final presentation being deferred till the accounts should be made up. This was done in June 1846, on the occasion of a public dinner at which were assembled Rowland Hill's aged father, his only son—then a lad of fourteen—and his brothers, in addition to many of those good friends who had done yeoman service for the reform. The idea of the testimonial originated with Mr John Estlin,[235] an eminent surgeon of Bristol, and was speedily taken up in London by *The Inquirer*, the article advocating it being written by the editor, the Rev. Wm. Hinks. The appeal once started was responded to by the country cordially and generously.

Many pleasant little anecdotes show how heartily the poorer classes appreciated both reform and reformer. Being, in 1853, on a tour in Scotland, my father one day employed a poor journeyman tailor of Dunoon to mend a torn coat. Somehow the old man found out who was its wearer, and no amount of persuasion would induce him to accept payment for the rent he so skilfully made good. A similar case occurred somewhat earlier, when we were staying at Beaumaris; while a "humble admirer" who gave no name wrote, a few years later than the presentation of the National Testimonial, to say that at the time he had been too poor to subscribe, but now sent a donation, which he begged my father to accept. His identity was never revealed. Another man wrote a letter of thanks from a distant colony, and not knowing the right address, inscribed the cover "To him who gave us all the Penny Post." Even M. Grasset, when in a similar difficulty, directed his envelope from Paris to "Rowland Hill—where he is." That these apologies for addresses can be reproduced is proof that the missives reached their destination.[236]

It would be easy to add to these stories; their name is legion.

Tributes like these touched my father even more deeply than the bestowal of public honours, although he also prized these as showing that his work was appreciated in all grades of life. Moreover, in those now far-off days, "honours" were bestowed more sparingly and with greater discrimination than later came to be the case; and merit was considered of more account than money-bags. Thus in 1860 Rowland Hill was made a K.C.B., the suggestion of that step being understood to lie with Lords Palmerston and Elgin (the then Postmaster-General), for the recipient had not been previously sounded, and the gift came as a surprise.

After my father's retirement, the bestowal of honours recommenced, though he did *not* assume the title of "Lord Queen's head," as Mr Punch suggested he should do were a peerage offered to him—which was not at all likely to be done. At Oxford he received the honorary degree of D.C.L.,[237] and a little later was presented by the then Prince of Wales with the first Albert Gold Medal issued by the Society of Arts. The following year, when Rowland Hill was dining at Marlborough House, the Prince reminded him of the presentation. Upon which the guest told his host a little story which was news to H.R.H., and greatly amused him. The successive blows required for obtaining high relief on the medal had shattered the die before the work was completed. There was not time to make another die, as it was found impossible to postpone the ceremony. At the moment of presentation, however, the recipient only, and not the donor, was aware that it was an empty box which, with much interchange of compliments, passed from the royal hands into those of the commoner.

From Longton, in the Staffordshire Potteries, came a pair of very handsome vases. When the workmen engaged in making them learned for whom they were intended, they bargained that, by way of contribution to the present, they should give their labour gratuitously.

An address to Rowland Hill was voted at a town's meeting at Liverpool, and this was followed by the gift of some valuable pictures. Their selection being left to my father himself, he chose three, one work each, by friends of long standing—his ex-pupil Creswick, and Messrs Cooke and Clarkson Stanfield, all famous Royal Academicians. Three statues of the postal reformer have been erected, the first at Birmingham, where, soon after his resignation, a town's meeting was held to consider how to do honour to the man whose home had once been there, the originator of the movement being another ex-pupil, Mr James Lloyd of the well-known banking family. From Kidderminster his fellow-townsmen sent my father word that they were about to pay him the same compliment they had already paid to another Kidderminster man, the famous preacher, Richard Baxter. But this newer statue, like the one by Onslow Ford in London,[238] was not put up till after the reformer's death. Of the three, the Kidderminster statue, by Thomas Brock, R.A., is by far the best, the portrait being good and the pose characteristic. Mr Brock has also done justice to his subject's strongest point, the broad, massive head suggestive of the large, well-balanced brain within. That the others were not successful as likenesses is not surprising. Even when living he was difficult to portray, a little bust by Brodie, R.S.A., when Rowland Hill was about fifty, being perhaps next best to Brock's. The small bust in Westminster Abbey set up in the side chapel where my father lies is absolutely unrecognisable. Another posthumous portrait was the engraving published by Vinter (Lithographer to the Queen). It was taken from a photograph then quite a quarter-century old. Photography in the early 'fifties was comparatively a young art. Portraits were often woeful caricatures; and the photograph in our possession was rather faded, so that the lithographer had no easy task before him. Still, the likeness was a fair one, though the best of all—and they were admirable—were an engraving published by Messrs Kelly of the "Post Office Directory," and one which appeared in the *Graphic*.

THE STATUE, KIDDERMINSTER.
By Thomas Brock, R.A.
From a Photograph by the late T. Ball.

In June 1879, less than three months before his death, the Freedom of the City of London was bestowed upon the veteran reformer. By this time he had grown much too infirm to go to the Guildhall to receive the honour in accordance with long-established custom. The Court of Common Council therefore considerately waived precedent, and sent to Hampstead a deputation of five gentlemen,[239] headed by the City Chamberlain, who made an eloquent address, briefly describing the benefits achieved by the postal reform, while offering its dying author "the right hand of fellowship in the name of the Corporation." My father was just able to sign the Register, but the autograph is evidence of the near approach to dissolution of the hand that traced it.

On the 27th of August in the same year he passed away in the presence of his devoted wife, who, barely a year his junior, had borne up bravely and hardly left his bedside, and of one other person. Almost his last act of consciousness was, while holding her hand in his, to feel for the wedding ring he had placed upon it nearly fifty-two years before.

My father's noblest monument is his reform which outlives him, and which no reactionary Administration should be permitted to sweep away. The next noblest is the "Rowland Hill Benevolent Fund," whose chief promoters were Sir James Whitehead and Mr R. K. Causton, and was the fruit of a subscription raised soon after the postal reformer's death, doubled, eleven years later, by the proceeds of the two Penny Postage Jubilee celebrations, the one at the Guildhall and the other at the South Kensington Museum, in 1890. Had it been possible to consult the dead man's wishes as to the use to be made of this fund, he would certainly have given his voice for the purpose to which it is dedicated—the relief of those among the Post Office employees who, through ill-health, old age, or other causes, have broken down, and are wholly or nearly destitute. For, having himself graduated in the stern school of poverty, he too had known its pinch, and could feel for the poor as the poor are ever readiest to feel.

My father's fittest epitaph is contained in the following poem which appeared in *Punch* soon after his death. His family have always, and rightly, considered that no more eloquent or appreciative obituary notice could have been penned.

In Memoriam

ROWLAND HILL

ORIGINATOR OF CHEAP POSTAGE

Born at Kidderminster, 3rd December 1795. Died at Hampstead, 27th August 1879. Buried in Westminster Abbey, by the side of James Watt, Thursday, 4th September.

No question this of worthy's right to lie

With England's worthiest, by the side of him

Whose brooding brain brought under mastery

The wasted strength of the Steam giant grim.

Like labours—his who tamed by sea and land

Power, Space, and Time, to needs of human kind,

That bodies might be stronger, nearer hand,

And his who multiplied mind's links with mind.

Breaking the barriers that, of different height

For rich and poor, were barriers still for all;

Till "out of mind" was one with "out of sight,"

And parted souls oft parted past recall.

Freeing from tax unwise the interchange

Of distant mind with mind and mart with mart;

Releasing thought from bars that clipped its range;

Lightening a load felt most i' the weakest part.

What if the wings he made so strong and wide
Bear burdens with their blessings? Own that all
For which his bold thought we oft hear decried,
Of laden bag, too frequent postman's call,

Is nothing to the threads of love and light
Shot, thanks to him, through life's web dark and wide,
Nor only where he first unsealed men's sight,
But far as pulse of time and flow of tide!

Was it a little thing to think this out?
Yet none till he had hit upon the thought;
And, the thought brought to birth, came sneer and flout
Of all his insight saw, his wisdom taught.

All office doors were closed against him—hard;
All office heads were closed against him too.
He had but worked, like others, for reward.
"The thing was all a dream." "It would not do."

But this was not a vaguely dreaming man,
A windbag of the known Utopian kind;
He had thought out, wrought out, in full, his plan;
'Twas the far-seeing fighting with the blind.

And the far-seeing won his way at last,
Though pig-headed Obstruction's force died hard;
Denied his due, official bitters cast,
Into the cup wrung slowly from their guard.

But not until the country, wiser far
Than those who ruled it, with an angry cry,
Seeing its soldiers 'gainst it waging war,

At last said resolutely, "Stand you by!

"And let him in to do what he has said,
And you do not, and will not let him do."
And so at last the fight he fought was sped,
Thought at less cost freer and further flew.

And all the world was kindlier, closer knit,
And all man's written word can bring to man
Had easier ways of transit made for it,
And none sat silent under poortith's ban

When severed from his own, as in old days.
And this we owe to one sagacious brain,
By one kind heart well guided, that in ways
Of life laborious sturdy strength had ta'en.

And his reward came, late, but sweeter so,
In the wide sway that his wise thought had won:
He was as one whose seed to tree should grow,
Who hears him blest that sowed it 'gainst the sun.

So love and honour made his grey hairs bright,
And while most things he hoped to fulness came,
And many ills he warred with were set right,
Good work and good life joined to crown his name.

And now that he is dead we see how great
The good work done, the good life lived how brave,
And through all crosses hold him blest of fate,
Placing this wreath upon his honoured grave!

—*Punch*, 20th September 1879

FOOTNOTES:

[226] On leaving office he drew up a short paper entitled, "Results of Postal Reform," a copy of which appears in the Appendix.

[227] He was, indeed, never likely to err as once did the unpopular Postmaster-General who summoned to his presence the head of one of the departments to give an explanation of some difficult matter that was under consideration. The interview was bound to be lengthy, but the unfortunate man was not invited to take a chair, till Rowland Hill, who was also present, rose, and, by way of silent protest against an ill-bred action, remained standing. Then both men were asked to sit down.

[228] "Life," ii. 411-414.

[229] "Life," ii. 363, 400.

[230] It is well to reproduce these remarks of one who could remember the old postal system, because among the younger generations who know nothing of it, a belief seems to be prevalent that the plan of penny postage was merely an elaboration of the little local posts. Gladstone was thirty when the great postal reform was established, and was therefore fully qualified to speak of it as he did.

[231] His love for "the Queen of all the Sciences" was gratified one cloudless day in the late autumn of his life by following through his telescope the progress of a transit of Mercury, which he enjoyed with an enthusiasm that was positively boyish. An early lesson in astronomy had been given him one wintry night by his father, who, with the little lad, had been taking a long walk into the country. On their return, young Rowland, being tired, finished the journey seated on his father's back, his arms clasped round the paternal neck. Darkness came on, and in the clear sky the stars presently shone out brilliantly. The two wayfarers by and by passed beside a large pond, in which, the evening being windless, the stars were reflected. Seeing how admirable an astral map the placid waters made, the father stopped and pointed out the constellations therein reproduced, naming them to his little son. The boy eagerly learned the lesson, but his joy was somewhat tempered by the dread lest he should fall into what, to his childish fancy, looked like a fathomless black abyss. Happily, his father had a firm grasp of Rowland's clinging arms, and no accident befell him.

[232] "Life," ii. 401.

[233] A more recent instance of killing a man before he is dead, and raising his spirit to talk at a *séance*, was that of Mr Sherman, the American statesman. His ghost expatiated eloquently on the beauties and delights of Heaven—with which region, as he was still in the land of the living, he

could hardly have made acquaintance—and altogether uttered much unedifying nonsense. The following veracious anecdotes show what hazy views on history, postal or otherwise, some children, and even their elders, entertain. A school mistress who had recently passed with honours through one of our "Seminaries of Useless Knowledge," was asked by a small pupil if Rowland Hill had not invented the penny post. "No, my dear," answered the learned instructress. "The penny post has been established in this country for hundreds of years. All that Rowland Hill did was to put the Queen's head on to a penny stamp." The other story is of a recent *viva voce* examination in English history at one of our large public schools. "Who was Rowland Hill?" was the question. "Rowland Hill," came without hesitation the reply, though not from the grand-nephew who was present and is responsible for the tale, "was a man who was burned for heresy." Could the boy have been thinking of Rowland Taylor, a Marian martyr? The fact that my father was not exactly orthodox, lends piquancy to the story.

[234] While we were children our father used often to read aloud to us—as a schoolmaster and elocutionist he was a proficient in that comparatively rare art—and in course of time we thus became acquainted with nearly all these books. He probably missed the occasional lengthy introductory chapters and other parts which well bear pruning, for memory holds no record of their undeniable tediousness. We certainly did not find Scott "dry." Why should we? Through him we came to know chivalric Saladin, David of Huntingdon, and tawny-haired Richard of the Lion's heart; to love the noble Rebecca, and to assist at the siege of Torquilstone Castle; to look on at the great fight between the Clan Chattan and the Clan Quhele, and to mourn over Rothesay's slow, cruel doing to death; to know kings and queens, and companies of gallant knights and lovely ladies, and free-booters like Rob Roy and Robin Hood, and wits and eccentric characters who were amusing without being vulgar or impossible. Also was it not Sir Walter who "discovered" Scotland for our delight, and through that discovery contributed largely to his native land's prosperity?

[235] The Mercantile Committee suggested a National Testimonial in March 1844, but Mr Estlin's proposal was yet earlier.

[236] A third letter to the postal reformer, also delivered, came directed to the General Post Office to "Mr Owl O Neill." Owing to the present spread of education, the once numerous (and genuine) specimens of eccentric spelling are yearly growing fewer, so that the calling of "blind man"—as the official decipherer of illegible and ill-spelled addresses is not very appropriately termed—is likely to become obsolete. It would surely have given any ordinary mortal a headache to turn "Uncon" into Hong-Kong, "Ilawait" into Isle of Wight, "I Vicum" into High Wycombe, "Searhoo

Skur" into Soho Square, or "Vallop a Razzor" into Valparaiso. Education will also deprive us of insufficiently addressed letters. "Miss Queene Victoria of England" did perhaps reach her then youthful Majesty from some Colonial or American would-be correspondent; but what could have been done with the letter intended for "My Uncle Jon in London," or that to "Mr Michl Darcy in the town of England"? The following pair of addresses are unmistakably Hibernian. "Dennis Belcher, Mill Street, Co. Cork. As you turn the corner to Tom Mantel's field, where Jack Gallavan's horse was drowned in the bog-hole," and "Mr John Sullivan, North Street, Boston. He's a man with a crutch. Bedad, I think that'll find him." That the French Post Office also required the services of "blind man" these strange addresses, taken from Larouse's "Dictionnaire du XIXe Siècle," vol. xii. p. 1,497, demonstrate. The first, "À monsieur mon fils à Paris," reached its destination because it was called for at the chief office, where it had been detained, by a young man whose explanation satisfied the enquiring official. Whether the letter addressed to Lyon, and arriving at a time of thaw, "À M. M., demeurant dans la maison auprès de laquelle il y a un tas de neige" was delivered is not so certain.

[237] He had long before added to his name the justly-prized initials of F.R.S. and F.R.A.S.

[238] This last statue had not long been unveiled when the street boys—so reported one of our newspapers—began to adorn the pedestal with postage stamps.

[239] These were Mr Washington Lyon, mover of the resolution; Sir John Bennett, the seconder; Mr Peter M'Kinley, the Chairman of General Purposes Committee; Mr (afterwards Sir Benjamin) Scott, F.R.A.S., the City Chamberlain; and Mr (afterwards Sir John) Monckton, F.S.A., the Town Clerk.

APPENDIX

RESULTS OF POSTAL REFORM

BEFORE stating the results of Postal Reform it may be convenient that I should briefly enumerate the more important organic improvements effected. They are as follows:

1. A very large reduction in the Rates of Postage on all correspondence, whether Inland, Foreign, or Colonial. As instances in point, it may be stated that letters are now conveyed from any part of the United Kingdom to any other part—even from the Channel Islands to the Shetland Isles—at one-fourth of the charge previously levied on letters passing between post towns only a few miles apart;[240] and that the rate formerly charged for this slight distance—viz. 4d.—now suffices to carry a letter from any part of the United Kingdom to any part of France, Algeria included.

2. The adoption of charge by weight, which, by abolishing the charge for mere enclosures, in effect largely extended the reduction of rates.

3. Arrangements which have led to the almost universal resort to prepayment of correspondence, and that by means of stamps.

4. The simplification of the mechanism and accounts of the department generally, by the above and other means.

5. The establishment of the Book Post (including in its operation all printed and much M.S. matter), at very low rates; and its modified extension to our Colonies, and to many foreign countries.

6. Increased security in the transmission of valuable letters afforded, and temptation to the letter-carriers and others greatly diminished, by reducing the Registration Fee from 1s. to 4d., by making registration of letters containing coin compulsory, and by other means.

7. A reduction to about one-third in the cost—including postage—of Money Orders, combined with a great extension and improvement of the system.

8. More frequent and more rapid communication between the Metropolis and the larger provincial towns; as also between one provincial town and another.

9. A vast extension of the Rural Distribution—many thousands of places, and probably some millions of inhabitants having for the first time been included within the Postal System.

10. A great extension of free deliveries. Before the adoption of Penny Postage, many considerable towns, and portions of nearly all the larger towns, had either no delivery at all, or deliveries on condition of an extra charge.

11. Greatly increased facilities afforded for the transmission of Foreign and Colonial Correspondence; by improved treaties with foreign countries, by a better arrangement of the Packet service, by sorting on board and other means.

12. A more prompt dispatch of letters when posted, and a more prompt delivery on arrival.

13. The division of London and its suburbs into Ten Postal Districts, by which, and other measures, communication within the 12-miles circle has been greatly facilitated, and the most important delivery of the day has, generally speaking, been accelerated as much as two hours.

14. Concurrently with these improvements, the condition of the employees has been materially improved; their labours, especially on the Sunday, having been very generally reduced, their salaries increased, their chances of promotion augmented, and other important advantages afforded them.

RESULTS

My pamphlet on "Post Office Reform" was written in the year 1836. During the preceding twenty years—viz., from 1815 to 1835 inclusive— *there was no increase whatever in the Post Office revenue, whether gross or net*, and therefore, in all probability, none in the number of letters; and though there was a slight increase in the revenue, and doubtless in the number of letters, between 1835 and the establishment of Penny Postage early in 1840—an increase chiefly due, in my opinion, to the adoption of part of my plan, viz., the establishment of Day Mails to and from London—yet, during the whole period of twenty-four years immediately preceding the adoption of Penny Postage, the revenue, whether gross or net, and the number of letters, were, in effect, stationary.

Contrast with this the rate of increase under the new system which has been in operation during a period of about equal length. In the first year of Penny Postage the letters more than doubled, and though since then the increase has, of course, been less rapid, yet it has been so steady that, notwithstanding the vicissitudes of trade, every year, without exception, has shown a considerable advance on the preceding year, and the first year's number is now nearly quadrupled. As regards revenue, there was, of course, at first a large falling off—about a million in gross and still more in net revenue. Since then, however, the revenue, whether gross or net, has rapidly advanced, till now it even exceeds its former amount, the rate of increase, both of letters and revenue, still remaining undiminished.

In short, a comparison of the year 1863 with 1838 (the last complete year under the old system) shows that the number of chargeable letters has risen from 76,000,000 to 642,000,000; and that the revenue, at first so much impaired, has not only recovered its original amount, but risen, the gross from £2,346,000 to about £3,870,000, and the net from £1,660,000 to about £1,790,000.[241]

The expectations I held out before the change were, that eventually, under the operation of my plans, the number of letters would increase fivefold, the gross revenue would be the same as before, while the net revenue would sustain a loss of about £300,000. The preceding statement shows that the letters have increased, not fivefold, but nearly eight-and-a-half-fold; that the gross revenue, instead of remaining the same, has increased by about £1,500,000; while the net revenue, instead of falling £300,000, has risen more than £100,000.

While the revenue of the Post Office has thus more than recovered its former amount, the indirect benefit to the general revenue of the country arising from the greatly increased facilities afforded to commercial transactions, though incapable of exact estimate, must be very large. Perhaps it is not too much to assume that, all things considered, the vast benefit of cheap, rapid, and extended postal communication has been obtained, even as regards the past, without fiscal loss. For the future there must be a large and ever-increasing gain.

The indirect benefit referred to is partly manifested in the development of the Money Order System, under which, since the year 1839, the annual amount transmitted has risen from £313,000 to £16,494,000, that is, fifty-two-fold.

An important collateral benefit of the new system is to be found in the cessation of that contraband conveyance which once prevailed so far that habitual breach of the postal law had become a thing of course.

It may be added that the organisation thus so greatly improved and extended for postal purposes stands available for other objects; and, passing over minor matters, has already been applied with great advantage to the new system of Savings Banks.

Lastly, the improvements briefly referred to above, with all their commercial, educational, and social benefits, have now been adopted, in greater or less degree—and that through the mere force of example—by the whole civilised world.

I cannot conclude this summary without gratefully acknowledging the cordial co-operation and zealous aid afforded me in the discharge of my arduous duties. I must especially refer to many among the superior officers of the department—men whose ability would do credit to any service, and whose zeal could not be greater if their object were private instead of public benefit.

ROWLAND HILL.

HAMPSTEAD,
23rd February 1864.

Milton Keynes UK
Ingram Content Group UK Ltd.
UKHW010702080324
439098UK00004B/248